CHICKASAW BY BLOOD ENROLLMENT CARDS 1898-1914

VOLUME IV

TRANSCRIBED BY
JEFF BOWEN

NATIVE STUDY
Gallipolis, Ohio
USA

Originally published:
Baltimore, Maryland
2010

Reprinted by:

Native Study LLC
Gallipolis, OH
www.nativestudy.com

Library of Congress Control Number: 2020915583

ISBN: 978-1-64968-042-6

Made in the United States of America.

This whole series is dedicated to my wife and best friend, Kathy.

ENROLLMENT CARDS FOR THE
FIVE CIVILIZED TRIBES
1898-1914

On 93 rolls of this microfilm publication are reproduced the enrollment cards that were prepared by the staff of the Commission to the Five Civilized Tribes between 1898 and 1914. These records are part of Records of the Bureau of Indian Affairs, Record Group (RG) 75, and are housed in the Archives Branch of the Federal Archives and Records Center, Fort Worth, Tex. An act of Congress approved March 3, 1893 (27 Stat. 645), authorized the establishment of the Commission to negotiate agreements with the Cherokee, Choctaw, Chickasaw, Creek, and Seminole tribes providing for the dissolution of the tribal governments and the allotment of land to each tribal member. Senator Henry L. Dawes of Massachusetts was appointed Chairman of this Commission on November 1, 1893, after which it has commonly been referred to as the Dawes Commission. The Commission was authorized by an act of Congress approved June 28, 1898 (30 Stat. 495), to prepare citizenship (tribal membership) rolls for each tribe. These final rolls were the basis for allotment. Under this act, subsequent acts, and resulting agreements negotiated with each tribe, the Commission received applications for membership covering more than 250,000 people and enrolled more than 101,000. The tribal membership rolls were closed on March 4, 1907, by an act of Congress approved on April 26, 1906 (34 Stat. 370), although an additional 312 persons were enrolled under an act approved August 1, 1914. The Commission enrolled individuals as "citizens" of a tribe under the following categories: Citizens By Blood, Citizens by Marriage, New Born Citizens By Blood (enrolled under an act of Congress approved March 3, 1905), Minor Citizens By Blood (enrolled under an act of Congress approved April 26, 1906), Freedmen (former black slaves of Indians, later freed and admitted to tribal citizenship), New Born Freedmen, and Minor Freedmen. Delaware Indians adopted by the Cherokee tribe were enrolled as a separate group within the Cherokee. Within each enrollment category, the Commission generally maintained three types of cards: "Straight" cards for persons whose applications were approved, "D" cards for persons whose applications were considered doubtful and subject to question, and "R" cards for persons whose applications were rejected. Persons listed on "D" cards were subsequently transferred to either "Straight" or "R" cards depending on the Commission's decisions. All decisions of the Commission were sent to the Secretary of the Interior for final approval.

    An enrollment card, sometimes referred to by the Commission as a "census card," records the information provided by individual applications submitted by members of the same family group or household and includes notation of the actions taken. The information given for each applicant includes name, roll number (individual's number if enrolled), age, sex, degree of Indian blood, relationship to the head of the family group, parents' names, and references to enrollment on earlier rolls used by the Commission for verification of eligibility. The card often includes references to kin-related enrollment cards and notations about births, deaths, changes in marital status, and actions taken by the Commission and the Secretary of the Interior. Within each enrollment category, the cards are arranged numerically by a "field" or "census card" number, which is separate from the roll number. The index to the final rolls, which is reproduced on roll 1 of this publication, provides the roll number for each person while the final rolls themselves provide the census card numbers for each enrollee. No indexes have been located for the majority of the "D" and "R" cards. There are a few Mississippi Choctaw "Identified" and "Field Cards" as well as some Chickasaw "Cancelled" that refer to person never finally enrolled.

National Archives and Records Administration
American Indians Catalogue, p. 41

INTRODUCTION

The following Introduction describes the considerations employed in transcribing the Chickasaw enrollment cards that comprise the basis for this series. The Chickasaw by Blood enrollment cards, sometimes called "census cards" by the Dawes Commission, were pre-printed cards or loose sheets of paper labeled **Chickasaw Nation. Chickasaw Roll (Not Including Freedmen) with Residence County**. The heading **Post Office** appeared on the left side of each card, and **Card No., Field No.** on the right. The cards were further broken down into the categories *Dawes No., Name, Relationship to Person First Named, Age, Sex, Blood, Tribal Enrollment (Year, Town, Page), Name of Father, Year, Town, Name of Mother, Year, Town*, as well as *Tribal Enrollments of Parents*. For whatever reason, no card numbers were recorded in the corresponding field on any of the cards.

This and subsequent volumes have been transcribed from National Archives microfilm series M-1186: Roll 67, 1-662 and Roll 68, 663-1424. The page format of this transcription does not follow the microfilm exactly, owing to the space restrictions of the book format, but I have endeavored to include all categories of information supplied in the original. Also, the Dawes Roll No. has been relegated to the Notes area of each transcribed page. The notes section also contains information such as, Other name listings, Transfers to different cards, Birth dates, Death dates, listings on various payrolls with years, even sometimes a mention of a spouse in the doubtful category with card number, spouse possibly from another tribe, or a marriage license and certificate that was on file along with location. Sometimes the notes contain revealing information such as the following, "5/31/99. It is reported that Wm. Washington has this woman on his place and had parties to marry and they have never lived together—Investigate." Interestingly, this tidbit was found not under the representation of Wm. Washington but under that of Head of Household "Frank Osavior." Finally, the category "County" indicates the status of Non-Citizen, ethnicity, or Creek Roll, Cherokee Roll, Chocktaw Roll, etc.

Jeff Bowen
Gallipolis, OH
NativeStudy.com

RESIDENCE: Panola   COUNTY   CARD NO.

POST OFFICE: Colbert, Ind. Ter.   FIELD NO.

	NAME	RELATION-SHIP TO PERSON FIRST NAMED	AGE	SEX	BLOOD	TRIBAL ENROLLMENT		
						YEAR	COUNTY	PAGE
1	Smith, Jourdan Anderson	NAMED	68	M	I.W.	1897	Panola	76
2	" Nancy	Wife	55	F	3/4	1897	"	5
3	" Jordan Cutchentubby	Son	17	M	3/8	1897	"	5

TRIBAL ENROLLMENT OF PARENTS

	NAME OF FATHER	YEAR	COUNTY	NAME OF MOTHER	YEAR	COUNTY
1	Thomas Smith	Dead	Non-Citizen	Nancy Smith	Dead	Non-Citizen
2	Sloan Love	"	Chickasaw Roll	Lottie Love	"	Chickasaw Roll
3	No. 1			No. 2		

(NOTES)

No. 1 On Chickasaw Roll as J.A. Smith   *(No. 1 Dawes' Roll No. 172)*

No. 3 "   "   "   " Canchentubby Smith

See affidavits of Peter Love, Charity Love and H.C. Hamblin relative to the marriage between
    Nos. 1 and 2 filed April 14, 1903.

(Notation illegible)

P.O. Marietta, I.T. 10/30/02   Oct. 10/98.

RESIDENCE: Choctaw Nation 3rd Dist.   ~~COUNTY~~   CARD NO.

POST OFFICE: Stringtown, Ind. Ter.   FIELD NO.

	NAME	RELATION-SHIP TO PERSON FIRST NAMED	AGE	SEX	BLOOD	TRIBAL ENROLLMENT		
						YEAR	COUNTY	PAGE
1	Watson, Edna	NAMED	16	F	1/2			
2	" Jonas J	Son	3,p	M	1/4			

TRIBAL ENROLLMENT OF PARENTS

	NAME OF FATHER	YEAR	COUNTY	NAME OF MOTHER	YEAR	COUNTY
1	Jesse Bond		Jacks Fork County Choctaw Roll	Mary Bond	1897	Chick residing in Choctaw N. 3rd Dist.
2	Julius Watson		" "	No. 1		

(NOTES)

No. 1 On Choctaw Census Record No. 2 Page 487; transferred to Chickasaw Roll by Dawes Com.

No. 1 On Choctaw Roll 1896 Jacks Fork County No. 14085

No. 1 is wife of Julius J. Watson on Choctaw Roll Card #1895.

Oct. 10/98.

CANCELLED Stamped across card

RESIDENCE: Pickens **COUNTY**   **CARD NO.**
POST OFFICE: Chickasha, Ind. Ter.   **FIELD NO.**

	NAME	RELATION-SHIP TO PERSON FIRST NAMED	AGE	SEX	BLOOD	TRIBAL ENROLLMENT		
						YEAR	COUNTY	PAGE
1	Scarlett, Richard James	NAMED	54	M	I.W.	1897	Pontotoc	81
2	" Louisa	Wife	62	F	Full	1897	"	65
3	" Jefferson D.	Son	18	M	1/2	1897	"	65
4	" Edward J.	"	16	"	1/2	1897	"	66
5	" Richard J, Jr.	"	14	"	1/2	1897	"	66

TRIBAL ENROLLMENT OF PARENTS

	NAME OF FATHER	YEAR	COUNTY	NAME OF MOTHER	YEAR	COUNTY
1	Edward Scarlett	Dead	Non-Citizen	Penelope Scarlett	Dead	Non-Citizen
2	(Name Illegible)	"	Chickasaw Roll	Chohonah	"	Chickasaw Roll
3	No. 1			No. 2		
4	No. 1			No. 2		
5	No. 1			No. 2		

(NOTES)

No. 1 See decision of June 13 '04.   (No. 1 Dawes' Roll No. 396)
No. 1 Affidavit of witnesses to marriage to be supplied. Certified copy of record received Oct. 21/98.
   " " Judge who issued marriage license to be supplied. Received Oct. 21/98.
No. 1 On Chickasaw Roll as R.J. Scarlett
No. 3 " " " " J.D. "
No. 4 " " " " E.J. "
No. 5 " " " " R.J. " Jr.
No. 3 Died Oct. 9, 1899. Evidence of Death filed March 23, 1901.
   See testimony of No. 1 taken Oct. 17, 1902.
Certified copy of divorce proceedings between No. 2 and her former husband filed March 19/03.

Oct. 6/98.

RESIDENCE: Choctaw Nation 3rd Dist. ~~COUNTY~~   **CARD NO.**
POST OFFICE: Sitre, Ind. Ter.   **FIELD NO.**

	NAME	RELATION-SHIP TO PERSON FIRST NAMED	AGE	SEX	BLOOD	TRIBAL ENROLLMENT		
						YEAR	COUNTY	PAGE
1	Johnson, Frances	NAMED	21	F	Full	1893	Pontotoc	P.R.#2 122

TRIBAL ENROLLMENT OF PARENTS

	NAME OF FATHER	YEAR	COUNTY	NAME OF MOTHER	YEAR	COUNTY
1	Ah-wan-tan-tubby	Dead	Chickasaw Roll	Chim-ho-che	Dead	Chickasaw Roll

Chickasaw Enrollment Cards 1898-1914
Chickasaw by Blood   Volume IV

(NOTES)

No. 1 Also on 1896 Choctaw Roll Page 367? #13999, as Frances Watson.
On Chickasaw Roll as Francis Johnson.
    Cancelled and transferred to Choctaw Card No. 5683 Aug. 15/98.   8/20/04.

Oct. 5/98.

RESIDENCE: Choctaw Nation 1st Dist.   **COUNTY**   **CARD NO.**
POST OFFICE: Russellville, Ind. Ter.   **FIELD NO.**

	NAME	RELATIONSHIP TO PERSON FIRST NAMED	AGE	SEX	BLOOD	TRIBAL ENROLLMENT YEAR	COUNTY	PAGE
1	Hancock, Robert M	FIRST NAMED	18	M	1/4	1893	Chick residing in Choctaw N. 1st Dist.	No. 2 191
2	" Flora Viola	Dau	10mo	F	1/8			
3	" Katie	Wife	20	F	I.W.			

TRIBAL ENROLLMENT OF PARENTS

	NAME OF FATHER	YEAR	COUNTY	NAME OF MOTHER	YEAR	COUNTY
1	Jarvis Hancock	Dead	Pickens	Grace Hancock	Dead	Non-Citizen
2	No. 1			Katie Hancock		" "
3	Charlie Margaret		non-citz	Mollie Margaret		non-citz

(NOTES)

No. 1 On Chickasaw Roll, Census Page ??
No. 1 On Chickasaw Roll as Robt M. Handcock
No. 1 Husband of Katy Hancock, non-citizen; Certificate of marriage filed June 1st 1902
No. 2 Born Aug. 26th 1901; Enrolled June 1st 1902
No. 3 transferred from Chickasaw card #D451 April 1, 1903   *(No. 3 Dawes' Roll No. 50)*
   See decision of March *(illegible)*

Oct. 5/98.

RESIDENCE: Pickens   **COUNTY**   **CARD NO.**
POST OFFICE: Lebanon, Ind. Ter.   **FIELD NO.**

	NAME	RELATIONSHIP TO PERSON FIRST NAMED	AGE	SEX	BLOOD	TRIBAL ENROLLMENT YEAR	COUNTY	PAGE
1	Archerd, John William	NAMED	34	M	1/32	1897	Pickens	8
2	" Lillian G.	Dau	1mo	F	1/64			
3	" Pineo	Son	11mo	M	1/64			
4	" Cassoe	Wife	25	F	I.W.			

	TRIBAL ENROLLMENT OF PARENTS					
NAME OF FATHER	YEAR	COUNTY	NAME OF MOTHER	YEAR	COUNTY
1	Pineo Archerd (I.W.)	1897	Pickens	Martha Archerd	1897	Pickens
2	No. 1			Cassie Archerd		
3	No. 1			" "		
4	W.J. Banks		non citizen	Sarah Banks		non citizen

(NOTES)

Admitted by Dawes Com Case No. 5 as John Archerd, and no appeal taken
On Chickasaw Roll as John Archard
No. 1 Wife on Chickasaw Card No. D.140
No. 2 Enrolled 6/13/1900
No. 2 Died Aug. 16, 1900; Proof of Death filed Nov. 10, 1902
No. 3 Born Oct. 24th 1901; Enrolled Sept 30th 1902
No. 4 transferred from Chickasaw Card #D140.   *(No. 4 Dawes' Roll No. 289)*
　　See decision of March 5, 1904   Mar. 23, 1904

P.O. Kingston, I.T. 11/6/02   Oct. 5/98.

RESIDENCE: Pickens *COUNTY*　　　　　　　　CARD NO.

POST OFFICE:　　Lebanon, Ind. Ter. (Orphan Home)　　FIELD NO.

	NAME	RELATION-SHIP TO PERSON FIRST NAMED	AGE	SEX	BLOOD	TRIBAL ENROLLMENT		
						YEAR	COUNTY	PAGE
1	Folsome, Isaac	NAMED	17	M	Full	1897	Panola	5
2	" Minnie	Sister	15	F	"	1897	"	5
3	" Willie	Brp	10	M	"	1897	"	5

	TRIBAL ENROLLMENT OF PARENTS					
NAME OF FATHER	YEAR	COUNTY	NAME OF MOTHER	YEAR	COUNTY
1	Henry Folsome	Dead	Chickasaw Roll	Mary Folsome	Dead	Chickasaw Roll
2	" "	"	" "	" "	"	" "
3	" "	"	" "	" "	"	" "

(NOTES)

No. 1 On Chickasaw Roll as [sic], Pickens County, Page 18.
No. 3 "   "   "   [sic],   "   "   "   "

Oct. 5/98.

Chickasaw Enrollment Cards 1898-1914
Chickasaw by Blood   Volume IV

RESIDENCE: Pickens   COUNTY   CARD NO.
POST OFFICE: Linn, Ind. Ter.   FIELD NO.

	NAME	RELATION-SHIP TO PERSON FIRST NAMED	AGE	SEX	BLOOD	TRIBAL ENROLLMENT		
						YEAR	COUNTY	PAGE
1	Irvin, Emmie Elizabeth	NAMED	18	F	1/16	1897	Pickens	25
2	" Walter	Husb	26	M	I.W.			

TRIBAL ENROLLMENT OF PARENTS

	NAME OF FATHER	YEAR	COUNTY	NAME OF MOTHER	YEAR	COUNTY
1	William Archard (I.W.)	1897	Pickens	Nancy Archard	1897	Poclems
2	Mack Irvin		non citizen	Willie Irvin		non citizen

(NOTES)

No. 1 Admitted by Commission in 1891; Chickasaw Card #289
No. 1 Admitted as Emily E. Archard
    On Chickasaw Roll as Rena E. Archard
No. 1 is wife of Walter Irvin on Chickasaw #D137
No. 2 transferred from Chickasaw card #D.137   *(No. 2 Dawes' Roll No. 288)*
    See decision of March 5, 1904 March 23rd 1904.

Oct. 5/98.

RESIDENCE: Pickens   COUNTY   CARD NO.
POST OFFICE: Powell, Ind. Ter.   FIELD NO.

	NAME	RELATION-SHIP TO PERSON FIRST NAMED	AGE	SEX	BLOOD	TRIBAL ENROLLMENT		
						YEAR	COUNTY	PAGE
1	McGee, Alen	NAMED	30	M	3/4	1897	Pickens	12
2	" Maggie	Wife	26	F	I.W.	1897	"	78
3	" Eula	Dau	10	"	3/8	1897	"	12
4	" Willie	"	8	"	3/8	1897	"	12
5	" Dollie	"	6	"	3/8	1897	"	12
6	" Imon	"	3	"	3/8	1897	"	12
7	" Annie	"	10mo	"	3/8			
8	" Frank	Son	5mo	M	3/8			

TRIBAL ENROLLMENT OF PARENTS

	NAME OF FATHER	YEAR	COUNTY	NAME OF MOTHER	YEAR	COUNTY
1	Alen McGee	Dead	Chickasaw Roll	*(Name Illegible)*	Dead	Chickasaw Roll
2	Shu?ley Culp	"	Non citizen	Mary Culp		Non citizen
3	No. 1			No. 2		
4	No. 1			No. 2		
5	No. 1			No. 2		

5

Chickasaw Enrollment Cards 1898-1914
Chickasaw by Blood   Volume IV

6	No. 1			No. 2	
7	No. 1			No. 2	
8	No. 1			No. 2	

(NOTES)

No. 4 On Chickasaw Roll as Willis McGee   *(No. 2 Dawes' Roll No. 836)*
No. 5 Died Oct. 5th 1901; Proof of Death filed Oct. 13th 1902
No. 6 On Chickasaw Roll as Ainon McGee
No. 7 Affidavit of attending physician to be supplied. Received Oct. 5/98.

Oct. 5/98.

RESIDENCE: Pickens   COUNTY   CARD NO.
POST OFFICE: Willis, Ind. Ter.   FIELD NO.

NAME	RELATION-SHIP TO PERSON FIRST NAMED	AGE	SEX	BLOOD	TRIBAL ENROLLMENT		
					YEAR	COUNTY	PAGE
1 Hardwick, David	FIRST NAMED	19	M	1/16	1897	Chick residing in Choctaw N. 3rd Dist.	75
2 " Mattie	Dau	1mo	F	1/32			
3 " Frank H.	Son	2wks	M	1/32			

TRIBAL ENROLLMENT OF PARENTS

	NAME OF FATHER	YEAR	COUNTY	NAME OF MOTHER	YEAR	COUNTY
1	Joe Hardwick	Dead	Pickens	Sally Hardwick	Dead	Non-Citizen
2	No. 1			Mary Hardwick		" "
3	No. 1			" "		" "

(NOTES)
Marriage license and certificate filed June 30, 1902.
No. 2 Enrolled June 30th 1900
No. 3 Born Aug. 23rd 1902; Enrolled Sept. 12, 1902.

Oct. 4/98.

RESIDENCE: Pickens   COUNTY   CARD NO.
POST OFFICE: Linn, Ind. Ter.   FIELD NO.

NAME	RELATION-SHIP TO PERSON FIRST NAMED	AGE	SEX	BLOOD	TRIBAL ENROLLMENT		
					YEAR	COUNTY	PAGE
1 Archerd, William	NAMED	47	M	I.W.	1897	Pickens	78
2 Archerd, Nancy Jane	Wife	35	F	1/8	1897	"	25
3 Gray, Ada B.	Dau	12	"	1/16	1897	"	25
4 Archerd, J. William	Son	10	M	1/16	1897	"	25
5 " Sydney E.	"	8	"	1/16	1897	"	25

TRIBAL ENROLLMENT OF PARENTS

	NAME OF FATHER	YEAR	COUNTY	NAME OF MOTHER	YEAR	COUNTY
1	John W Archard		Non-Citizen	Elizabeth Archard	Dead	Non-Citizen
2	David Burney	Dead	Chickasaw Roll	Emily Burney	"	Chickasaw Roll
3	No. 1			No. 2		
4	No. 1			No. 2		
5	No. 1			No. 2		

(NOTES)

All admitted by Commission in 1896, Chickasaw Case #239.   *(No. 1 Dawes' Roll No. 834)*
No. 2 On Chickasaw Roll as Mary J. Archard
No. 4 "   "   "   " Willie   "
No. 3 is now the wife of Chas Gray, non citizen. Evidence of marriage filed *(illegible)*

Oct. 4/98.

RESIDENCE: Pickens   COUNTY   CARD NO.
POST OFFICE: Marietta, Ind. Ter.   FIELD NO.

	NAME	RELATION- SHIP TO PERSON FIRST NAMED	AGE	SEX	BLOOD	TRIBAL ENROLLMENT		
						YEAR	COUNTY	PAGE
1	Short, Lizzie	NAMED	21	F	1/16	1897	Pickens	13
2	" Maury	Son	18mo	M	1/32	1897	"	86
3	" Morris L.	"	1	M	1/32			

TRIBAL ENROLLMENT OF PARENTS

	NAME OF FATHER	YEAR	COUNTY	NAME OF MOTHER	YEAR	COUNTY
1	Wm F. Morris	Dead	Non-Citizen	Annie Love Morris	Dead	Pickens
2	Falen J. Short	" "	No. 1		
3	" " "	" "	No. 1		

(NOTES)

No. 2 On Chickasaw Roll as Maury Short.   *(No. 2 Dawes' Roll No. 4179)*
No. 2 Proof of Birth received and filed Sept. 25, 1902
No. 3 Enrolled June 8th 1901.

Oct. 4/98.

RESIDENCE: Pickens   COUNTY   CARD NO.
POST OFFICE: Marietta, Ind. Ter.   FIELD NO.

	NAME	RELATION- SHIP TO PERSON FIRST NAMED	AGE	SEX	BLOOD	TRIBAL ENROLLMENT		
						YEAR	COUNTY	PAGE
1	Love, Overton	NAMED	75	M	1/8	1897	Pickens	12
2	" Harriet	Wife	56	F	1/16	1897	"	12

3	"	Ruby Belle		Dau	18	F	3/32	1897	"	12
4	"	Hattie Byrd		"	16	"	3/32	1897	"	12
5	"	Jodie Jessie Menota		"	13	"	3/32	1897	"	12
6	"	Henry O.		Son	27	M	3/8	1897	"	12
7	Hill, Nellie Pynum		Void	Dau	22	F	3/8	1897	"	12
8	"	Mamie	Void	Gr.Dau	4	"	3/16	1897	"	13

TRIBAL ENROLLMENT OF PARENTS

	NAME OF FATHER	YEAR	COUNTY	NAME OF MOTHER	YEAR	COUNTY
1	Henry Love	Dead	Chickasaw Roll	Sallie Love	Dead	Non Citizen
2	John Byrd	"	non citizen	Mary Byrd	"	Chickasaw Roll
3	No. 1			No. 2		
4	No. 1			No. 2		
5	No. 1			No. 2		
6	No. 1			Martha Love	Dead	Pickens
7	No. 1			" "	"	"
8	Allen Love Hill	Dead	Non Citizen	No. 7		

(NOTES)

No. 1 On Chickasaw Roll as O.   Love
No. 2 "   "   "   " Hattie   "
No. 3 "   "   "   " Ruby   "
No. 4 "   "   "   " Bridie "
No. 5 "   "   "   " Jadie   "
No. 7 "   "   "   " Nellie Hill
Nos, 7 & 8 Transferred to Card #1556 Sept. 12th 1899
No. 5 is 18 years old, see testimony of June 2, 1903.

Oct. 4/98.

RESIDENCE: Pickens COUNTY						CARD NO.			
POST OFFICE: Lebanon, Ind. Ter.						FIELD NO.			

	NAME	RELATION-SHIP TO PERSON FIRST NAMED	AGE	SEX	BLOOD	TRIBAL ENROLLMENT		
						YEAR	COUNTY	PAGE
1	Whitesel, Jerome	NAMED	49	M	I.W.	1897	Pickens	77
2	" Mary Elizabeth	Wife	36	F	1/16	1897	"	9
3	" Katie May	Dau	12	"	1/32	1897	"	9
4	" Freddie Jerome	Son	4	M	1/32	1897	"	9
5	" Willis Love	"	2	"	1/32	1897	"	9
6	" Zulah	Dau	3mo	F	1/32			

	NAME OF FATHER	YEAR	COUNTY	NAME OF MOTHER	YEAR	COUNTY
			TRIBAL ENROLLMENT OF PARENTS			
1	George Whitesel	Dead	Non citizen	Lydia Whitesel	Dead	Non citizen
2	John Stubbefield	"	" "	Caroline Stubbefield now Ayers	1897	Pickens
3	No. 1			No. 2		
4	No. 1			No. 2		
5	No. 1			No. 2		
6	No. 1			No. 2		

(NOTES)

No. 2 On Chickasaw Roll as M.E. Whitsell   *(No. 1 Dawes' Roll No. 148)*
No. 3 "   "   " " Hattie "
No. 4 "   "   " " Freddie "
No. 5 "   "   " " Willie "
No. 6 Enrolled Nov. 4, 1899
Affidavit as to marriage between Nos. 1 and 2 *(remainder illegible).*

P.O. Sulphur, I.T. 9/23/02   Oct. 4/98.

RESIDENCE: Tishomingo COUNTY				CARD NO.			
POST OFFICE: Tishomingo, Ind. Ter.				FIELD NO.			

	NAME	RELATION-SHIP TO PERSON FIRST NAMED	AGE	SEX	BLOOD	TRIBAL ENROLLMENT		
						YEAR	COUNTY	PAGE
1	McSwain, Laura	NAMED	10	F	3/8	1897	Tishomingo	34
2	" Charles	Father	36	M	I.W.	1897	Pickens	79

	NAME OF FATHER	YEAR	COUNTY	NAME OF MOTHER	YEAR	COUNTY
			TRIBAL ENROLLMENT OF PARENTS			
1	Charles McSwain		White man	Amanda McSwain	Dead	Tishomingo
2	Moses S. McSwain	dead	Non citizen	Cynthia McSwain		Non citizen

(NOTES)

No. 2 formerly the husband of Amanda McSwain, formerly Myers, a recognized citizen by blood of the Chickasaw Nation, now deceased. Later, No. 2 married Belle McSwain (nee Brown) a recognized and enrolled citizen by blood of the Chickasaw Nation on Chickasaw card #1710, Chick roll #4848.
No. 2 originally listed for enrollment Oct. 4/98 on Chickasaw card #D.133; transferred to this card Dec. 15, 1904.
     See decision of Nov. 29, 1904.

                                               Oct. 4/98.

RESIDENCE: Pickens COUNTY   CARD NO.
POST OFFICE: Ardmore, Ind. Ter.   FIELD NO.

NAME	RELATION-SHIP TO PERSON FIRST NAMED	AGE	SEX	BLOOD	TRIBAL ENROLLMENT		
					YEAR	COUNTY	PAGE
1 Harrison, Maud	NAMED	19	F	1/32	1897	Pickens	13
2 " ~~Robert Lee Rankins~~	~~Son~~	~~1mo~~	M	~~1/64~~	DIED PRIOR TO SEPTEMBER 25 1902		
3 " Emma Eviline	Dau	8mo	F	1/64			
4 " George William	husband	25	M	I.W.			

TRIBAL ENROLLMENT OF PARENTS

NAME OF FATHER	YEAR	COUNTY	NAME OF MOTHER	YEAR	COUNTY
1 Bill Watkins	Dead	non citizen	Bettie Watkins	Dead	Pickens
2 ~~George Harrison~~		~~white man~~	~~No.1~~		
3 " "		" "	No. 1		
4 James Harrison	Dead	Non-Citizen	Mary Harrison	Dead	Non-Citizen

(NOTES)

No. 1 Husband, George William Harrison, on Chickasaw D.132
No. 1 On Chickasaw Roll as Maude Watkins
No. 2 Died May 9th 1899. Proof of Death filed *(illegible)* 3, 1902
No. 3 Enrolled July 16th 1901
No. 4 transferred from Chickasaw Card #D132   *(No. 4 Dawes' Roll No. 194)*
See decision of May 5, 1902.

Oct. 4/1898.

RESIDENCE: Pickens COUNTY   CARD NO.
POST OFFICE: McMillan, Ind. Ter.   FIELD NO.

NAME	RELATION-SHIP TO PERSON FIRST NAMED	AGE	SEX	BLOOD	TRIBAL ENROLLMENT		
					YEAR	COUNTY	PAGE
1 Gardner, Benjamin Shannon	NAMED	39	M	I.W.	1897	Pickens	77
2 " Annie	Wife	28	F	1/2	1897	"	11
3 " John	Son	10	M	1/4	1897	"	11
4 " Cleveland	"	8	"	1/4	1897	"	11
5 " Sam	"	6	"	1/4	1897	"	11
6 " Maggie	Dau	1mo	F	1/4			
7 " Albert	Son	1 1/2mo	M	1/4			

TRIBAL ENROLLMENT OF PARENTS

NAME OF FATHER	YEAR	COUNTY	NAME OF MOTHER	YEAR	COUNTY
1 Albert Gardner		non citizen	Malinda Gardner	Dead	Non Citizen
2 McGee	Dead		McGee	Dead	

3	No. 1			No. 2	
4	No. 1			No. 2	
5	No. 1			No. 2	
6	No. 1			No. 2	
7	No. 1			No. 2	

(NOTES)

No. 1 On Chickasaw Roll as *(Illegible)* Gardner

No. 1 Enrolled January 3rd 1901

(No. 1 Dawes' Roll No. 147)

Oct. 4/98.

RESIDENCE: Pickens   COUNTY   CARD NO.

POST OFFICE: Kingston, Ind. Ter.   FIELD NO.

NAME	RELATION-SHIP TO PERSON FIRST NAMED	AGE	SEX	BLOOD	TRIBAL ENROLLMENT		
					YEAR	COUNTY	PAGE
1 Sealy, Willie		19	M	Full	1897	Pickens	23

TRIBAL ENROLLMENT OF PARENTS

NAME OF FATHER	YEAR	COUNTY	NAME OF MOTHER	YEAR	COUNTY
1 Dave Sealy	1897	Pickens	Nancy Sealy	Dead	Pickens

(NOTES)

Susie Sealy, wife of No. 1 on Chickasaw Card R #82. Marriage license and certificate between
Willie Sealy and Susie Morton, filed this date on Chickasaw R. #82.

Oct. 4/98.

RESIDENCE: Pickens   COUNTY   CARD NO.

POST OFFICE: Brownville, Ind. Ter.   FIELD NO.

NAME	RELATION-SHIP TO PERSON FIRST NAMED	AGE	SEX	BLOOD	TRIBAL ENROLLMENT		
					YEAR	COUNTY	PAGE
1 Kaney, Harmon		37	M	Full	1897	Pickens	25
2 " Ida Belle	Dau	12	F	1/2	1897	"	25
3 " ~~Amos~~	~~Son~~	~~10~~	~~M~~	~~1/2~~	~~1893~~	"	~~130~~
4 " ~~Ada~~	"	~~6~~	"	~~1/2~~	~~1893~~	"	

TRIBAL ENROLLMENT OF PARENTS

NAME OF FATHER	YEAR	COUNTY	NAME OF MOTHER	YEAR	COUNTY
1 Wilson Kaney	Dead	Pickens	Cassie Kaney	Dead	Pickens
2 No. 1			Belle Kaney	"	Non-Citizen
3 ~~No. 1~~			" "	"	" "
4 ~~No. 1~~			" "	"	" "

11

(NOTES)

No. 1 On Chickasaw Roll as H. Kaney

No. 1 now the Husband of Mary Long on Chickasaw Card #506. Evidence of marriage filed July 22nd 1902.

No. 2 On Chickasaw Roll as Ida Kaney

No. 3 "   "   " " Amos "

No. 3 Died March 20th 1899. Proof of Death filed Nov. 6, 1902;

No. 4 On Chickasaw Roll as Edith Kaney

No. 4 Died Oct. 29th 1900; Proof of Death filed Nov. 6th 1902

P.O. Woodville, I.T.   Oct. 4/98.

RESIDENCE: Pickens COUNTY		CARD NO.					
POST OFFICE: Woodville, Ind. Ter.		FIELD NO.					

	NAME	RELATION-SHIP TO PERSON FIRST NAMED	AGE	SEX	BLOOD	TRIBAL ENROLLMENT		
						YEAR	COUNTY	PAGE
1	Mutz, Jake	NAMED	36	M	I.W.	1897	Pickens	77
2	" Lizzie	Wife	25	F	1/16	1897	"	11
3	" Mamie Frances	Dau	9	"	1/32	1897	"	11
4	" James Henry	Son	4	M	1/32	1897	"	11
5	" Joe Franklin	"	2	"	1/32			
6	" Edwin Willis	"	2mo	"	1/32			
7	" Jesse Lee	"	2mo	"	1/32			

	TRIBAL ENROLLMENT OF PARENTS						
	NAME OF FATHER	YEAR	COUNTY	NAME OF MOTHER	YEAR	COUNTY
1	Jacob Mutz		Non citizen	Margaret Mutz	Dead	Non-citizen
2	Henry Earls	Dead	" "	Katie O'Brien	1897	Panola
3	No. 1			No. 2		
4	No. 1			No. 2		
5	No. 1			No. 2		
6	No. 1			No. 2		
7	No. 1			No. 2		

(NOTES)

No. 3 On Chickasaw Roll as Mamie Mutz   *(No. 1 Dawes' Roll No. 146)*

No. 4 "   "   " " James "

No. 5 Affidavit of attending physician to be supplied. Received Oct. 21/98.

No. 6 Enrolled Mar. 6/99

No. 7 Enrolled July 27th 1901

No. 5 Affidavits relative to the enrollment of Joe Franklin Mead in 1896 filed January 27, 1903

P.O. Ninnekah, I.T.   Oct. 4/98.

Chickasaw Enrollment Cards 1898-1914
Chickasaw by Blood   Volume IV

RESIDENCE: Pickens   COUNTY
POST OFFICE: Lebanon, Ind. Ter.

CARD NO.
FIELD NO.

NAME	RELATION-SHIP TO PERSON FIRST NAMED	AGE	SEX	BLOOD	TRIBAL ENROLLMENT		
					YEAR	COUNTY	PAGE
1 McLish, Millie	NAMED	40	F	Full	1897	Pickens	25
2 Pratt, Robert	Son	18	M	"	1897	"	25
3 McLish, Alice	Dau	9	F	"	1897	"	25
4 " Allie	"	6	"	"	1897	"	25
5 " Rosie	"	4	"	"	1897	"	25

TRIBAL ENROLLMENT OF PARENTS

	NAME OF FATHER	YEAR	COUNTY	NAME OF MOTHER	YEAR	COUNTY
1	Okchantubby	Dead	Chickasaw Roll	Eu-thli-ke	Dead	Chickasaw Roll
2	Henry Pratt	"	Tishomingo	No. 1		
3	Frazier McLish	1897	Pickens	No. 1		
4	" "	1897	"	No. 1		
5	" "	1897	"	No. 1		

(NOTES)

No. 1 On Chickasaw Roll as Mollie McLish
No. 4 "   "   " " Eli   "
No. 5 "   "   " " Ruthie "
(Notation illegible)

Oct. 4/98.

RESIDENCE: Pickens   COUNTY
POST OFFICE: Lebanon, Ind. Ter.

CARD NO.
FIELD NO.

NAME	RELATION-SHIP TO PERSON FIRST NAMED	AGE	SEX	BLOOD	TRIBAL ENROLLMENT		
					YEAR	COUNTY	PAGE
1 Archerd, Pineo	NAMED	45	M	I.W.	1897	Pickens	77
2 " Martha	Wife	46	F	1/16	1897	"	8
3 " Henry Adolphus	Son	20	M	1/32	1897	"	8
4 " James Edward	"	18	"	1/32	1897	"	8
5 " Charlie Vernon	"	11	"	1/32	1897	"	8
6 " Effie Jane	Dau	9	F	1/32	1897	"	8
7 " Cora Maude	"	7	"	1/32	1897	"	8
8 " Max	Son	5	M	1/32	1897	"	8

TRIBAL ENROLLMENT OF PARENTS

	NAME OF FATHER	YEAR	COUNTY	NAME OF MOTHER	YEAR	COUNTY
1	John W. Archer		non-citizen	Elizabeth Archer	Dead	Non-citizen

13

2	Christopher Moore	Dead	"	"	Catherine Moore	"	Chickasaw Roll
3	No. 1				No. 2		
4	No. 1				No. 2		
5	No. 1				No. 2		
6	No. 1				No. 2		
7	No. 1				No. 2		
8	No. 1				No. 2		

(NOTES)

All admitted by Dawes Com. Case No. 5 and No Appeal taken.

No. 1 On Chickasaw Roll as Pinea Archer   *(No. 1 Dawes' Roll No. 436)*
No. 3 "   "   "   " Henry Archard
No. 4 "   "   "   " Edward   "
No. 5 "   "   "   " Charley   "
No. 6 "   "   "   " Effy   "
No. 7 "   "   "   " Cora   "

P.O. Madill, I.T.   Oct. 4/98.

RESIDENCE: Pickens   COUNTY   CARD NO.
POST OFFICE: Willis Ind. Ter.   FIELD NO.

NAME	RELATION-SHIP TO PERSON FIRST NAMED	AGE	SEX	BLOOD	TRIBAL ENROLLMENT		
					YEAR	COUNTY	PAGE
1 Massey, Marietta	NAMED	20	F	1/32	1897	Pickens	11

TRIBAL ENROLLMENT OF PARENTS

NAME OF FATHER	YEAR	COUNTY	NAME OF MOTHER	YEAR	COUNTY
1 John Huff	Dead	Non-Citizen	Nannie Huff	Dead	Pickens

(NOTES)
No. 1 is now the wife of Enoch L. Massey on Chickasaw Card #D368, Sept. 20 1902.

Oct. 4/98

RESIDENCE: Pickens   COUNTY   CARD NO.
POST OFFICE: Cliff, Ind. Ter.   FIELD NO.

NAME	RELATION-SHIP TO PERSON FIRST NAMED	AGE	SEX	BLOOD	TRIBAL ENROLLMENT		
					YEAR	COUNTY	PAGE
1 Mutz, Ida	NAMED	21	F	3/8	1897	Pickens	8
2 " Ada	Dau	3	"	3/16	1897	"	8
3 " Fred	Son	2wks	M	3/16			
4 " Henry Overton	"	2mo	"	3/16			

14

| 5 | " George | husband | 36 | M | I.W, | | |

TRIBAL ENROLLMENT OF PARENTS

	NAME OF FATHER	YEAR	COUNTY	NAME OF MOTHER	YEAR	COUNTY
1	Dave Hardwick	Dead	Pickens	Crecy Merriman	1897	Pickens
2	George Mutz		white man	No. 1		
3	" "		" "	No. 1		
4	" "		" "	No. 1		
5	Jake Mutz		non citz	Margaret Mutz	Dead	non citz

(NOTES)

No. 1 Husband, George Mutz, on Chickasaw Card D.129
No. 3 Enrolled Nov. 21/98
No. 4 Enrol;led April 9, 1901
No. 5 transferred from Chickasaw Card #D.129 April 6, 1903.   *(No. 5 Dawes' Roll No. 49)*
   See decision of March 6, 1903.

Oct. 4/98.

RESIDENCE: Pickens   **COUNTY**   **CARD NO.**
POST OFFICE: Marietta, Ind. Ter.   **FIELD NO.**

NAME	RELATION-SHIP TO PERSON FIRST NAMED	AGE	SEX	BLOOD	TRIBAL ENROLLMENT		
					YEAR	COUNTY	PAGE
1 Washington, Jeremiah Calvin	NAMED	13	M	1/8	1897	Pickens	11
2 " Russell Love	Bro	10	"	1/8	1897	"	11

TRIBAL ENROLLMENT OF PARENTS

	NAME OF FATHER	YEAR	COUNTY	NAME OF MOTHER	YEAR	COUNTY
1	F.C. Washington		non-citizen	Mabel Washington	Dead	Pickens
2	" "		" "	" "	"	"

(NOTES)

No. 1 On Chickasaw Roll as Cal Washington
No. 2 "   "   "   " Love   "
Nos. 1 & 2 also on Chickasaw Card C.67. Admitted by U.S. Court, Ardmore, Dec. 22, 1898. Court Case #8;
   May 17 1900

CANCELLED Stamped across card
Duplicate of Nos. 2 & 3[sic] on #C.67

Chickasaw Enrollment Cards 1898-1914
Chickasaw by Blood   Volume IV

RESIDENCE: Pickens COUNTY CARD NO.
POST OFFICE: Cliff, Ind. Ter. FIELD NO.

	NAME	RELATION-SHIP TO PERSON FIRST NAMED	AGE	SEX	BLOOD	TRIBAL ENROLLMENT		
						YEAR	COUNTY	PAGE
1	Merriman, Tate	FIRST NAMED	36	M	I.W.	1893	Pickens	P.R. #2 150
2	" Crecy	Wife	38	F	1/2	1897	"	8
3	Hardwick, Brit	StepSon	18	M	3/8	1897	"	8
4	" Eastman	" "	15	"	3/8	1897	"	8
5	" Janie	" Dau	12	F	3/8	1897	"	8
6	" Mayetta	Dau of No. 3	1yr 5mo	"	3/16			

TRIBAL ENROLLMENT OF PARENTS

	NAME OF FATHER	YEAR	COUNTY	NAME OF MOTHER	YEAR	COUNTY
1	(Name Illegible)	Dead	Non Citizen	(Name Illegible)	Dead	Non Citizen
2	Will Harney	"	" " "	Maulsie Harney	"	Chickasaw Roll
3	Dave Hardwick	"	Pickens	No. 2		
4	" "	"	"	No. 2		
5	" "	"	"	No. 2		
6	No. 3			Minnie Hardwick		Non-citizen

(NOTES)
Affidavit of R.B. Willis as to marriage of Nos. 1 & 2 filed Nov. 6th 1902
No. 3 now the Husband of Minnie Snellgood, non-citizen, Evidence of marriage filed July 17th 1902
No. 5 On Chickasaw Roll as Jincy Hardwick
No. 6 Born Feb. 16th 1901. Enrolled July 17th 1902
No. 1 in penitentiary at Ada
11/2/02 Mother of No. 6 living at Ego, I.T. Father in Ft. Leavenworth Penitentiary.

Oct. 4th/98.

RESIDENCE: Pickens COUNTY CARD NO.
POST OFFICE: Willis, Ind. Ter. FIELD NO.

	NAME	RELATION-SHIP TO PERSON FIRST NAMED	AGE	SEX	BLOOD	TRIBAL ENROLLMENT		
						YEAR	COUNTY	PAGE
1	Hardwick, Lilburn	FIRST NAMED	16	M	1/16	1897	Chick residing in Choctaw N. 3rd Dist.	15

TRIBAL ENROLLMENT OF PARENTS

	NAME OF FATHER	YEAR	COUNTY	NAME OF MOTHER	YEAR	COUNTY
1	Joe Hardwick	Dead	Pickens	Sally Hardwick	Dead	Non Citizen

(NOTES)
No. 1 On Chickasaw Roll as Lilburn Hardwick.

Oct. 4/98.

Chickasaw Enrollment Cards 1898-1914
Chickasaw by Blood   Volume IV

RESIDENCE: Pickens COUNTY   CARD NO.
POST OFFICE: Willis, Ind. Ter.   FIELD NO.

	NAME	RELATIONSHIP TO PERSON FIRST NAMED	AGE	SEX	BLOOD	TRIBAL ENROLLMENT		
						YEAR	COUNTY	PAGE
1	Hays, Jesse S.	NAMED	46	M	I.W.			
2	" Amelia	Wife	38	F	1/16	1897	Pickens	12
3	" ~~John Benjamin~~	~~Son~~	~~23~~	~~M~~	~~1/32~~	~~1897~~	~~"~~	~~12~~
4	" Willie	"	19	"	1/32	1897	"	12
5	" James Osa	"	9	"	1/32	1897	"	12
6	" Viola	Dau	5	F	1/32	1897	"	12
7	" Eula	"	2wks	"	1/32			

TRIBAL ENROLLMENT OF PARENTS

	NAME OF FATHER	YEAR	COUNTY	NAME OF MOTHER	YEAR	COUNTY
1	John A. Hays	Dead	Non-Citizen	Eliza Hays	Dead	Non-Citizen
2	J.H. Willis	"	" "	Elvira Willis	"	Pickens
3	~~No. 1~~			~~No. 2~~		
4	No. 1			No. 2		
5	No. 1			No. 2		
6	No. 1			No. 2		
7	No. 1			No. 2		

(NOTES)

No. 3 Transferred to Chickasaw Card *(remainder illegible)*   *(No. 1 Dawes' Roll No. 383)*
No. 3 On Chickasaw Card as Ben Hays
No. 5 "   "   "   " Osie "
No. 7 Enrolled Nov. 4th 1899

                                                    Oct. 4/98.

RESIDENCE: Pickens COUNTY   CARD NO.
POST OFFICE: Holder, Ind. Ter.   FIELD NO.

	NAME	RELATIONSHIP TO PERSON FIRST NAMED	AGE	SEX	BLOOD	TRIBAL ENROLLMENT		
						YEAR	COUNTY	PAGE
1	Holder, Lottie	NAMED	43	F	1/2	1897	Pickens	8
2	" Ed DEAD	Son	15	M	1/4	1897	"	8
3	" Eula	Dau	13	F	1/4	1897	"	8
4	" Ardie	"	7	"	1/4	1897	"	8
5	" Daisy	"	3	"	1/4	1897	"	8

17

	TRIBAL ENROLLMENT OF PARENTS					
NAME OF FATHER	YEAR	COUNTY	NAME OF MOTHER	YEAR	COUNTY
1 *(Illegible)* Love	Dead	Pickens	Sarah Love	Dead	Pickens
2 Geo. W. Holder		non-citizen	No. 1		
3 " " "		" "	No. 1		
4 " " "		" "	No. 1		
5 " " "		" "	No. 1		

(NOTES)
No. 1 Husband, George Washington Holder, on Chickasaw D.128
No. 2 Died Dec. 8th 1900; See testimony of Geo. W. Holder May 20th 1902.

Oct. 4/98.

RESIDENCE: Tishomingo   COUNTY   CARD NO.
POST OFFICE: Ravia, Ind. Ter.   FIELD NO.

NAME	RELATION-SHIP TO PERSON FIRST NAMED	AGE	SEX	BLOOD	TRIBAL ENROLLMENT		
					YEAR	COUNTY	PAGE
1 Hamilton, Henderson	NAMED	21	M	Full	1893	Tishomingo	119

	TRIBAL ENROLLMENT OF PARENTS					
NAME OF FATHER	YEAR	COUNTY	NAME OF MOTHER	YEAR	COUNTY
1 Amos Hamilton	Dead	Tishomingo	Sealy Hamilton	Dead	Tishomingo

(NOTES)
On 1897 Chickasaw Census Roll Page 97,

Oct. 4/98.

RESIDENCE: Pickens   COUNTY   CARD NO.
POST OFFICE: Woodville, Ind. Ter.   FIELD NO.

NAME	RELATION-SHIP TO PERSON FIRST NAMED	AGE	SEX	BLOOD	TRIBAL ENROLLMENT		
					YEAR	COUNTY	PAGE
1 Coffee, Thomas Jefferson	NAMED	35	M	I.W.	1897	Pickens	18
2 " Luella	Wife	25	F	1/32	1897	"	9
3 " John Lewis	Son	8	M	1/64	1897	"	9
4 " Cora	Dau	3	F	1/64	1897	"	9
5 " Mamie	"	6mo	"	1/64			

	TRIBAL ENROLLMENT OF PARENTS					
NAME OF FATHER	YEAR	COUNTY	NAME OF MOTHER	YEAR	COUNTY
1 Samuel Coffee	Dead	Non Citizen	Harriet Coffee	Dead	Non Citizen
2 *(Name Illegible)*	"	" " "	Ellen *(Illegible)*	1897	Pickens

18

3	No. 1			No. 2		
4	No. 1			No. 2		
5	No. 1			No. 2		

(NOTES)

No. 1 On Chickasaw Roll as Tom Coffee
No. 3 "   "   " " John "
No. 5 Enrolled 6/14/1900

P.O. Helen, I.T. 11/5/02   Oct. 4/98.

RESIDENCE:	Pickens	COUNTY				CARD NO.		
POST OFFICE:	Marietta, Ind. Ter.					FIELD NO.		

	NAME	RELATION-SHIP TO PERSON FIRST NAMED	AGE	SEX	BLOOD	TRIBAL ENROLLMENT		
						YEAR	COUNTY	PAGE
1	King, Robert Oliver		18	M	1/8	1897	Pickens	
2	" Lou May	Sister	16	F	1/8	1897	"	

	TRIBAL ENROLLMENT OF PARENTS							
	NAME OF FATHER	YEAR	COUNTY	NAME OF MOTHER		YEAR	COUNTY	
1	Lee King		Non-Citizen	Maude King		Dead	Pickens	
2	" "		" "	" "		"	"	

(NOTES)

No. 1 On Chickasaw Roll as R.O. King
Nos. 1 & 2 were admitted by U.S. Court, Ardmore, December 22nd 1897; Court Case #7
No. 2 *(remainder illegible)*

CANCELLED Stamped across card
transferred to C.91

Oct. 4/98.

RESIDENCE:	Pickens	COUNTY				CARD NO.		
POST OFFICE:	Grantham, Ind. Ter.					FIELD NO.		

	NAME	RELATION-SHIP TO PERSON FIRST NAMED	AGE	SEX	BLOOD	TRIBAL ENROLLMENT		
						YEAR	COUNTY	PAGE
1	Monday, Alexander Elson		38	M	I.W.	1897	Pickens	78
2	" Mary	Wife	24	F	1/32	1897	"	16
3	" Jim	Son	7	M	1/64	1897	"	16
4	" Everet	"	5	"	1/64	1897	"	16

19

Chickasaw Enrollment Cards 1898-1914
Chickasaw by Blood   Volume IV

	TRIBAL ENROLLMENT OF PARENTS					
	NAME OF FATHER	YEAR	COUNTY	NAME OF MOTHER	YEAR	COUNTY
1	Wm Monday	Dead	Non-Citizen	Viney F. Monday	Dead	Non-Citizen
2	Brit Willis	1897	Pickens	Margaret Willis	1897	Pickens
3	No. 1			No. 2		
4	No. 1			No. 2		

(NOTES)

No. 1 On Chickasaw Roll as A.E. Monday.

(No. 1 Dawes' Roll No. 145)

P.O. Madill, I.T. 11/10/02

Oct. 4/98.

RESIDENCE: Pickens   COUNTY   CARD NO.

POST OFFICE: Powell, Ind. Ter.   FIELD NO.

	NAME	RELATION-SHIP TO PERSON FIRST NAMED	AGE	SEX	BLOOD	TRIBAL ENROLLMENT		
						YEAR	COUNTY	PAGE
1	Hardwick, Joe B.	NAMED	18	M	1/16	1897	Chick residing in Choctaw N. 3rd Dist.	75
2	" Montia B.	Dau	2mo	F	1/32	DIED PRIOR TO SEPTEMBER 25 1902		

	TRIBAL ENROLLMENT OF PARENTS					
	NAME OF FATHER	YEAR	COUNTY	NAME OF MOTHER	YEAR	COUNTY
1	Joe Hardwick	Dead	Pickens	Sally Hardwick	Dead	Non Citizen
2	No. 1			Alma Bell Hardwick		" "

(NOTES)

No. 1 is the husband of Alma Bell Hardwick, non citizen. Evidence of marriage filed Nov. 9th 1901

No. 2 Born Aug. 29, 1901; Enrolled Nov. 7th 1901

No. 2 Died Dec 12, 1901; Proof of Death filed Nov. 11th

Oct. 4/98.

RESIDENCE: Pickens   COUNTY   CARD NO.

POST OFFICE: Ardmore, Ind. Ter.   FIELD NO.

	NAME	RELATION-SHIP TO PERSON FIRST NAMED	AGE	SEX	BLOOD	TRIBAL ENROLLMENT		
						YEAR	COUNTY	PAGE
1	Bonner, Margaret	NAMED	49	F	1/16	1897	Pickens	31
2	" James	Husband	38	M	I.W.			

	TRIBAL ENROLLMENT OF PARENTS					
	NAME OF FATHER	YEAR	COUNTY	NAME OF MOTHER	YEAR	COUNTY
1	Jim Boyd	Dead	Non Citizen	Nancy Boyd	Dead	Pickens
2	F?? Bonner	Dead	" "	*(Name Illegible)*	Dead	non citizen

20

(NOTES)

No. 1 is wife of James Bonner on Chickasaw Card #D.127
Nos. 1 & 2 were separated in 1898
No. 2 originally listed for enrollment on Chickasaw card D.127 Oct. 4/98
transferred to the card Feb. 5, 1905. See decision *(remainder illegible)*

Oct. 4/98.

RESIDENCE: Pickens COUNTY					CARD NO.			
POST OFFICE: Cumberland, Ind. Ter.					FIELD NO.			
	RELATION-SHIP TO PERSON FIRST NAMED	AGE	SEX	BLOOD	TRIBAL ENROLLMENT			
NAME					YEAR	COUNTY	PAGE	
1 Ross, James F.	NAMED	43	M	I.W.	1897	Pickens	77	
2 " Joseph F.	Son	8	"	1/32	1897	"	9	

TRIBAL ENROLLMENT OF PARENTS							
NAME OF FATHER	YEAR	COUNTY	NAME OF MOTHER	YEAR	COUNTY		
1 Alen Ross	Dead	Non Citizen	Jane Ross		Non-Citizen		
2 No. 1			Ella Ross	Dead	Pickens		

(NOTES)

No. 1 Admitted as an intermarried citizen and   *(No. 1 Dawes' Roll No. 435)*
No. 2 as a citizen by Blood by Dawes Commission in 1896 Chickasaw Case #78   *(No. 2 Dawes' Roll No. 4178)*
No. 1 Marriage license and certificate to be supplied. Received Oct. 3/98.
No. 1 On Chickasaw Roll as James Ross
No. 2 " " " " Joseph "
No. 1 is father of Arvilla Ross on Chickasaw Card D #388

Oct. 4/98

RESIDENCE: Pickens COUNTY					CARD NO.			
POST OFFICE: Woodville, Ind. Ter.					FIELD NO.			
	RELATION-SHIP TO PERSON FIRST NAMED	AGE	SEX	BLOOD	TRIBAL ENROLLMENT			
NAME					YEAR	COUNTY	PAGE	
1 Ayers, Caroline	NAMED	63	F	1/16	1897	Pickens	13	

TRIBAL ENROLLMENT OF PARENTS							
NAME OF FATHER	YEAR	COUNTY	NAME OF MOTHER	YEAR	COUNTY		
1 J.H. Willis	Dead	Non Citizen	Amanda Willis	Dead	Pickens		

(NOTES)

Sirname on Chickasaw Roll as Ayes
No. 1 Died in December, 1899.

Oct. 4/98.

CANCELLED Stamped across card

RESIDENCE: Pickens COUNTY   CARD NO.
POST OFFICE: Woodville, Ind. Ter.   FIELD NO.

	NAME	RELATION-SHIP TO PERSON FIRST NAMED	AGE	SEX	BLOOD	TRIBAL ENROLLMENT		
						YEAR	COUNTY	PAGE
1	Moore, Ellen	NAMED	54	F	1/16	1897	Pickens	12
2	Christian, Holmes	Son	18	M	1/32	1897	"	12
3	" Maude	Dau	12	F	1/32	1897	"	12

TRIBAL ENROLLMENT OF PARENTS

	NAME OF FATHER	YEAR	COUNTY	NAME OF MOTHER	YEAR	COUNTY
1	J.H. Willis	Dead	Non-Citizen	Amanda Willis	Dead	Pickens
2	John Christian	"	" "	No. 1		
3	" "	"	" "	No. 1		

(NOTES)
No. 1 is wife of Ransom Moore on Chickasaw Card #D.124.

Oct. 4/98.

RESIDENCE: Pickens COUNTY   CARD NO.
POST OFFICE: Woodville, Ind. Ter.   FIELD NO.

	NAME	RELATION-SHIP TO PERSON FIRST NAMED	AGE	SEX	BLOOD	TRIBAL ENROLLMENT		
						YEAR	COUNTY	PAGE
1	Christian, Walter	NAMED	25	M	1/32	1897	Pickens	13

TRIBAL ENROLLMENT OF PARENTS

	NAME OF FATHER	YEAR	COUNTY	NAME OF MOTHER	YEAR	COUNTY
1	James Christian	Dead	Non Citizen	Caroline Ayers	1897	Pickens

(NOTES)
11/5/02 Said to be incompetent and that Jerome Whitsell is looking after him.
P.O. of Jerome Whitsell is Sulphur, I.T.

Oct. 4/98.

RESIDENCE: Pickens COUNTY   CARD NO.
POST OFFICE: Woodville, Ind. Ter.   FIELD NO.

	NAME	RELATION-SHIP TO PERSON FIRST NAMED	AGE	SEX	BLOOD	TRIBAL ENROLLMENT		
						YEAR	COUNTY	PAGE
1	~~Hicks, Amanda~~	NAMED	~~37~~	~~F~~	~~1/16~~	~~1897~~	~~Pickens~~	~~15~~
2	Christian, Lee	Dau	13	"	1/32	1897	"	15
3	" John	Son	9	M	1/32	1897	"	15
4	" Lottie	Dau	6	F	1/32	1897	"	15

5	Hicks, Tom	Son	3	M	1/32	1897	"	15
6	~~" Charley~~	"	~~3mo~~	"	~~1/32~~			
7	" Daniel L.	"	2mo	"	1/32			

TRIBAL ENROLLMENT OF PARENTS

	NAME OF FATHER	YEAR	COUNTY	NAME OF MOTHER	YEAR	COUNTY
~~1~~	~~Ed. McLaughlin~~	~~Dead~~	~~Pickens~~	~~Lottie McLoughlin now Vann~~	~~1897~~	~~Pickens~~
2	Walter Christian	"	Non-Citizen	No. 1		
3	" "	"	" "	No. 1		
4	" "	"	" "	No. 1		
5	Walter Hicks		" "	No. 1		
6	" "		" "	~~No. 1~~		
7	" "		" "	No. 1		

(NOTES)

No. 1 Died Dec. 23, 1900; Proof of Death filed Nov. 6, 1902
No. 2 is now the wife of J.F. Dowdy, non-Citizen; Evidence of Marriage filed Nov. 6, 1902.
No. 6 Affidavit of physician to be supplied. Received *(remainder illegible)*
No. 6 Died Jan. 1900; Proof of Death filed Nov. 6, 1902.
No. 7 Enrolled 6/14/1900

Oct. 4/98.

RESIDENCE: Pickens	*COUNTY*		*CARD NO.*	
POST OFFICE: Willis, Ind. Ter.			*FIELD NO.*	

	NAME	RELATION-SHIP TO PERSON FIRST NAMED	AGE	SEX	BLOOD	TRIBAL ENROLLMENT		
						YEAR	COUNTY	PAGE
1	Willis, Raleigh Britton		45	M	1/16	1897	Pickens	9
2	" Margaret	Wife	42	F	I.W.	1897	"	77
3	" Holmes Ulysses	Son	18	M	1/32	1897	"	9

TRIBAL ENROLLMENT OF PARENTS

	NAME OF FATHER	YEAR	COUNTY	NAME OF MOTHER	YEAR	COUNTY
1	Hamp Willie	Dead	Non Citizen	Elvira Love Willis	Dead	Pickens
2	Jim Page		" "	Minerva Page		Non-Citizen
3	No. 1			No. 2		

(NOTES)

No. 1 On Chickasaw Roll as Brit Willis
No. 2 " " " " Maggie "
No. 3 " " " " Holmes " Jr.

(No. 2 Dawes' Roll No. 332)

Oct. 4/98.

Chickasaw Enrollment Cards 1898-1914
Chickasaw by Blood Volume IV

RESIDENCE: Pickens COUNTY

POST OFFICE: Burneyville, Ind. Ter.

CARD NO.

FIELD NO.

	NAME	RELATION-SHIP TO PERSON FIRST	AGE	SEX	BLOOD	TRIBAL ENROLLMENT		
						YEAR	COUNTY	PAGE
1	Burney, Albert Sydney	NAMED	27	M	1/2	1897	Pickens	21
2	" Sydney Guy	Son	3	"	1/4	1897	"	21
3	" Joseph	"	2	"	1/4			
4	" Jams[sic] Bixby	"	1mo	"	1/4			
5	" Geraldine	Dau	2wks	F	1/4			
6	" Lillie May	Wife	25	"	I.W.	1897	"	21

TRIBAL ENROLLMENT OF PARENTS

	NAME OF FATHER	YEAR	COUNTY	NAME OF MOTHER	YEAR	COUNTY
1	W.B. Burney	1897	Pickens	Mary Burney	Dead	Pickens
2	No. 1			Lillie Burney		white woman
3	No. 1			" "		" "
4	No. 1			" "		" "
5	No. 1			" "		" "
6	Joseph Wood		non Citizen	Emily Wood		non Citizen

(NOTES)

No. 1 On Chickasaw Roll as A.S. Burney

No. 1 Wife, Lillie Burney, on Chickasaw D.122.

No. 4 Enrolled Nov. 23, 1898

No. 5 Born May 31st 1902' Enrolled June 16, 1902

No. 6 On Chickasaw roll, Pickens Co, (by blood) Page 21 by mistake.   *(No. 6 Dawes' Roll No. 395)*

No. 6 transferred from Chick. card D-122 July 7th 1904. See decision of June 21, 1904.

P.O. Marietta, I.T. 10/27/02

Oct. 4/98.

RESIDENCE: Pickens COUNTY

POST OFFICE: Woodville, Ind. Ter.

CARD NO.

FIELD NO.

	NAME	RELATION-SHIP TO PERSON FIRST	AGE	SEX	BLOOD	TRIBAL ENROLLMENT		
						YEAR	COUNTY	PAGE
1	Christian, Tom	NAMED	27	M	1/32	1897	Pickens	12

TRIBAL ENROLLMENT OF PARENTS

	NAME OF FATHER	YEAR	COUNTY	NAME OF MOTHER	YEAR	COUNTY
1	John Christian	Dead	Non-Citizen	Ellen Christian now Moore	1897	Pickens

(NOTES)

Oct. 4/98.

RESIDENCE: Pickens   COUNTY   CARD NO.

POST OFFICE: Powell, Ind. Ter.   FIELD NO.

NAME	RELATION-SHIP TO PERSON FIRST NAMED	AGE	SEX	BLOOD	TRIBAL ENROLLMENT		
					YEAR	COUNTY	PAGE
1 Brown, Ben W.	NAMED	57	M	I.W.	1897	Pickens	77
2 ' Melton Perry	Son	14	"	1/16	1897	"	12

TRIBAL ENROLLMENT OF PARENTS

NAME OF FATHER	YEAR	COUNTY	NAME OF MOTHER	YEAR	COUNTY
1 W.H. Brown	Dead	Non Citizen	Caroline Brown	Dead	non-Citizen
2 No. 1			Lizzie Brown	"	Pickens

(NOTES)

No. 1 See decision of June 13 '??   *(No. 1 Dawes' Roll No. 394)*

No. 1 On Chickasaw Roll as Ben Brown

No. 2 "   "   "   " M.P.   "

Oct. 4/98.

RESIDENCE: Pickens   COUNTY   CARD NO.

POST OFFICE: Woodville, Ind. Ter.   FIELD NO.

NAME	RELATION-SHIP TO PERSON FIRST NAMED	AGE	SEX	BLOOD	TRIBAL ENROLLMENT		
					YEAR	COUNTY	PAGE
1 McDuffee, Edward Harvey	NAMED	35	M	I.W.	1897	Pickens	77
2 " Rebecca	Wife	27	F	1/8	1897	"	11
3 " Myrtle May	Dau	5	"	1/16	1897	"	11
4 " Morey Emily	"	2	"	1/16	1897	"	11
5 " Juzan Ben	Son	2mo	M	1/16			
6 " Indiola	Dau	1mo	F	1/16			

TRIBAL ENROLLMENT OF PARENTS

NAME OF FATHER	YEAR	COUNTY	NAME OF MOTHER	YEAR	COUNTY
1 W.G. McDuffee	Dead	Non-Citizen	Nancy A. McDuffee	Dead	Non-Citizen
2 Thomas Juzan	1897	Pickens	Eliza Juzan (I.W.)	1897	Pickens
3 No. 1			No. 2		
4 No. 1			No. 2		
5 No. 1			No. 2		
6 No. 1			No. 2		

(NOTES)

No. 1 On Chickasaw Roll as Harvey McDuffy   *(No. 1 Dawes' Roll No. 331)*

No. 2 "   "   " " Rebecca   "

No. 3 "   "   " " Myrth May "

No. 4 "   "   " " Maria E   "

25

No. 5 Enrolled March 6/99
No. 6 Enrolled Sept. 16, 1901

Oct. 4/98.

RESIDENCE: Pickens *COUNTY*						*CARD NO.*		
POST OFFICE: Woodville, I.T.						*FIELD NO.*		
NAME	RELATION-SHIP TO PERSON FIRST NAMED	AGE	SEX	BLOOD	TRIBAL ENROLLMENT			
					YEAR	COUNTY		PAGE
1 Brooks, Alexander	NAMED	23	M	3/8	1897	Pickens		8
2 " Steven	Son	8mo	M	3/16				
TRIBAL ENROLLMENT OF PARENTS								
NAME OF FATHER	YEAR	COUNTY		NAME OF MOTHER		YEAR	COUNTY	
1 John Brooks	Dead	Non Citizen		Elizabeth Brooks		1897	Pickens	
2 No. 1				Mary Brooks			White woman	

(NOTES)

No. 1 On Chickasaw Roll as Alex Brooks
No. 2 enrolled Dec. 16, 1899; Subject to *(illegible)* of evidence of marriage of parents. Same requested;
Same received and filed June 21, '02.

Oct. 4/98.

RESIDENCE: Pickens *COUNTY*						*CARD NO.*		
POST OFFICE: Woodville, I.T.						*FIELD NO.*		
NAME	RELATION-SHIP TO PERSON FIRST NAMED	AGE	SEX	BLOOD	TRIBAL ENROLLMENT			
					YEAR	COUNTY		PAGE
1 Brooks, Elizabeth	NAMED	67	F	3/4	1897	Pickens		8
2 Russell, Stephen	Son	34	M	3/8	1897	"		8
TRIBAL ENROLLMENT OF PARENTS								
NAME OF FATHER	YEAR	COUNTY		NAME OF MOTHER		YEAR	COUNTY	
1 Charles Colbert	Dead	Chick Roll		Mississippi Juzan		Dead	Chick Roll	
2 John Russell	"	Non Citizen		No. 1				

(NOTES)

No. 2 in penitentiary at Columbus *(Illegible)*

Oct. 4, 1898.

RESIDENCE: Pickens   **COUNTY**   **CARD NO.**

POST OFFICE: Woodville, I.T.   **FIELD NO.**

	NAME	RELATION-SHIP TO PERSON FIRST NAMED	AGE	SEX	BLOOD	TRIBAL ENROLLMENT		
						YEAR	COUNTY	PAGE
1	Juzan, Thomas	NAMED	51	M	1/4	1897	Pickens	11
2	" Eliza	Wife	45	F	I.W.	1897	"	77
3	Steele, Amelia	Dau	24	"	1/16	1897	"	8
4	" Willie	Gr.Dau	6	"	"	1897	"	8
5	" Thomas	Gr.Son	4	M	"	1897	"	8
6	" Overton	" "	2	"	"	1897	"	8

TRIBAL ENROLLMENT OF PARENTS

	NAME OF FATHER	YEAR	COUNTY	NAME OF MOTHER	YEAR	COUNTY
1	Jackson Juzan	Dead	Choc. Roll	Mississippi Juzan	Dead	Chick Roll
2	John Brooks	"	Non Citizen	Jane Brooks	"	Non Citizen
3	No. 1			No. 2		
4	W.G. Steele	Dead	Non Citizen	No. 3		
5	" " "	"	" "	No. 3		
6	" " "	"	" "	No. 3		

(NOTES)

No. 1 on Chickasaw Roll as Tom Juzan
Copy of marriage certificate to be supplied.
No. 2 married in 1874.

(No. 2 Dawes' Roll No. 330)
Oct. 4, 1898.

RESIDENCE: Tishomingo   **COUNTY**   **CARD NO.**

POST OFFICE: Sulphur, Ind. Ter.   **FIELD NO.**

	NAME	RELATION-SHIP TO PERSON FIRST NAMED	AGE	SEX	BLOOD	TRIBAL ENROLLMENT		
						YEAR	COUNTY	PAGE
1	Parker, John Wesley	NAMED	50	M	Full	1897	Tishomingo	29
2	" Ella Rennie	Dau	3	F	1/2	1897	"	29
3	" Emily Frazier	"	1	"	1/2	1897	"	88
4	" ~~Clarence Hubbard~~	~~Son~~	~~5mo~~	~~M~~	~~1/2~~			
5	" Douglas H.J.	"	4 "	"	1/2			
6	" ~~Mala C~~	~~Dau~~	~~1 "~~	~~F~~	~~1/2~~			
7	" Alice I.	Wife	32	F	I.W.			

TRIBAL ENROLLMENT OF PARENTS

	NAME OF FATHER	YEAR	COUNTY	NAME OF MOTHER	YEAR	COUNTY
1	Parker	Dead	Chickasaw Roll	Siney	Dead	Chickasaw Roll

27

2	No. 1			Alice Parker		white woman
3	No. 1			" "		" "
4	~~No. 1~~			" "		" "
5	No. 1			" "		" "
6	No. 1			" "		" "
7	Jim Smith	dead	non citz	Melinda Smith		non-citz

(NOTES)

Wife of No. 1 is on Chickasaw Card D#121
No. 2 On Chickasaw roll as Ella R. Parker
No. 3 "   "   " " Emily F. "   *(No. 3 Dawes' Roll No. 4755)*
No. 1 "   "   " " J. Wesley "
Alice 1 Parker wife of No. 1 Chickasaw D121
No. 6 Died June 4, 1902; Proof of death filed Dec. 24, 1902.
No. 6 Enrolled Sept. 12, 1901.
No. 7 transferred from Chickasaw Card #D121, April 1, 1903.   *(No. 7 Dawes' Roll No. 48)*
   See decision of March 16, 1903.
No. 3 proof of death filed March 24, 1903.
No. 4 Transferred to Choctaw card No. 5254
No. 4 do not issue *(illegible)*
   See *(illegible)* Dec. 31/03   No. 4 enrolled Mar. 6/99
                                                                   No. 5 enrolled Nov. 3/99
                                                                   Oct. 4/98.

RESIDENCE: Choctaw Nation ~~COUNTY~~				CARD NO.				
POST OFFICE:				FIELD NO.				

NAME	RELATION-SHIP TO PERSON	AGE	SEX	BLOOD	TRIBAL ENROLLMENT		
					YEAR	COUNTY	PAGE
1 Bourland, John B.	FIRST NAMED	47	M	1/16	1897	Chick residing in Choc. N. 1st Dist.	70

TRIBAL ENROLLMENT OF PARENTS

NAME OF FATHER	YEAR	COUNTY	NAME OF MOTHER	YEAR	COUNTY
1 Reuben R. Bourland (I.W.)	1897	Chick residing in Choc. N. 1st Dist.	Eliza Bourland	Dead	Chick. Roll

(NOTES)

No. 1 died Nov. 28, 1901; Proof of death filed July 30, 1902.

Oct. 4, 1898.

CANCELLED Stamped across card

Chickasaw Enrollment Cards 1898-1914
Chickasaw by Blood   Volume IV

RESIDENCE: Choctaw Nation ~~COUNTY~~   CARD NO.

POST OFFICE: McAlester, I.T.   FIELD NO.

NAME	RELATION-SHIP TO PERSON	AGE	SEX	BLOOD	TRIBAL ENROLLMENT		
					YEAR	COUNTY	PAGE
1 Bourland, Reuben R.	FIRST NAMED	78	M	I.W.	1897	Chick residing in Choc. N. 1st Dist.	82

TRIBAL ENROLLMENT OF PARENTS

NAME OF FATHER	YEAR	COUNTY	NAME OF MOTHER	YEAR	COUNTY
1 Benj. Bourland	Dead	Non Citizen	Nancy Bourland	Dead	Non Citizen

(NOTES)

No. 1 died Dec. 17, 1900; Proof of death filed July 30, 1902.

Oct. 4, 1898.

CANCELLED Stamped across card

RESIDENCE: Pontotoc   COUNTY   CARD NO.

POST OFFICE: Wynnewood, I.T.   FIELD NO.

	NAME	RELATION-SHIP TO PERSON FIRST	AGE	SEX	BLOOD	TRIBAL ENROLLMENT		
						YEAR	COUNTY	PAGE
1	Long, Samuel D.	NAMED	30	M	I.W.			
2	" Lydia Caroline	Wife	19	F	1/32	1897	Pickens	9
3	" Jewell V.	Dau	?mo	"	1/64			
4	" Harry Jerome	Son	?mo	M	1/64			
5	" Paul Edward	"	3wks	"	1/64			

TRIBAL ENROLLMENT OF PARENTS

	NAME OF FATHER	YEAR	COUNTY	NAME OF MOTHER	YEAR	COUNTY
1	H.T. Long		Non Citizen	Nancy J. Long		Non-Citizen
2	Jerome Whitsell (I.W.)	1897	Pickens	Mollie Whitsell	1897	Pickens
3	No. 1			No. 2		
4	No. 1			No. 2		
5	No. 1			No. 2		

(NOTES)

No. 2 on Chickasaw Roll as L.C. Whitsell

No. 3 died Nov. 8, 1899. Proof of death filed Nov. 1, 1902.

No. 4 Enrolled May 22, 1900

No. 5 Born Aug. 27, 1902; Enrolled Sept. 12, 1902.

As to degree of Chickasaw blood possessed by No. 2, See affidavits of
J. *(Illegible)*Willis and Martha Martin filed Oct. 10, 1902.

No. 3 Enrolled Nov. 3, 1899.

(No. 1 Dawes' Roll No. 144)
(No. 2 Dawes' Roll No. 4175)
(No. 4 Dawes' Roll No. 4176)
(No. 5 Dawes' Roll No. 4177)

P.O. Sulphur, I.T.   Oct. 3, 1898.

RESIDENCE: Pickens   COUNTY   CARD NO.
POST OFFICE: Holder, Ind. Ter.   FIELD NO.

NAME	RELATION-SHIP TO PERSON FIRST NAMED	AGE	SEX	BLOOD	TRIBAL ENROLLMENT		
					YEAR	COUNTY	PAGE
1 Stewart. Calvin	NAMED	26	M	1/16	1897	Pickens	8
2 " Ben	Bro	21	"	1/16	1897	"	8

TRIBAL ENROLLMENT OF PARENTS

NAME OF FATHER	YEAR	COUNTY	NAME OF MOTHER	YEAR	COUNTY
1 George Stewart	Dead	Non Citizen	Lottie Holder	1897	Pickens
2 " "	"	" "	" "	"	"

(Notes)

Oct. 3, 1898.

RESIDENCE: Pickens   COUNTY   CARD NO.
POST OFFICE: Willis, I.T.   FIELD NO.

NAME	RELATION-SHIP TO PERSON FIRST NAMED	AGE	SEX	BLOOD	TRIBAL ENROLLMENT		
					YEAR	COUNTY	PAGE
1 Smith, Mollie	NAMED	33	F	1/16	1897	Pickens	9
2 " Tom	husband	42	M	I.W.			

TRIBAL ENROLLMENT OF PARENTS

NAME OF FATHER	YEAR	COUNTY	NAME OF MOTHER	YEAR	COUNTY
1 Doffey Colbert	Dead	Panola	Mary Colbert	Dead	Non Citizen
2 Eph. Smith	Dead	non-citizen	Ophelia Smith	Dead	" "

(NOTES)

No. 1 is wife of Tom Smith on Chickasaw Card #D,120
No. 2 transferred from Chickasaw card #D120, April 1, 1903. See decision of March 16, 1903.

Oct. 3, 1898.

RESIDENCE: Pickens   COUNTY   CARD NO.
POST OFFICE: Willis, I.T.   FIELD NO.

NAME	RELATION-SHIP TO PERSON FIRST NAMED	AGE	SEX	BLOOD	TRIBAL ENROLLMENT		
					YEAR	COUNTY	PAGE
1 Overton, Ruel Joseph	NAMED	24	M	1/32	1897	Pickens	9
2 " Viola	Wife	19	F	1/32	1897	"	9
3 " Jewel	Dau	4	"	1/32	1897	"	9
4 " Frank	Son	16mo	M	1/32	1897	"	86
5 " Stella M	Dau	4mo	F	1/32			

	TRIBAL ENROLLMENT OF PARENTS					
	NAME OF FATHER	YEAR	COUNTY	NAME OF MOTHER	YEAR	COUNTY
1	B.F. Overton	Dead	Pickens	Bettie Overton	Dead	Non Citizen
2	Brit Willis	1897	"	Mag Willis, I.W.	1897	Pickens
3	No. 1			No. 2		
4	No. 1			No. 2		
5	No. 1			No. 2		

(NOTES)

No. 1 On Chickasaw Roll as R.J. Overton
No. 2 Enrolled March 12, 1901
No. 4 Proof of birth received and filed Sept. 30, 1902.

(No. 4 Dawes' Roll No. 4174)
Oct. 3, 1898.

RESIDENCE: Pickens   COUNTY   CARD NO.
POST OFFICE: Oakland, I.T.   FIELD NO.

	NAME	RELATION-SHIP TO PERSON FIRST NAMED	AGE	SEX	BLOOD	TRIBAL ENROLLMENT		
						YEAR	COUNTY	PAGE
1	Thompson, William Ashley	NAMED	35	M	I.W.	1897	Pickens	77
2	" Flora Mary	Wife	25	F	1/16	1897	"	11
3	" James Willis	Son	8	M	1/32	1897	"	11
4	" Eula	Dau	5	F	1/32	1897	"	11
5	" Lillian	"	2	F	1/32	1897	"	11
6	~~" Halaw Guy~~	~~Son~~	~~9mo~~	~~M~~	~~1/32~~	DIED PRIOR TO SEPTEMBER 25 1902		
7	Dickerson, Amanda	Sister in law	17	F	1/16	1897	Pickens	11
8	Thompson, Stell	Dau	3mo	F	1/32			

	TRIBAL ENROLLMENT OF PARENTS					
	NAME OF FATHER	YEAR	COUNTY	NAME OF MOTHER	YEAR	COUNTY
1	W.A. Thompson	Dead	Non Citizen	Orra Thompson	Dead	Non Citizen
2	Willis Dickerson	"	" "	Mary Dickerson	"	Pickens
3	No. 1			No. 2		
4	No. 1			No. 2		
5	No. 1			No. 2		
6	~~No. 1~~			~~No. 2~~		
7	Willis Dickerson	Dead	Non Citizen	Mary Dickerson	Dead	Pickens
8	No. 1			No. 2		

(NOTES)

No. 1 On Chickasaw Roll as Bill Thompson
No. 2 "   "   " " F.M.   "

31

No. 3 " " " " J.W. "
No. 4 " " " " Ella "
No. 8 Enrolled February 13, 1901
No. 6 Died Nov. 21, 1900; Proof of death filed Nov. 7, 1902.
Nol 6 See affidavit, as to death filed Feby. 9, 1903.

P.O. Willis, I.T.

Oct. 3, 1898.

RESIDENCE: Pickens COUNTY CARD NO.
POST OFFICE: Lebanon, I.T. FIELD NO.

	NAME	RELATIONSHIP TO PERSON FIRST NAMED	AGE	SEX	BLOOD	TRIBAL ENROLLMENT YEAR	COUNTY	PAGE
1	Keel, Colbert		21	M	Full	1897	Pickens	9
2	" Caroline	Wife	27	F	"	1897	"	9
3	" Minnie	S.Dau	4	"	"	1897	"	9
4	" Belton	" Son	3	M	"	1897	"	9
5	" Bennie	Son	2mo	"	"			
6	~~" Gary Floyd~~	"	~~3mo~~	"	"	DIED	PRIOR TO SEPTEMBER 25 1902	

TRIBAL ENROLLMENT OF PARENTS

	NAME OF FATHER	YEAR	COUNTY	NAME OF MOTHER	YEAR	COUNTY
1	Johnson Keel	Dead	Pickens	Winey Keel	1897	Pickens
2	Ephraim Alexander	"	Pontotoc	Jennie Alexander	Dead	Pontotoc
3	Ivison Keel	"	Pickens	No. 2		
4	" "	"	"	No. 2		
5	No. 1			No. 2		
6	No. 1			No. 2		

(NOTES)

No. 6 Enrolled June 21, 1901
No. 6 Died Feby. 10, 1902; Proof of death filed Nov. 7, 1902.
No. 6 Died Feb. 10, 1902. Enrollment cancelled *(remainder illegible)*

Oct. 3, 1898.

RESIDENCE: Pickens COUNTY CARD NO.
POST OFFICE: Kingston, I.T. FIELD NO.

	NAME	RELATIONSHIP TO PERSON FIRST NAMED	AGE	SEX	BLOOD	TRIBAL ENROLLMENT YEAR	COUNTY	PAGE
1	Peter, Martha		32	F	1/2	1897	Pickens	23
2	" Ella	Dau	9	"	1/4	1897	"	23

3	" Noel	Son	3	M	1/4	1897	"	23
4	" Enos	"	1	"	1/4			
5	" Jesse	Son	1	M	1/4			

TRIBAL ENROLLMENT OF PARENTS

	NAME OF FATHER	YEAR	COUNTY	NAME OF MOTHER	YEAR	COUNTY
1	O-loue-by	Dead	Choc. Roll	Shi-ho-lo	1897	Pickens
2	Stephen Peter	1896	Choc. residing in Chic District	No. 1		
3	" "	"	"	No. 1		
4	" "	"	"	No. 1		
5	" "	"	"	No. 1		

(NOTES)

No. 1 wife of Stephen Peter, Choctaw Roll Card No. 340
No. 3 On Chickasaw Roll as Hall Peter
No. 5 Born Dec. 1, 1901; Enrolled Nov. 20, 1902.   *(No. 5 Dawes' Roll No. 4173)*
No. 4 Enrolled Dec. 16, 1899.

Oct. 3, 1898.

RESIDENCE: Tishomingo **COUNTY**   **CARD NO.**
POST OFFICE: Ravia, I.T.   **FIELD NO.**

	NAME	RELATION-SHIP TO PERSON FIRST NAMED	AGE	SEX	BLOOD	TRIBAL ENROLLMENT		
						YEAR	COUNTY	PAGE
1	Brown, Martin		17	M	Full	1897	Tishomingo	37

TRIBAL ENROLLMENT OF PARENTS

	NAME OF FATHER	YEAR	COUNTY	NAME OF MOTHER	YEAR	COUNTY
1	Major Brown	Dead	Tishomingo	Sophie Brown	Dead	Tishomingo

(NOTES)

No. 1 is the husband of Mamie Brown on Chickasaw Roll Card #818.
   See affidavit filed with papers with Chickasaw Card #818. Aug. 13, 1901.

Oct. 3, 1898.

RESIDENCE: Pickens **COUNTY**   **CARD NO.**
POST OFFICE: Oakland, I.T.   **FIELD NO.**

	NAME	RELATION-SHIP TO PERSON FIRST NAMED	AGE	SEX	BLOOD	TRIBAL ENROLLMENT		
						YEAR	COUNTY	PAGE
1	Kennedy, Maulsie		27	F	1/16	1897	Pickens	26
2	Paul, Joe M.	Son	5	M	3/8	1897	"	26
3	" William Ikard	"	3	"	3/8	1897	"	26

4	Kennedy, W.J. Bryan	"	2mo	"	1/32		
5	" George W.	"	2wks	M	1/32		

	TRIBAL ENROLLMENT OF PARENTS						
	NAME OF FATHER	YEAR	COUNTY	NAME OF MOTHER	YEAR	COUNTY	
1	Ben Stewart (I.W.)	1897	Pickens	Mary F. Stewart	1897	Pickens	
2	Joe Paul	Dead	"	No. 1			
3	" "	"	"	No. 1			
4	John Kennedy		Non Citizen	No. 1			
5	" "		" "	No. 1			

(NOTES)

No. 1 On Chickasaw Roll as Maulsie Paul
No. 3 "   "   "   " Ikard   "
No. 5 enrolled Sept. 19, 1900.

Oct. 3, 1898.

RESIDENCE: Tishomingo   COUNTY   CARD NO.
POST OFFICE: Regan. I.T.   FIELD NO.

	NAME	RELATION-SHIP TO PERSON FIRST NAMED	AGE	SEX	BLOOD	TRIBAL ENROLLMENT		
						YEAR	COUNTY	PAGE
1	Brown, Sampson	NAMED	25	M	Full	1897	Tishomingo	28
2	" Patsey	Wife	23	F	"	1897	"	28
3	" Flora Belle	Dau	4	"	"	1897	"	28
4	Chisholm, Sallie	Sister in law	15	"	"	1897	"	28
5	Hunnatubby, Delphia	"	19	"	"	1897	"	28
6	Jimmy, Rena	S.Dau	12	"	"	1897	"	28
7	McLish, Annie	" "	10	"	"	1897	"	28
8	Wilson, Icy	Sister	20	"	"	1897	"	28
9	Newberry, Martha	1/2 "	17	"	"	1897	"	28
10	Brown, Lily	Dau	6mo	"	"			
11	" Ben	Son	2mo	M	"			
12	~~Wilson, Owenby~~	~~Son of No. 8~~	~~2mo~~	~~"~~	~~3/4~~			
13	Gaddis, George	Son of No. 5	2 1/2	"	9/16			

	TRIBAL ENROLLMENT OF PARENTS						
	NAME OF FATHER	YEAR	COUNTY	NAME OF MOTHER	YEAR	COUNTY	
1	Ben Brown	Dead	Tishomingo	(Name Illegible)	Dead	Tishomingo	
2	Aaron Benton	"	Pickens	Louisa Benton	"	Pickens	

3	No. 1			No. 2		
4	Chisholm Impatubby	Dead	Pickens	Louisa Benton	Dead	Pickens
5	Jim Watson	"	"	" "	"	"
6	William Jimmy	1897	Tishomingo	No. 2		
7	Frank McLish	Dead	Pickens	No. 2		
8	Ben Brown	"	Tishomingo	Nan-no-ye	Dead	Tishomingo
9	Levi Newberry	1896	"	" " "	"	"
10	No. 1			No. 2		
11	No. 1			No. 2		
~~12~~	~~Newton Wilson~~	~~1897~~	~~Tishomingo~~	~~No. 8~~		
13	George L. Gaddis	1897	Pickens	No. 5		

(NOTES)

No. 3 On Chickasaw Roll as Belle Brown
No. 4 "　　"　　"　" Sally Chison
No. 6 "　　"　　"　" Loucina Jimmie
No. 7 "　　"　　"　" Annie　"
No. 9 "　　"　　"　" Martha Brown
No. 5 "　　"　　"　" Delphie Watson
No. 5 Also on 1897 Roll, Page 28, Tishomingo Co. as Delphia Benton
No. 10 Enrolled Nov. 3, 1899
No. 11 Enrolled May 23, 1901.
No. 12 Enrolled Sept. 10, 1901.
No. 13 Born Jan. 30, 1900; Enrolled Nov. 7, 1902.　　　　　*(No. 13 Dawes' Roll No. 4172)*
No. 8 is now the wife of Newton Wilson on Chickasaw Card #905. Evidence of marriage filed Sept. 10, 1901.
No. 5 is now the wife of Isum Hunnatubby on Chickasaw Care #829;
　　See affidavit of Isum Hunnatubby filed Nov. 8, 1901.

P.O. Tishomingo, I.T. 1/25-04　　　　　　　　　　　　　　　　　　　Oct. 3, 1898.

RESIDENCE:	Pickens	*COUNTY*				CARD NO.		
POST OFFICE:		Lebanon, I.T.				FIELD NO.		

NAME	RELATION-SHIP TO PERSON FIRST NAMED	AGE	SEX	BLOOD	TRIBAL ENROLLMENT		
					YEAR	COUNTY	PAGE
1	Pershica, Ben		35	M	Full	1897	Pickens	23
2	"　McLane	Son	8	"	"	1897	"	23
3	"　Fred	"	5	"	"	1897	"	23
4	"　~~(Illegible)~~	~~Dau~~	3	F	"	~~1897~~	"	~~23~~

TRIBAL ENROLLMENT OF PARENTS

	NAME OF FATHER	YEAR	COUNTY	NAME OF MOTHER	YEAR	COUNTY
1	Pershica	Dead	Chick Roll	Siley Pershica	Dead	Pontotoc

35

2	No. 1			Rhody Pershica	"	Pickens
3	No. 1			" "	"	"
4	~~No. 1~~			" "	-	-

(NOTES)

No. 2 On Chickasaw Roll as McLene
No. 4 "   "   "   " Pearl
No. 4 Died June 3, 1900; Proof of death filed Nov. 8, 1902.
No. 4 Died June 3, 1900. Enrollment cancelled by Dept. *(remainder illegible)*

Oct. 3, 1898.

RESIDENCE: Tishomingo COUNTY CARD NO.
POST OFFICE: Ravia, I.T. FIELD NO.

NAME	RELATIONSHIP TO PERSON FIRST NAMED	AGE	SEX	BLOOD	TRIBAL ENROLLMENT		
					YEAR	COUNTY	PAGE
1 Clayboun, Celia		25	F	Full	1897	Tishomingo	33

TRIBAL ENROLLMENT OF PARENTS

	NAME OF FATHER	YEAR	COUNTY	NAME OF MOTHER	YEAR	COUNTY
1	Clayboun Allen	Dead	Tishomingo	Hollie Allen	Dead	Tishomingo

(NOTES)

On Chickasaw Roll as Sealy Thomas

Oct. 3, 1898.

RESIDENCE: Pickens COUNTY CARD NO.
POST OFFICE: Kingston, I.T. FIELD NO.

NAME	RELATIONSHIP TO PERSON FIRST NAMED	AGE	SEX	BLOOD	TRIBAL ENROLLMENT		
					YEAR	COUNTY	PAGE
1 Willis, J. hamp.		25	M	1/2	1897	Pickens	21
2 " Emma	Wife	23	F	3/4	1897	Tishomingo	35
3 " Helen Robinia	Dau	8mo	"	3/8			

TRIBAL ENROLLMENT OF PARENTS

	NAME OF FATHER	YEAR	COUNTY	NAME OF MOTHER	YEAR	COUNTY
1	Brit Willis	1897	Pickens	Margaret Willis (I.W.)	1897	Pickens
2	R.M. Harris	1897	Tishomingo	Lucy Harris	Dead	Tishomingo
3	No. 1			No. 2		

(NOTES)

No. 2 On Chickasaw Roll as Emma Harris.
No. 3 Affidavit of Attending Physician to be supplied. Affidavit of mother substituted and received Oct. 4, 1898.

Oct. 3, 1898

Chickasaw Enrollment Cards 1898-1914
Chickasaw by Blood   Volume IV

RESIDENCE: Pickens   COUNTY   CARD NO.

POST OFFICE: Pike, I.T.   FIELD NO.

	NAME	RELATION-SHIP TO PERSON FIRST NAMED	AGE	SEX	BLOOD	TRIBAL ENROLLMENT		
						YEAR	COUNTY	PAGE
1	Alexander, Ella	NAMED	16	F	1/4	1897	Pickens	22
2	" (Illegible) Lee	Son	1mo	M	1/8			
3	" ~~Felix Sidney~~	"	~~2wks~~	"	~~1/8~~	DIED PRIOR TO SEPTEMBER 25 1902		

TRIBAL ENROLLMENT OF PARENTS

	NAME OF FATHER	YEAR	COUNTY	NAME OF MOTHER	YEAR	COUNTY
1	Pike Coyle	Dead	Pickens	Clara Coyle (I.W.)	1897	Pickens
2	D.L. Alexander		Non Citizen	No. 1		
3	" "		" "	~~No. 1~~		

(NOTES)

No. 1 is now the wife of Dan Lee Alexander a United States Citizen, Aug. 31, 1900.
   Evidence of marriage filed Oct. 11, 1901.
No. 2 enrolled Sept. 1, 1900.
No. 3   "   Oct. 11, 1901
No. 3 died Feby. 18, 1902. Proof of death filed Nov. 1, 1902.

Oct. 3, 1898.

RESIDENCE: Pickens   COUNTY   CARD NO.

POST OFFICE: Oakland, I.T.   FIELD NO.

	NAME	RELATION-SHIP TO PERSON FIRST NAMED	AGE	SEX	BLOOD	TRIBAL ENROLLMENT		
						YEAR	COUNTY	PAGE
1	Sacra, Mattie	NAMED	36	F	5/16	1897	Pickens	8
2	" Lillie	Dau	11	"	3/32	1897	"	8
3	" Estelle	"	9	"	5/32	1897	"	8
4	" Edward	Son	6	M	5/32	1897	"	8
5	" Marie	Dau	4	F	5/32	1897	"	8
6	" Leston	Son	8wks	M	5/32			
7	Shelton, Clemmie	Dau	17	F	3/16	1897	Pickens	8
8	Overton, Frankie	"	15	"	3/16	1897	"	8
9	Sacra, Mattie Loyce	Dau	1mo	"	5/32			
10	" Malachia	Dau	3wks	"	5/32			
11	" Ed	Husb	42	M	I.W.	1897	Pickens	77

TRIBAL ENROLLMENT OF PARENTS

	NAME OF FATHER	YEAR	COUNTY	NAME OF MOTHER	YEAR	COUNTY
1	Colbert Carter	Dead	Panola	Elizabeth Carter	Dead	Panola

37

2	Ed Sacra		White man	No. I		
3	" "		" "	No. I		
4	" "		" "	No. I		
5	" "		" "	No. I		
6	" "		" "	No. I		
7	B.F. Overton	Dead	Pickens	No. I		
8	" " "	"	"	No. I		
9	Ed. Sacra		White man	No. I		
10	" "		" "	No. I		
11	" "		non citizen	Mary Sacra		non citizen

(NOTES)

No. 3 On Chickasaw Roll as Stella Sacra
No. 4 "   "   "   " Ed   "
No. 5 "   "   "   " Maria   "
No. 9 Enrolled April 6, 1901.
No. I is now wife of Ed Sacra Chickasaw D.II9
No. 7 is wife of William J. Shelton on Chickasaw Card #D.276.
No. 10 Born Sept. 23, 1902 enroled[sic] Oct. 17, 1902.   *(No. 10 Dawes' Roll No. 4171)*
No. 11 transferred from Chickasaw card #D.II9.   *(No. 11 Dawes' Roll No. 287)*
See decision of March 5, 1904. Mar. 23, 1904.

Oct. 3, 1898.

RESIDENCE: Pickens COUNTY					CARD NO.		
POST OFFICE: Lebanon, I.T.					FIELD NO.		

NAME	RELATION-SHIP TO PERSON FIRST NAMED	AGE	SEX	BLOOD	TRIBAL ENROLLMENT		
					YEAR	COUNTY	PAGE
1 Okchantubby, Winey		53	F	Full	1897	Pickens	9
2 Keel, Sanders	Son	17	M	"	1897	"	9
3 " Simon, Jr.	"	15	"	"	1897	"	9

	TRIBAL ENROLLMENT OF PARENTS						
NAME OF FATHER	YEAR	COUNTY	NAME OF MOTHER		YEAR	COUNTY	
1 Okchantubby	Dead	Chick Roll	*(Name Illegible)*		Dead	Chick Roll	
2 Johnson Keel	"	Pickens	No. I				
3 " "	"	"	No. I				

(NOTES)

No. I on Chickasaw Roll as Winnie Keel.

Oct. 3, 1898.

RESIDENCE: Pickens COUNTY   CARD NO.

POST OFFICE: Kingston, I.T.   FIELD NO.

NAME	RELATION-SHIP TO PERSON FIRST NAMED	AGE	SEX	BLOOD	TRIBAL ENROLLMENT		
					YEAR	COUNTY	PAGE
1 Anoatubby, Atchison	NAMED	37	M	Full	1897	Pickens	22
2 " Minnie	Wife	19	F	"	1897	Tishomingo	34
3 " Lee	Son	11	M	"	1897	Pickens	22
4 " McKinzie	"	6	"	"	1897	"	22
5 " Zola	Dau	6	F	"			
6 " Richman	Son	9mo	M	"			
7 " Elsie	Dau	5mo	F	"			

	TRIBAL ENROLLMENT OF PARENTS					
	NAME OF FATHER	YEAR	COUNTY	NAME OF MOTHER	YEAR	COUNTY
1	Anoatubby	Dead	Chick Roll	Wa-nah-sha	Dead	Chick Roll
2	Daniel Pusheahly	"	" "	Delphie Benton	1897	Tishomingo
3	No. 1			Elizabeth	Dead	Pickens
4	No. 1			"	"	"
5	No. 1			No. 2		
6	No. 1			No. 2		
7	No. 1			No. 2		

(NOTES)

No. 1 on Chickasaw Roll as "Atchinson"
No. 2 "   "   " " Minnie Colbert
No. 3 "   "   " " Lee Atchinson
No. 4 "   "   " " McKinney "
No. 6 Enrolled July 5, 1901
No. 7 Born June 16, 1902; Enrolled Nov. 10, 1902.

(No. 7 Dawes' Roll No. 4170)
Oct. 3, 1898.

RESIDENCE: Pickens COUNTY   CARD NO.

POST OFFICE: Willis, I.T.   FIELD NO.

NAME	RELATION-SHIP TO PERSON FIRST NAMED	AGE	SEX	BLOOD	TRIBAL ENROLLMENT		
					YEAR	COUNTY	PAGE
1 Martin, Charles Benjamin	NAMED	45	M	I.W.	1897	Pickens	77
2 " Martha	Wife	22	F	1/32	1897	"	11
3 " Stonewall Jackson	Son	2	M	1/64	1897	"	11

39

Chickasaw Enrollment Cards 1898-1914
Chickasaw by Blood   Volume IV

	TRIBAL ENROLLMENT OF PARENTS					
NAME OF FATHER	YEAR	COUNTY	NAME OF MOTHER	YEAR	COUNTY	
1	Albert Martin		Non Citizen	Fannie Martin		Non Citizen
2	R.?. Willis	1897	Pickens	Mag Willis (I.W.)	1897	Pickens
3	No. 1			No. 2		

(NOTES)

No. 1 on Chickasaw Roll as Dr. C.B. Martin   *(No. 1 Dawes' Roll No. 143)*
No. 3 "   "   "   " S.J.   "
Affidavit of L.V. Colbert together with copy of license and marriage certificate of Nos. 1 & 2, also affidavits of
Isaac D. Lewis County Clerk with Elizabeth H. Colbert and Benjamin Bean witnesses to marriage received and
filed March 20, 1903.

P.O. Helen, I.T. 11/6/02   Oct. 3, 1898.

RESIDENCE: Pickens   COUNTY   CARD NO.
POST OFFICE: Willis, I.T.   FIELD NO.

	NAME	RELATION-SHIP TO PERSON FIRST NAMED	AGE	SEX	BLOOD	TRIBAL ENROLLMENT		
						YEAR	COUNTY	PAGE
1	Willis, Holmes	NAMED	41	M	1/16	1897	Pickens	14
2	" Viola	Wife	38	F	I.W.	1897	"	78
3	" William	Son	18	M	1/32	1897	"	14
4	" Sydney	"	14	"	1/32	1897	"	14
5	" Hortense	Dau	8	F	1/32	1897	"	14
6	" Overton Love	Son	3	M	1/32	1897	"	14

	TRIBAL ENROLLMENT OF PARENTS					
NAME OF FATHER	YEAR	COUNTY	NAME OF MOTHER	YEAR	COUNTY	
1	J.H. Willis	Dead	Non Citizen	Elvira Willis	Dead	Pickens
2	William Gibson	"	" "	Martha Gibson		Non Citizen
3	No. 1			No. 2		
4	No. 1			No. 2		
5	No. 1			No. 2		
6	(This line blank)			No. 2		

(NOTES)

No. 5 on Chick. Roll as Hense Willis   *(No. 2 Dawes' Roll No. 142)*
No. 5[sic] "   "   " " Overton L. "
Affidavit of W.R. Hiser as to marriage between between No. 1 and 3[sic] filed Nov. 7, 1902.

                                                            Oct. 3, 1898.

Chickasaw Enrollment Cards 1898-1914
Chickasaw by Blood   Volume IV

RESIDENCE: Pickens   COUNTY   CARD NO.
POST OFFICE: Brownsville, I.T.   FIELD NO.

NAME	RELATION-SHIP TO PERSON FIRST NAMED	AGE	SEX	BLOOD	TRIBAL ENROLLMENT		
					YEAR	COUNTY	PAGE
1 Polomishtubby, Wesley	NAMED	41	M	Full	1897	Pickens	25
2　　"　　Dhahhyyah	Wife	40	F	"	1897	"	23
3 Ward, Houston	S.Son	18	M	"	1897	"	23

TRIBAL ENROLLMENT OF PARENTS

	NAME OF FATHER	YEAR	COUNTY	NAME OF MOTHER	YEAR	COUNTY
1	Polomishtubby	Dead	Chick Roll	Stone-a-he-che	Dead	Chick. Roll
2	Ah-wal-in-stubby	"	" "	Polly	"	" "
3	Wallis Ward	"	Pickens	No. 2		

(NOTES)

No. 1 on Chickasaw Roll as Wesley Hays
No. 2 "　　"　　"　" *(Illegible)* Hamilton

Oct. 3, 1898.

RESIDENCE: Pickens   COUNTY   CARD NO.
POST OFFICE: Lebanon, I.T.   FIELD NO.

NAME	RELATION-SHIP TO PERSON FIRST NAMED	AGE	SEX	BLOOD	TRIBAL ENROLLMENT		
					YEAR	COUNTY	PAGE
1 Brown, Calvin	NAMED	24	M	Full	1897	Pickens	9
2 Woody, Ada	Wife	18	F	"	1897	"	9
3 Jefferson, Edmon	Bro in Law	11	M	"	1897	"	9
4 Brown, Neta	Dau	4mo	F	"			
5 Woody, Guy	Son of No. 2	3wks	M	1/2			
6　　"　　Brice	Son of No. 2	2wks	M	1/2			
7 Brown, Susi	Wife	22	F	I.W.			

TRIBAL ENROLLMENT OF PARENTS

	NAME OF FATHER	YEAR	COUNTY	NAME OF MOTHER	YEAR	COUNTY
1	Houston Brown	Dead	Pickens	Jane Brown	Dead	Pickens
2	Edmon Jefferson	"	Panola	Mary Jefferson	"	Panola
3	" "	"	"	" "	"	"
4	No. 1			No. 2		
5	C.H. Woody			No. 2		
6	" "			No. 2		

41

| 7 | James Woody | | Non Citz | Elizabeth Woody | | Non Citz. |

(NOTES)

No. 7 license dated Nov. 25/99 and certificate dated Nov. 27/99   *(No. 7 Dawes' Roll No. 547)*

No. 2 now wife of Charles H. Woody, on Card D.290 Nov. 20, 1899

No. 1 is now husband of Susie Brown nee Woody, Dec. 15, 1899, Card No. D.297

No. 5 Enrolled Sept. 10, 1900

No. 6 Born April 3, 1902; Enrolled April 22, 1902

No. 4 Enrolled March 22, 1899

　　　Copy of divorce proceedings between No. 4 and J.P. Thomas received and filed March 24, 1903

No. 7 originally listed for enrollment on Chickasaw Card #D.297 Dec. 15/99

　　　Transferred to this card Nov. 26, 1904. See decision of Nov. 10, 1904.

Oct. 3, 1898.

RESIDENCE: Pickens **COUNTY**　　**CARD NO.**

POST OFFICE: Lebanon, I.T.　　**FIELD NO.**

NAME	RELATION-SHIP TO PERSON FIRST NAMED	AGE	SEX	BLOOD	TRIBAL ENROLLMENT		
					YEAR	COUNTY	PAGE
1 Pratt, Thomas	NAMED	20	M	Full	1897	Pickens	25
2 " Alice	Wife	20	F	I.W.			
3 " Robert	Son	1mo	M	1/2			

	TRIBAL ENROLLMENT OF PARENTS					
NAME OF FATHER	YEAR	COUNTY	NAME OF MOTHER	YEAR	COUNTY	
1 Henry Pratt	Dead	Pickens	Millie McLish	1897	Pickens	
2 Sam Williford		Non Citizen	Kate Williford		Non Citizen	
3 No. 1			No. 2			

(NOTES)

No. 3 Born Dec. 13, 1901; Enrolled Jany 12, 1902.　　*(No. 2 Dawes' Roll No. 141)*

Oct. 3, 1898.

RESIDENCE: Pickens **COUNTY**　　**CARD NO.**

POST OFFICE: McMillan, I.T.　　**FIELD NO.**

NAME	RELATION-SHIP TO PERSON FIRST NAMED	AGE	SEX	BLOOD	TRIBAL ENROLLMENT		
					YEAR	COUNTY	PAGE
1 Pickens, *(Illegible)*	NAMED	54	M	Full	1897	Pickens	9
2 " Annie	Wife	45	F	"	1897	"	9
3 Tyubby, Leah	Dau	22	"	"	1893	"	181
4 Pickens, Leona	"	20	"	"	1893	"	181
5 " Eli	Son	18	M	"	1897	"	11

6	" Shumpahcha	Dau	16	F	"	1897	"	12
7	" Joseph	Son	12	M	"	1897	"	12
8	" Apsie	Dau	9	F	"	1897	"	12
9	" Hallie	"	7	"	"	1897	"	12
10	" Janel	"	4	"	"	1897	"	12
11	Tyubby, Nicey	Gr.Dau	2mo	F	"			
12	Pickens, Mina	Gr.Dau	4mo	F	1/2			

TRIBAL ENROLLMENT OF PARENTS

	NAME OF FATHER	YEAR	COUNTY	NAME OF MOTHER	YEAR	COUNTY
1	Chon-tub-by	Dead	Chick Roll	(Name Illegible)	Dead	Chick Roll
2	Bob Ned	"	" "	Shini-ho-kee	"	" "
3	No. 1			No. 2		
4	No. 1			No. 2		
5	No. 1			No. 2		
6	No. 1			No. 2		
7	No. 1			No. 2		
8	No. 1			No. 2		
9	No. 1			No. 2		
10	No. 1			No. 2		
11	Noel Tyubby	1897	Pickens	No. 3		
12	(Gilbert Pickens)		(Choctaw Roll)	(No. 4)		

(NOTES)

Nos. 3-4 also on 1896 Chickasaw Roll, Pickens County, Page 96

No. 2 on Chickasaw Roll as Anney Pickens

No. 6 "   "   " " Mary   "

No. 3 is now the wife of Noel Tyubby on Chickasaw Card #764. See letter of J.C. McCurtain relative to marriage filed July 17, 1901. Also affidavit of Noel Tyubby filed Sept. 5, 1901.

No. 11 enrolled July 17, 1901.

No. 6 died Sept. 16, 1900. Evidence of death filed Sept. 2, 1901.

No. 4 is now the wife of Gilbert Pickens on Choctaw Card #5605. Evidence of marriage requested Nov. 12, 1902.

No. 12 born July 26, 1902; enrolled Nov. 12, 1902.   *(No. 12 Dawes' Roll No. 4169)*

Father of No. 12, is Gilbert Pickens on Choctaw Census 1896 Roll, Page 208, #10166 Gaines Co.

Mother of No. 12 is No. 4.

Oct. 3, 1898.

RESIDENCE: Pickens   COUNTY   CARD NO.

POST OFFICE: Mansville, I.T.   FIELD NO.

NAME	RELATION-SHIP TO PERSON FIRST NAMED	AGE	SEX	BLOOD	TRIBAL ENROLLMENT		
					YEAR	COUNTY	PAGE
1 Colbert, Louis ?.		35	M	Full	1897	Pickens	23

2	"	Betsey	Wife	36	F	I.W.	1897	"		79
3	"	Eva Lou	Dau	8	"	1/2	1897	"		23
4	"	Elizabeth Honor	"	6	"	1/2	1897	"		23
5	"	Eula Emily	"	4	"	1/2	1897	"		23
6	"	Amy	"	14mo	"	1/2				
7	"	Julia May	Dau	4mo	"	1/2				

TRIBAL ENROLLMENT OF PARENTS

	NAME OF FATHER	YEAR	COUNTY	NAME OF MOTHER	YEAR	COUNTY
1	Vann Colbert	Dead	Chick Roll	(Name Illegible)	Dead	Chick Roll
2	Ben Bean		Non Citizen	Honor Bean	"	Non Citizen
3	No. 1			No. 2		
4	No. 1			No. 2		
5	No. 1			No. 2		
6	No. 1			No. 2		
7	No. 1			No. 2		

(NOTES)

No. 4 on Chickasaw Roll as Elizabeth H. Colbert   *(No. 2 Dawes' Roll No. 140)*
No. 5 "   "   " " Eula H   "
No. 7 Enrolled July 16, 1900.

Oct. 3, 1898.

RESIDENCE: Pickens COUNTY						CARD NO.			
POST OFFICE: Brownsville, I.T.						FIELD NO.			

	NAME	RELATION-SHIP TO PERSON FIRST NAMED	AGE	SEX	BLOOD	TRIBAL ENROLLMENT		
						YEAR	COUNTY	PAGE
1	Holo?ubby, Chohota	NAMED	80	F	Full	1897	Pickens	23
2	Chester, Joel	Gr.Son	19	M	"	1897	"	23
3	King, Elie	Dau	47	F	"			

TRIBAL ENROLLMENT OF PARENTS

	NAME OF FATHER	YEAR	COUNTY	NAME OF MOTHER	YEAR	COUNTY
1	Elijah	Dead	Chick Roll	Sla ho yo	Dead	Chick Roll
2	Thompson Chester	"	Panola	Gillen Chester	"	Panola
3	Moloubby	"	"	No. 1		

(NOTES)

No. 1 on Chickasaw Roll as Mrs. Hollauby
No. 2 "   "   " " Joel Chester
No. 3 " Choctaw Census Record No. 2, Blue Co, Page 322, transferred to Chickasaw Roll by Dawes Commission
No. 2 is now the husband of Jinsie Burris on Chickasaw Card #965.
        Evidence of marriage requested July 17, 1901.

Oct. 3, 1898.

Chickasaw Enrollment Cards 1898-1914
Chickasaw by Blood   Volume IV

RESIDENCE: Pickens   COUNTY   CARD NO.

POST OFFICE: McMillan, I.T.   FIELD NO.

	NAME	RELATION-SHIP TO PERSON FIRST NAMED	AGE	SEX	BLOOD	TRIBAL ENROLLMENT		
						YEAR	COUNTY	PAGE
1	Burns, Charles Ambron	NAMED	34	M	I.W.	1897	Pickens	77
2	" Mollie	Wife	24	F	Full	1897	"	9
3	" Annie	Dau	3	"	1/2	1897	"	9
4	" Charley Frances	Son	1	M	1/2			
5	" Ely Pickens	Son	2mo	M	1/2			

TRIBAL ENROLLMENT OF PARENTS

	NAME OF FATHER	YEAR	COUNTY	NAME OF MOTHER	YEAR	COUNTY
1	G.W. Burns	Dead	Non Citizen	Carrie Burns	Dead	Non Citizen
2	Thunder Pickens	1897	Pickens	Anna Pickens	1897	Pickens
3	No. 1			No. 2		
4	No. 1			No. 2		
5	No. 1			No. 2		

(NOTES)

No. 1 on Chickasaw Roll as Charley Burns   *(No. 1 Dawes' Roll No. 329)*

Nos. 1, 2 and 3 admitted by Dawes Commission Case No. 19 and no appeal taken

No. 5 Enrolled May 24, 1900

Oct. 3, 1898.

RESIDENCE: Pickens   COUNTY   CARD NO.

POST OFFICE: Foster, I.T.   FIELD NO.

	NAME	RELATION-SHIP TO PERSON FIRST NAMED	AGE	SEX	BLOOD	TRIBAL ENROLLMENT		
						YEAR	COUNTY	PAGE
1	Lomer, Adam	NAMED	24	M	Full	1897	Pickens	24
2	" Malinda	Mother	45	F	"	1897	"	24
3	" Wesley	Bro	21	M	"	1897	"	24
4	" ~~Elizabeth~~	~~Sister~~	~~17~~	~~F~~	~~"~~	DIED PRIOR TO SEPTEMBER 25 1902 ~~1897~~	~~"~~	~~24~~
5	" Amanda	"	13	"	"	1897	"	24
6	" Susan	"	10	"	"	1897	"	24
7	" Sophia	"	8	"	"	1897	"	24
8	" Lillie	"	5	"	"	1897	"	24
9	" ~~Morris~~	~~S.Son~~	~~1~~	~~M~~	~~"~~	DIED PRIOR TO SEPTEMBER 25 1902		

	TRIBAL ENROLLMENT OF PARENTS					
	NAME OF FATHER	YEAR	COUNTY	NAME OF MOTHER	YEAR	COUNTY
1	Tecumseh Lomer	Dead	Pickens	Malinda Lomer {No. 2}	1897	Pickens
2	*(Name Illegible)*	"	Chick Roll	*(Name Illegible)*	Dead	Chick Roll
3	Tecumseh Lomer	Dead	Pickens	No. 2		
4	~~" "~~	~~"~~	~~"~~	~~No. 2~~		
5	" "	"	"	No. 2		
6	" "	"	"	No. 2		
7	" "	"	"	No. 2		
8	⟨Illegitimate⟩			No. 2		
9	~~"~~			~~No. 2~~		

(NOTES)

No. 4 Died Aug. 14, 1900; Enrollment *(remainder illegible)*
No. 4 on Chickasaw Roll as Lisburt Lomer
No. 5 " " " " Mandy "
No. 7 " " " " Sounie "
No. 9 Died Feb, 1899. Enrollment cancelled by Dept *(remainder illegible)*
No. 1 is now husband of Emely Pettigrew, on Chickasaw Card #897; April 17, 1902
No. 9 Died in February 1899; Proof of death filed Nov. 18, 1902
No. 4 died Aug. 14, 1900; Proof of death filed Nov. 18, 1902
Transferred Dec. 13, 1898, from white card No. D.118.

Oct. 3, 1898.

RESIDENCE: Tishomingo *COUNTY* *CARD NO.*
POST OFFICE: *(Illegible)* I.T. *FIELD NO.*

	NAME	RELATION-SHIP TO PERSON FIRST NAMED	AGE	SEX	BLOOD	TRIBAL ENROLLMENT		
						YEAR	COUNTY	PAGE
1	Colbert, Willie		32	M	3/4	1897	Tishomingo	27
2	~~" Agnes~~	~~Wife~~	~~23~~	~~F~~	~~Full~~	DIED ~~1897~~	PRIOR TO SEPTEMBER 25 1902 "	~~27~~
3	" *(Illegible)*	Dau	10mo	"	7/8			
4	Thomas, Heck	Nephew	8	M	7/8	1897	Pickens	18
5	~~" Edmon~~	"	~~9~~	"	~~7/8~~	DIED ~~1897~~	PRIOR TO SEPTEMBER 25 1902 "	~~18~~
6	Colbert, Maud	Wife	18	F	I.W.			

	TRIBAL ENROLLMENT OF PARENTS					
	NAME OF FATHER	YEAR	COUNTY	NAME OF MOTHER	YEAR	COUNTY
1	Edward Colbert	Dead	Chick Roll	Elsie Colbert	Dead	Chick Roll
2	~~Alex Russell~~	"	~~" "~~	~~Mary Russell~~	"	~~" "~~
3	No. 1			No. 2		

4	Isaac Thomas	Dead	Tishomingo	Eliza Thomas	Dead	Tishomingo
5	" "	"	"	" "	"	"
6	(Illegible) Harris	Dead	Non Citizen	Mag Harris		Non Citizen

(NOTES)

No. 2 died Aug. 22, 1899; Proof of death filed Nov. 10, 1902.

No. 5 "   " 23. 1902;   " " " " Nov. 10. 1902.

No. I is now husband of Maud Colbert on Chickasaw Card #E.382. Nov. 6,'02.

No. 6 transferred from Chickasaw Card #D.382   *(No. 6 Dawes' Roll No. 193)*

   See decision of May 31st/02

Oct. 3, 1898.

RESIDENCE: Pickens   COUNTY   CARD NO.

POST OFFICE: Russell, I.T.   FIELD NO.

NAME	RELATION-SHIP TO PERSON FIRST NAMED	AGE	SEX	BLOOD	TRIBAL ENROLLMENT		
					YEAR	COUNTY	PAGE
1 McGuire, Sam		25	M	Full	1897	Pickens	11

TRIBAL ENROLLMENT OF PARENTS

	NAME OF FATHER	YEAR	COUNTY	NAME OF MOTHER	YEAR	COUNTY
1	Nuck nech ubby	Dead	Panola	Anne	Dead	Panola

(NOTES)

Oct. 3, 1898.

RESIDENCE: Pickens   COUNTY   CARD NO.

POST OFFICE: Brownsville, I.T.   FIELD NO.

	NAME	RELATION-SHIP TO PERSON FIRST NAMED	AGE	SEX	BLOOD	TRIBAL ENROLLMENT		
						YEAR	COUNTY	PAGE
1	Burris, Joe H.	NAMED	24	M	Full	1897	Pickens	20
2	" Nina	Wife	40	F	"	1897	"	23
3	" Walsie	Son	1	M	"			
4	McLish, Esau	S.Son	9	"	"	1897	Pickens	23
5	Russell, Arthur	" "	5	"	"	1897	"	23
6	Parker, Louis	Ward	10	"	"	1897	"	23
7	Chester, Jinsie	Sister	18	F	"	1893	"	P.R.#2 41
8	DIED PRIOR TO SEPTEMBER 25 1902 Chester, Fulton Arbian	Nephew	1	M	"			

47

	TRIBAL ENROLLMENT OF PARENTS					
	NAME OF FATHER	YEAR	COUNTY	NAME OF MOTHER	YEAR	COUNTY
1	Aaron Burris	Dead	Pickens	Sylvie Burris	Dead	Pickens
2	Aaron Brown	"	Chick Roll	Malinda Brown	"	Chick Roll
3	No. 1			No. 2		
4	Frank McLish	Dead	Pickens	No. 2		
5	Nicholas Russell	"	"	No. 2		
6	Holmes Parker	"	"	May Halo Parker	Dead	Non Citizen
7	Aaron Burris	"	Pickens	Sylvie Burris	"	Pickens
8	Joel Chester	1897	Pickens	No. 1		

(NOTES)

No. 8 died in Oct. 1901; *(remainder illegible)*
No. 2 on Chickasaw Roll as Nina McLish
No. 5 "   "   "   " Arthur "
No. 3 Affidavit of attending Physician to be supplied. Affidavit of father susbtituted Oct. 3, 1898,
No. 7 is now the wife of Joel Chester on Chickasaw Card #970. Evidence of marriage requested July 17, 1901.
No. 8 Born Aug. 25, 1900; Enrolled Dec. 5, 1901.

P.O. Isom Spring, I.T. 1/6/03   Oct. 3, 1898.

RESIDENCE: Pickens COUNTY					CARD NO.		
POST OFFICE: Burneyville, I.T.					FIELD NO.		

	NAME	RELATION-SHIP TO PERSON FIRST NAMED	AGE	SEX	BLOOD	TRIBAL ENROLLMENT		
						YEAR	COUNTY	PAGE
1	Parker, Simeon		39	M	Full	1897	Pickens	15
2	" Birt	Son	12	"	1/2	1897	"	15
3	" Ed	"	9	"	1/2	1897	"	15
4	" Aley	Dau	7	F	1/2	1897	"	15
5	" Dovie	"	5	"	1/2	1897	"	15
6	" Katoolah	"	2 1/2	"	1/2	1897	"	15
7	" Claud	Son	2mo	M	1/2			
8	" Laura	Wife	33	F	I.W.			

	TRIBAL ENROLLMENT OF PARENTS					
	NAME OF FATHER	YEAR	COUNTY	NAME OF MOTHER	YEAR	COUNTY
1	Thomas Parker	Dead	Pickens	Lalatia Parker	Dead	Pickens
2	No. 1			Laura Parker		White woman
3	No. 1			" "		" "
4	No. 1			" "		" "
5	No. 1			" "		" "

48

Chickasaw Enrollment Cards 1898-1914
Chickasaw by Blood   Volume IV

				" "				" "
6	No. 1			" "				" "
7	No. 1			" "				" "
8	J.T. Greenwood		non-citizen	Ann Greenwood			non-citizen	

(NOTES)

No. 5 on Chickasaw Roll as Davis Parker
No. 6 " " " " Kaloolah "
No. 7 Born Feby 9, 1902. Enrolled April 8, 1902.
No. 1 is husband of Laura Parker on Chickasaw Card #D.117.
No. 8 transferred from Chickasaw card #D117 April 1, 1903.   *(No. 8 Dawes' Roll No. 46)*
    See decision of March 16, 1903.

Oct. 3, 1898.

RESIDENCE: Pickens   *COUNTY*   *CARD NO.*
POST OFFICE: Darwood, I.T.   *FIELD NO.*

	NAME	RELATIONSHIP TO PERSON FIRST NAMED	AGE	SEX	BLOOD	TRIBAL ENROLLMENT		
						YEAR	COUNTY	PAGE
1	Russell, Ellis	NAMED	32	M	Full	1897	Pickens	19
2	" Hattie	Dau	10	F	1/2	1897	"	19
3	" Edmund	Son	8	M	1/2	1897	"	19
4	" Eula	Dau	2	F	1/2	1897	"	19
5	" Richard	Son	4mo	M	1/2			
6	Calhoune, Charles	Ward	16	"	Full	1897	Pickens	
7	Russell, Lula Myrtle	Dau	2mo	F	1/2			
8	" Cleoleen	Wife	39	F	I.W.	1897	Pickens	77

TRIBAL ENROLLMENT OF PARENTS

	NAME OF FATHER	YEAR	COUNTY	NAME OF MOTHER	YEAR	COUNTY
1	Hardy Russell	Dead	Chick Roll	Ziley Pickens	1897	Pickens
2	No. 1			Cleoleen Russell		White woman
3	No. 1			" "		" "
4	No. 1			" "		" "
5	No. 1			" "		" "
6	Johnson Calhoune	Dead	Panola	Meloiney Calhoune	Dead	Pickens
7	No. 1			Cleoleen Russell		Non Citizen
8	Peter Potter		non citizen	Lizzie Potter		non citizen

(NOTES)

No. 3 on Chickasaw Roll as Edward Russell
No. 5 Affidavit of attending Physician to be supplied. Received Oct. 5, 1898.
No. 1 is husband of Cleoleen Russell, Chickasaw D.116
No. 7 Born May 11, 1902; Enrolled July 29, 1902

49

No. 8 transferred from Chickasaw Card #0116, April 1, 1903.   *(No. 8 Dawes' Roll No. 45)*
See decision of March 16, 1903.

P.O. Seems to be McMillan, I.T. 7/29/02   Oct. 3, 1898.

RESIDENCE: Pickens COUNTY					CARD NO.			
POST OFFICE: McMillan, I.T.					FIELD NO.			
NAME	RELATION-SHIP TO PERSON FIRST NAMED	AGE	SEX	BLOOD	TRIBAL ENROLLMENT			
					YEAR	COUNTY	PAGE	
1 Pickens, Clayburn	NAMED	30	M	Full	1897	Pickens	9	
2 " Anna	Wife	20	F	"	1897	"	9	
3 " Nonee	Dau	2wks	"	"				

	TRIBAL ENROLLMENT OF PARENTS						
NAME OF FATHER	YEAR	COUNTY	NAME OF MOTHER	YEAR	COUNTY		
1 I-a-han-ta Pickens	1897	Pickens	*(Name Illegible)*	Dead	Pickens		
2 Johnson Calhoune	Dead	Panola	Meloiney Calhoune	"	"		
3 No. 1			No. 2				

(NOTES)

No. 2 on Chickasaw Roll as Mary *(Illegible)*
No. 3 Enrolled March 21, 1899.

Oct. 3, 1898.

RESIDENCE: Pickens COUNTY					CARD NO.			
POST OFFICE: Brownsville, I.T.					FIELD NO.			
NAME	RELATION-SHIP TO PERSON FIRST NAMED	AGE	SEX	BLOOD	TRIBAL ENROLLMENT			
					YEAR	COUNTY	PAGE	
1 Brown, *(Illegible)*	NAMED	25!	M	Full	1897	Pickens	24	
2 " Lucy	Wife	22	F	"	1897	"	24	
3 " Carrie	Dau	5	"	"	1897	"	24	
4 " *(Illegible)*	"	3	"	"	1897	"	24	
5 " E?ta	"	1	"	"				

	TRIBAL ENROLLMENT OF PARENTS						
NAME OF FATHER	YEAR	COUNTY	NAME OF MOTHER	YEAR	COUNTY		
1 *(Illegible)* Brown	Dead	Pickens	*(Illegible)* Brown	Dead	Pickens		
2 *(Name Illegible)*	"	Chick Roll	Polly *(Illegible)*	"	Chick Roll		
3 No. 1			No. 2				
4 No. 1			No. 2				

5	No. 1			No. 2		

(NOTES)

No. 4 on Chickasaw Roll as Mary Brown

Oct. 3, 1898.

RESIDENCE: Pickens **COUNTY**   **CARD NO.**

POST OFFICE: Brownsville, I.T.   **FIELD NO.**

NAME	RELATION-SHIP TO PERSON FIRST NAMED	AGE	SEX	BLOOD	TRIBAL ENROLLMENT		
					YEAR	COUNTY	PAGE
1 lapahubby		74	M	Full	1897	Pickens	24

TRIBAL ENROLLMENT OF PARENTS

NAME OF FATHER	YEAR	COUNTY	NAME OF MOTHER	YEAR	COUNTY
1 Tallakoye	Dead	Chick Roll	Docey	Dead	Chick Roll

(NOTES)

On Chickasaw Roll as lappyubby
No. 1 died March 17, 1901; Proof of death filed Jany 17, 1902.

Oct. 3, 1898.

CANCELLED Stamped across card

RESIDENCE: Pickens **COUNTY**   **CARD NO.**

POST OFFICE: Powell, I.T.   **FIELD NO.**

NAME	RELATION-SHIP TO PERSON FIRST NAMED	AGE	SEX	BLOOD	TRIBAL ENROLLMENT		
					YEAR	COUNTY	PAGE
1 Anoatubby, Lankford	NAMED	21	M	Full	1897	Pickens	25
2 " Jane	Wife	19	F	"	1897	Tishomingo	35
3 " Ida	Step.Dau	2	"	"	1897	"	35

TRIBAL ENROLLMENT OF PARENTS

NAME OF FATHER	YEAR	COUNTY	NAME OF MOTHER	YEAR	COUNTY
1 Archison Anoatubby	1897	Pickens	Elizabeth Anoatubby	Dead	Pickens
2 Johnson Case	Dead	"	Icy Case	"	"
3 ⟨Illegitimate⟩			No. 2		

(NOTES)

No. 1 on Chickasaw Roll as Lankford Atchinson
No. 2 "   "   "   " Jennie Fletcher
No. 3 "   "   "   " Julia   "

Oct. 3, 1898.

51

RESIDENCE: Pickens COUNTY					CARD NO.		
POST OFFICE: Oakland, I.T.					FIELD NO.		
NAME	RELATION-SHIP TO PERSON FIRST NAMED	AGE	SEX	BLOOD	TRIBAL ENROLLMENT		
					YEAR	COUNTY	PAGE
1 Love, Clifton Nathaniel	NAMED	34	M	1/4	1897	Pickens	21
2 " Nellie	Wife	42	F	I.W.			
3 " Mary Otina	Dau	4	F	1/8	1897	Pickens	21
4 " Bessie Inona	"	2	"	1/8	1897	"	21
5 " Ruby	Dau	4mo	F	1/8			

	TRIBAL ENROLLMENT OF PARENTS						
NAME OF FATHER		YEAR	COUNTY	NAME OF MOTHER	YEAR	COUNTY	
1 Cubby *(illegible)*		Dead	Tishomingo	Sophie Love	Dead	Tishomingo	
2 Buck Smith			non-citz	Mary Ellen Smith	Dead	non-citz	
3 No. 1				Nellie Love		White Woman	
4 No. 1				" "		" "	
5 No. 1				" "		" "	

(NOTES)

No. 1 on Chickasaw Roll as C.N. Love
No. 3 "   "   "   " Mary "
No. 4 "   "   "   " Bessie "

(No. 2 Dawes' Roll No. 44)

No. 2 transferred from Chickasaw card #D113, April 1, 1903. See decision of March 16, 1903.
    Evidence of marriage of Nathaniel Clifton Love and Nellie Love, attached to Chickasaw Card D.113.
No. 5 transferred from Chickasaw D.113 to this Card March 27, 1902.
No. 4 died January 13, 1899; Proof of death filed Nov. 8, 1902.

Oct. 3, 1898.

RESIDENCE: Pickens COUNTY					CARD NO.		
POST OFFICE: Kingston, I.T.					FIELD NO.		
NAME	RELATION-SHIP TO PERSON FIRST NAMED	AGE	SEX	BLOOD	TRIBAL ENROLLMENT		
					YEAR	COUNTY	PAGE
1 Burris, Sam	NAMED	32	M	Full	1897	Pickens	20
2 " Bettie	Wife	20	F	"	1897	"	20
3 " Isaac	Son	11	M	"	1897	"	20
4 " Eastman	"	6	"	"	1897	"	20
5 " James	"	2	"	"	1897	"	20
6 " Sarah	Dau	1	F	"			
7 " Nancy	Dau	8mo	F	"			

	TRIBAL ENROLLMENT OF PARENTS					
NAME OF FATHER	YEAR	COUNTY	NAME OF MOTHER	YEAR	COUNTY
1	Aaron Burris	Dead	Pickens	Sylvia Burris	Dead	Pickens
2	Morgan Sealy	"	"	Chemaihe Sealy	"	Pontotoc
3	No. 1			Sean Burris	"	Pickens
4	No. 1			Epsey "	"	Panola
5	No. 1			No. 2		
6	No. 1			No. 2		
7	No. 1			No. 2		

(NOTES)

No. 7 Enrolled July 17, 1901
No. 6 " Dec. 16, 1899

Oct. 3, 1898.

RESIDENCE: Tishomingo COUNTY   CARD NO.
POST OFFICE: Regan, I.T.   FIELD NO.

NAME	RELATION-SHIP TO PERSON FIRST NAMED	AGE	SEX	BLOOD	TRIBAL ENROLLMENT		
					YEAR	COUNTY	PAGE
1	~~Lewis, Albert~~	NAMED	44	M	~~Full~~	~~1897~~	~~Pickens~~	~~35~~
2	" Sallie	Wife	45	F	"	1897	"	35

TRIBAL ENROLLMENT OF PARENTS						
NAME OF FATHER	YEAR	COUNTY	NAME OF MOTHER	YEAR	COUNTY
1	~~Cha-fah-tubby Brown~~	~~Dead~~	~~Tishomingo~~	~~Jincy Brown~~	~~Dead~~	~~Tishomingo~~
2	Tish-a-hon-tubby	"	"	Ah-no-le-ho-ye	"	"

(NOTES)

No. 1 died in March 1900; Proof of death filed Nov. 24, 1902.

Oct. 3, 1898.

RESIDENCE: Pickens COUNTY   CARD NO.
POST OFFICE: Kingston, I.T.   FIELD NO.

NAME	RELATION-SHIP TO PERSON FIRST NAMED	AGE	SEX	BLOOD	TRIBAL ENROLLMENT		
					YEAR	COUNTY	PAGE
1	Brown, Jack	NAMED	24	M	Full	1897	Pickens	23

TRIBAL ENROLLMENT OF PARENTS						
NAME OF FATHER	YEAR	COUNTY	NAME OF MOTHER	YEAR	COUNTY
1	Loman Brown	Dead	Pickens	Sylvia Okayanubby	1897	Pickens

(NOTES)

Oct. 3, 1898.

Chickasaw Enrollment Cards 1898-1914
Chickasaw by Blood   Volume IV

RESIDENCE: Pickens   COUNTY

POST OFFICE: Kingston, I.T.

CARD NO.

FIELD NO.

	NAME	RELATIONSHIP TO PERSON FIRST NAMED	AGE	SEX	BLOOD	TRIBAL ENROLLMENT		
						YEAR	COUNTY	PAGE
1	Okayanubby, Isom	NAMED	55	M	Full	1897	Pickens	22
2	" Sylvia	Wife	40	F	"	1897	"	22
3	Brown, Susan	S.Dau	19	"	"	1897	"	22
4	Hays, Louisa	" "	18	"	"	1897	"	22
5	Okayanubby, Albert	Son	11	M	"	1897	"	22
6	" Liza	Dau	9	F	"	1897	"	22
7	Ned, Solomon	Son of No. 4	5mo	M	"			

TRIBAL ENROLLMENT OF PARENTS

	NAME OF FATHER	YEAR	COUNTY	NAME OF MOTHER	YEAR	COUNTY
1	Okayanubby	Dead	Pickens	Sno-mul-ney	Dead	Pickens
2	Jimpson Frazier	"	"	Shim-a-hoy-ya	"	"
3	Loman Brown	"	"	No. 2		
4	Solomon Hays	"	"	No. 2		
5	No. 1			No. 2		
6	No. 1			No. 2		
7	Watson Ned	1897	Pontotoc and Pickens	No. 4		

(NOTES)

No. 1 died Jan. 23, 1901; Proof of death filed Nov. 11, 1902.

No. 4 is now the wife of Watson Ned on Chickasaw Card No. 1500, Nov. 14, 1902.

No. 7 Born in June 1902; Enrolled Nov. 14, 1902.   *(No. 7 Dawes' Roll No. 4168)*

No. 7 is illegitimate. The notation relative to No. 4 being wife of Watson Ned is an error. See testimony of Nos. 2 and 3 of May 23, 1903.

P.O. Isony Springs 2/5/03

Oct. 3, 1898.

RESIDENCE: Pickens   COUNTY

POST OFFICE: Brownsville, I.T.

CARD NO.

FIELD NO.

	NAME	RELATIONSHIP TO PERSON FIRST NAMED	AGE	SEX	BLOOD	TRIBAL ENROLLMENT		
						YEAR	COUNTY	PAGE
1	Capey, Wallace	NAMED	25	M	Full	1897	Pickens	22
2	" Serena	Wife	61	F	"	DIED PRIOR TO SEPTEMBER 25 1902 1897	"	22
3	Ohahentubby, Malinda	Cousin	54	"	"	1897	"	24

54

4	Kaney, Willie	Step Gr.Son	17	M	"	1897	"	22

TRIBAL ENROLLMENT OF PARENTS

	NAME OF FATHER	YEAR	COUNTY	NAME OF MOTHER	YEAR	COUNTY
1	Capey	Dead	Chick Roll	(Name Illegible)	Dead	Chick Roll
2	Tik-ka-lahh-te	"	" "	Co-ik-key	"	" "
3	Pe-looh-ey	"	" "	Ho-ma-tey	"	" "
4	Harmon Kaney	1897	Pickens	Sophie Kaney	"	Pickens

(NOTES)

No. 3 On Chick Roll as Melisa (Illegible)
No. 2 died March 29, 1902; Proof of death filed Nov. 8, 1902.

Oct. 3, 1898.

RESIDENCE: Pickens COUNTY			CARD NO.			
POST OFFICE: Lynn, I.T.			FIELD NO.			

	NAME	RELATION-SHIP TO PERSON FIRST NAMED	AGE	SEX	BLOOD	TRIBAL ENROLLMENT		
						YEAR	COUNTY	PAGE
1	Tussy, Jane		68	F	3/4	1897	Pickens	26

TRIBAL ENROLLMENT OF PARENTS

	NAME OF FATHER	YEAR	COUNTY	NAME OF MOTHER	YEAR	COUNTY
1	Jas. McLaughlin	Dead	Chick Roll	Liza McLaughlin	Dead	Chick Roll

(NOTES)

Oct. 3/98.

RESIDENCE: Pickens COUNTY			CARD NO.			
POST OFFICE: Kingston, I.T.			FIELD NO.			

	NAME	RELATION-SHIP TO PERSON FIRST NAMED	AGE	SEX	BLOOD	TRIBAL ENROLLMENT		
						YEAR	COUNTY	PAGE
1	Falata, Kuneatcha		29	F	Full	1897	Pickens	23
2	" Liuho	Sister	30	"	"	1897	"	12

TRIBAL ENROLLMENT OF PARENTS

	NAME OF FATHER	YEAR	COUNTY	NAME OF MOTHER	YEAR	COUNTY
1	Falata	Dead	Pickens	Elecky	Dead	Pickens
2	"	"	"	"	"	"

(NOTES)

No. 1 on Chickasaw Roll as Lucy Falata
No. 2 " " " Liuco "

Oct. 3, 1898.

RESIDENCE: Pontotoc   COUNTY   CARD NO.

POST OFFICE: Hart, I.T.   FIELD NO.

NAME	RELATION-SHIP TO PERSON FIRST NAMED	AGE	SEX	BLOOD	TRIBAL ENROLLMENT		
					YEAR	COUNTY	PAGE
1 Davis, John Lowery	NAMED	22	M	1/4	1897	Pontotoc	27

TRIBAL ENROLLMENT OF PARENTS

NAME OF FATHER	YEAR	COUNTY	NAME OF MOTHER	YEAR	COUNTY
1 John Davis	Dead	Cherokee Citz.	Harriet Burnett	1897	Pontotoc

(NOTES)

On Chickasaw Roll as "J.L. Davis".

Oct. 1, 1898.

RESIDENCE: Pickens   COUNTY   CARD NO.

POST OFFICE: Cheek, I.T.   FIELD NO.

NAME	RELATION-SHIP TO PERSON FIRST NAMED	AGE	SEX	BLOOD	TRIBAL ENROLLMENT		
					YEAR	COUNTY	PAGE
1 Hare, Sarah	NAMED	50	F	1/2	1897	Pickens	19
2 " Walter	Son	20	M	1/4	1897	"	19
3 " Charles	"	25	"	"			
4 " Minnie F.	Wife of No. 3	18	F	I.W.			

TRIBAL ENROLLMENT OF PARENTS

NAME OF FATHER	YEAR	COUNTY	NAME OF MOTHER	YEAR	COUNTY
1 Noah Watkins	Dead	Non Citizen	Nicey Watkins	Dead	Chick resid'g in Choc. N. 3rd Dist.
2 Francis Hare	1897	Cherokee Citz	No. 1		
3 " "	"	" "	No. 1		
4 John D. Smith		non-citz	Conie Smith		non-citz

(NOTES)

No. 3 on Maytubby Pay Roll No. 205; One of the children in family of Francis Hare.

No. 3 in Penetentiary, Columbus Ohio.

No. 3 is husband of Minnie F. Hare on Chickasaw Card #D.109.

No. 4 transferred from Chickasaw Card #D.291 March 29. 1903.   *(No. 4 Dawes' Roll No. 43)*

See decision of March 13, 1903.

P.O. of No. 3 is Orr, I.T.   Oct. 1, 1898.

Chickasaw Enrollment Cards 1898-1914
Chickasaw by Blood   Volume IV

RESIDENCE: Tishomingo COUNTY   CARD NO.
POST OFFICE: Mill Creek, I.T.   FIELD NO.

	NAME	RELATION-SHIP TO PERSON FIRST NAMED	AGE	SEX	BLOOD	TRIBAL ENROLLMENT		
						YEAR	COUNTY	PAGE
1	Lewis, Ben	NAMED	21	M	Full	1897	Tishomingo	21
2	Underwood, Salina	Wife	19	F	"	1897	"	21
3	Lewis, Fannis	Dau	1	"	"			
4	Underwood, Matlain	Dau of No. 2	3mo	F	"			

TRIBAL ENROLLMENT OF PARENTS

	NAME OF FATHER	YEAR	COUNTY	NAME OF MOTHER	YEAR	COUNTY
1	Josiah Lewis	Dead	Tishomingo	Malinda Lewis	Dead	Tishomingo
2	Harry Austin	"	Pickens	Malinda Brown	"	"
3	No. 1			No. 2		
4	Elonzo Underwood		Tishomingo	No. 2		

(NOTES)

No. 2 is now the wife of Elonzo Underwood, on Chickasaw Cared #909.
No. 3 Affidavit of attending Physician to be supplied. Rec'd Oct. 11, 98   June 4, 1901.
No. 1 on Chickasaw Roll as Ben Lewis, Jr.
No. 4 enrolled June 4, 1901
No. 3 died Oct. 13, 1900. Proof of death filed Aug. 13, 1901.
No. 1 died   "   15, 1899;   "   "   "   "   Oct. 23, 1902.

P.O. Russett, I.T.   Oct. 1, 1898.

RESIDENCE: Tishomingo COUNTY   CARD NO.
POST OFFICE: Mill Creek, I.T.   FIELD NO.

	NAME	RELATION-SHIP TO PERSON FIRST NAMED	AGE	SEX	BLOOD	TRIBAL ENROLLMENT		
						YEAR	COUNTY	PAGE
1	Austin, Mattie	NAMED	11	F	Full	1897	Tishomingo	27

TRIBAL ENROLLMENT OF PARENTS

	NAME OF FATHER	YEAR	COUNTY	NAME OF MOTHER	YEAR	COUNTY
1	Harry Austin	Dead	Pickens	Malinda Brown	Dead	Tishomingo

(NOTES)

Oct. 1, 1898.

57

RESIDENCE: Pontotoc COUNTY					CARD NO.		
POST OFFICE: Wapanucka, I.T.					FIELD NO.		

NAME	RELATION-SHIP TO PERSON FIRST NAMED	AGE	SEX	BLOOD	TRIBAL ENROLLMENT		
					YEAR	COUNTY	PAGE
1 Fillmore, Isaac	NAMED	25	M	1/4	1897	Pontotoc	52
2 " Charles Wilson	Son	4	"	1/8	1897	"	52

TRIBAL ENROLLMENT OF PARENTS						
NAME OF FATHER	YEAR	COUNTY	NAME OF MOTHER	YEAR	COUNTY	
1 Wilson Fillmore	Dead	Pontotoc	Delphea W. Fillmore	1897	Pontotoc	
2 No. 1			Sallie Fillmore	1897	Non Citizen	

(NOTES)
No. 2 on Chickasaw Roll as Charles W. Fillmore
Surname on Chickasaw Roll Filmore

P.O. Fillmore, I.T. 1/31/02   Oct. 1, 1898.

RESIDENCE: Pontotoc COUNTY					CARD NO.		
POST OFFICE: Wapanucka, I.T.					FIELD NO.		

NAME	RELATION-SHIP TO PERSON FIRST NAMED	AGE	SEX	BLOOD	TRIBAL ENROLLMENT		
					YEAR	COUNTY	PAGE
1 Fillmore, Delphia W.	NAMED	60	F	1/2	1897	Pontotoc	52

TRIBAL ENROLLMENT OF PARENTS						
NAME OF FATHER	YEAR	COUNTY	NAME OF MOTHER	YEAR	COUNTY	
1 Wm McGillray	Dead	Pontotoc	Nancy McGillray	Dead	Pontotoc	

(NOTES)
No. 1 on Chickasaw Roll as Delphia W. Filmore
No. 1 died April 7, 1902; Proof of death filed Nov. 7, 1902.

Oct. 1, 1898

RESIDENCE: Pontotoc COUNTY					CARD NO.		
POST OFFICE: Stonewall, I.T.					FIELD NO.		

NAME	RELATION-SHIP TO PERSON FIRST NAMED	AGE	SEX	BLOOD	TRIBAL ENROLLMENT		
					YEAR	COUNTY	PAGE
1 Alberson, John	NAMED	10	M	Full	1893	Tishomingo	P.R. #1 107

TRIBAL ENROLLMENT OF PARENTS

	NAME OF FATHER	YEAR	COUNTY	NAME OF MOTHER	YEAR	COUNTY
1	Willie Alberson	Dead	Tishomingo	Sue Alberson	Dead	Tishomingo

(NOTES)

No. 1 also on 1893 Chickasaw Pay Roll #1, page 95.

Oct. 1, 1898.

RESIDENCE: Tishomingo COUNTY CARD NO.
POST OFFICE: Mill Creek, I.T. FIELD NO.

	NAME	RELATION-SHIP TO PERSON FIRST NAMED	AGE	SEX	BLOOD	TRIBAL ENROLLMENT		
						YEAR	COUNTY	PAGE
1	Cunnentubby, Palnier		19	M	Full	1897	Tishomingo	29

TRIBAL ENROLLMENT OF PARENTS

	NAME OF FATHER	YEAR	COUNTY	NAME OF MOTHER	YEAR	COUNTY
1	Ben Cunnetubby	Dead	Tishomingo	Sophie Cunnetubby	1897	Tishomingo

(NOTES)

On Chickasaw Roll as Cunnentubby.
No. 1 now husband of Lucy Gilbert, *(remainder illegible)*

P.O. Davis, I.T.

Oct. 1, 1898.

RESIDENCE: Tishomingo COUNTY CARD NO.
POST OFFICE: Tishomingo, I.T. FIELD NO.

	NAME	RELATION-SHIP TO PERSON FIRST NAMED	AGE	SEX	BLOOD	TRIBAL ENROLLMENT		
						YEAR	COUNTY	PAGE
1	Greenwood, Henry		27	M	Full	1897	Tishomingo	34

TRIBAL ENROLLMENT OF PARENTS

	NAME OF FATHER	YEAR	COUNTY	NAME OF MOTHER	YEAR	COUNTY
1	Cumanche Greenwood	Dead	Chick. Roll	Louisa Greenwood	Dead	Tishomingo

(NOTES)

See Chickasaw Card D.79 for enrollment of Mary Greenwood, his former wife, from whom he is now divorced. Nov. 1, 1900.

Oct. 1, 1898.

RESIDENCE: Tishomingo   **COUNTY**

POST OFFICE: Emmett, I.T.

CARD NO.

FIELD NO.

NAME	RELATION-SHIP TO PERSON FIRST NAMED	AGE	SEX	BLOOD	TRIBAL ENROLLMENT		
					YEAR	COUNTY	PAGE
1 Wolfe, Wilburn		18	M	Full	1897	Tishomingo	34

TRIBAL ENROLLMENT OF PARENTS

NAME OF FATHER	YEAR	COUNTY	NAME OF MOTHER	YEAR	COUNTY
1 John Wolfe	Dead	Panola	Mulsey Wolfe	Dead	Panola

(NOTES)

Oct. 1, 1898.

RESIDENCE: Chickasaw Nation   ~~COUNTY~~

POST OFFICE: Stewart, I.T.

CARD NO.

FIELD NO.

NAME	RELATION-SHIP TO PERSON FIRST NAMED	AGE	SEX	BLOOD	TRIBAL ENROLLMENT		
					YEAR	COUNTY	PAGE
1 Nelson, Phillip		19	M	1/1	1897	Chick resid'g in Chick. N. 1st Dist.	67

TRIBAL ENROLLMENT OF PARENTS

NAME OF FATHER	YEAR	COUNTY	NAME OF MOTHER	YEAR	COUNTY
1 Bill Nelson	Dead	Chic. Citizen	Annie Nelson	Dead	Chick resid'g in Choctaw Nation

(NOTES)

Also on 1896 Choctaw Roll, Page 249, No. 9834 Atoka Co.   *(No. 1 Dawes' Roll No. 4794)*

Is not No. 1 father of Joseph Nelson Chickasaw card #59

Oct. 1, 1898

RESIDENCE: Pontotoc   **COUNTY**

POST OFFICE: Stonewall, I.T.

CARD NO.

FIELD NO.

NAME	RELATION-SHIP TO PERSON FIRST NAMED	AGE	SEX	BLOOD	TRIBAL ENROLLMENT		
					YEAR	COUNTY	PAGE
1 ~~Brown, George~~		~~25~~	~~M~~	~~Full~~	~~1893~~	~~Pontotoc~~	~~P.R.#2~~ ~~46~~

TRIBAL ENROLLMENT OF PARENTS

NAME OF FATHER	YEAR	COUNTY	NAME OF MOTHER	YEAR	COUNTY
1 ~~Madison Brown~~	~~Dead~~	~~Pontotoc~~	~~Dana Brown~~	~~Dead~~	~~Pontotoc~~

(NOTES)

No. 1 is dead. See proof of death filed herein also

See Chickasaw Card No. 681.

See letter of Geo. D. Rodgers filed herein Nov. 19. 1902

Oct. 1, 1898.

RESIDENCE: Pontotoc COUNTY CARD NO.
POST OFFICE: Jeff, I.T. FIELD NO.

	NAME	RELATIONSHIP TO PERSON FIRST NAMED	AGE	SEX	BLOOD	TRIBAL ENROLLMENT		
						YEAR	COUNTY	PAGE
~~1~~	~~Underwood, Mollie~~		~~18~~	~~F~~	~~Full~~	~~1893~~	~~Pontotoc~~	~~P.R.#2 220~~

TRIBAL ENROLLMENT OF PARENTS

	NAME OF FATHER	YEAR	COUNTY	NAME OF MOTHER	YEAR	COUNTY
~~1~~	~~Gabriel Underwood~~	~~1897~~	~~Pontotoc~~	~~Sabrina Underwood~~	~~Dead~~	~~Pontotoc~~

(NOTES)

Cancelled Sept. *(remainder illegible)*
No. 1 is a cuplicate of No. 1 on Chick Card 1564.
Is not this a duplicate of No. 1 on Chickasaw card #1564?
see copy of letter of G.D. Rodgers, herein dated Nov. 12, 1902.

Oct. 1, 1898.

RESIDENCE: Tishomingo COUNTY CARD NO.
POST OFFICE: Ravia, I.T. FIELD NO.

	NAME	RELATIONSHIP TO PERSON FIRST NAMED	AGE	SEX	BLOOD	TRIBAL ENROLLMENT		
						YEAR	COUNTY	PAGE
1	Henderson, Campbell		30	M	Full	1897	Tishomingo	34
~~2~~	~~" Rhoda~~	~~Wife~~	~~19~~	~~F~~	~~"~~	~~1897~~	~~"~~	~~34~~
3	Palmer, Amanda	Dau	14	"	"	1897	"	34
4	Henderson, Francis	Dau	5	"	"	1897	"	34
5	" Norah	"	1	"	"			
6	Lavers, Maude	Son of No. 3	4mo	M	3/4			

TRIBAL ENROLLMENT OF PARENTS

	NAME OF FATHER	YEAR	COUNTY	NAME OF MOTHER	YEAR	COUNTY
1	Ishun-lub-by	Dead	Tishomingo	La-a-janet	Dead	Tishomingo
2	~~*(Name Illegible)*~~	~~"~~	~~"~~	~~*(Name Illegible)*~~	~~"~~	~~"~~
3	No. 1			Mulsey Henderson	"	"
4	No. 1			No. 2		
5	No. 1			No. 2		
6	Overton Lavers	1897	Tishomingo	No. 3		

(NOTES)

No. 2 Died April *(remainder illegible)*
No. 1 on Chickasaw Roll as Camel Henderson
No. 4 " " " " Francis "

No. 3 is the wife of Charles M. Palmer on Choctaw Card #D.385.
No. 6 Born June 8, 1902, enrolled Oct. 9, 1902   *(No. 6 Dawes' Roll No. 4467)*
No. 6 Illegitimate. Charles M. Palmer, husband of No. 3 is dead.
    See letter from A.A. Chapman in G.O. files #17300-1902.

Oct. 1, 1898.

	RESIDENCE: Tishomingo COUNTY					CARD NO.			
	POST OFFICE: Tishomingo, I.T.					FIELD NO.			
	NAME	RELATION-SHIP TO PERSON FIRST NAMED	AGE	SEX	BLOOD	TRIBAL ENROLLMENT			
						YEAR	COUNTY	PAGE	
1	Wolfe, Robinson	NAMED	15	M	3/4	1897	Tishomingo	34	
2	" Ida	Sister	11	F	"	1897	"	34	
3	" Johnnie	Brother	9	M	"	1897	"	34	

		TRIBAL ENROLLMENT OF PARENTS						
	NAME OF FATHER	YEAR	COUNTY	NAME OF MOTHER		YEAR	COUNTY	
1	Joe Wolfe	Dead	Tishomingo	Josephine Wolfe		Dead	Tishomingo	
2	" "	"	"	" "		"	"	
3	" "	"	"	" "		"	"	

(NOTES)

No. 2 on Chickasaw Roll as Ada Wolfe
No. 1 also on Page 18 as Robertson Wolfe
No. 2 " " " " " Ida "
No. 3 " " " " " John "

Oct. 1, 1898.

	RESIDENCE: Tishomingo COUNTY					CARD NO.			
	POST OFFICE: Davis, I.T.					FIELD NO.			
	NAME	RELATION-SHIP TO PERSON FIRST NAMED	AGE	SEX	BLOOD	TRIBAL ENROLLMENT			
						YEAR	COUNTY	PAGE	
1	McHardy, Wyatt	NAMED	53	M	1/2	1897	Tishomingo	27	

		TRIBAL ENROLLMENT OF PARENTS						
	NAME OF FATHER	YEAR	COUNTY	NAME OF MOTHER		YEAR	COUNTY	
1	Wyatt McHardy	Dead	Chick. Freedman	Sto-na-ho		Dead	Chick Roll	

(NOTES)

Oct. 1, 1898.

62

RESIDENCE:	Pickens	COUNTY				CARD NO.			
POST OFFICE:	Tishomingo, I.T.					FIELD NO.			

	NAME	RELATION-SHIP TO PERSON FIRST NAMED	AGE	SEX	BLOOD	TRIBAL ENROLLMENT		
						YEAR	COUNTY	PAGE
1	Burris, Ben	NAMED	20	M	Full	1897	Pickens	24

TRIBAL ENROLLMENT OF PARENTS

	NAME OF FATHER	YEAR	COUNTY	NAME OF MOTHER	YEAR	COUNTY
1	Siphen Burris	Dead	Pickens	Sukey Burris	Dead	Pickens

(NOTES)

Oct. 1, 1898.

RESIDENCE:	Pickens	COUNTY				CARD NO.			
POST OFFICE:	Tishomingo, I.T.					FIELD NO.			

	NAME	RELATION-SHIP TO PERSON FIRST NAMED	AGE	SEX	BLOOD	TRIBAL ENROLLMENT		
						YEAR	COUNTY	PAGE
1	Mule*, Joe	NAMED	27	M	Full	1897	Pickens	24
2	" Jeanna	Wife	16	F	"	1897	"	33
3	" ~~Solomon~~	~~Son~~	4	M	"	DIED PRIOR TO SEPTEMBER 25 1902 ~~1897~~	"	~~24~~
4	~~Long, Agnes~~	~~Neice[sic]~~	~~18~~	~~F~~	"	~~1897~~	"	~~24~~
5	~~Mule, Charley~~	~~Son~~	~~5mo~~	~~M~~	"	DIED PRIOR TO SEPTEMBER 25 1902		
6	" Amanda	Dau	2mo	F	"			

TRIBAL ENROLLMENT OF PARENTS

	NAME OF FATHER	YEAR	COUNTY	NAME OF MOTHER	YEAR	COUNTY
1	Charley Nule*	Dead	Pickens	(Name Illegible)	Dead	Pickens
2	Ben Colbert	1897	"	Susie Colbert	1897	Tishomingo
3	~~No. 1~~			~~(Illegible) Nule~~	~~Dead~~	~~Pickens~~
4	~~John Long~~	~~Dead~~	~~Pickens~~	~~Patsy Long~~	"	"
5	~~No. 1~~			~~No. 2~~		
6	No. 1			No. 2		

(NOTES)

(Name spelled both ways)*
No. 1 on Chickasaw Roll as Joe Wite
No. 2 "   "   "   " Jeanna Colbert
No. 3 "   "   "   " Solomon Wite
No. 4 died about May 1st, 1900
No. 5 Enrolled November 9, 1900
No. 4 died in April, 1899; Proof of death filed Nov. 11, 1902.
No. 5 "   Oct. 8, 1904   "   "   "   "   " 11, 1902

No. 3 " Dec. 6, 1899 " " " " " 11, 1902
No. 6 Born Sept. 19, 1902; Enrolled Nov. 28, 1902.   *(No. 6 Dawes' Roll No. 4166)*
                                                                              Oct. 1, 1898.

RESIDENCE: Choctaw Nation ~~COUNTY~~   **CARD NO.**
POST OFFICE: Fulsom, I.T.   **FIELD NO.**

NAME	RELATION-SHIP TO PERSON FIRST NAMED	AGE	SEX	BLOOD	TRIBAL ENROLLMENT		
					YEAR	COUNTY	PAGE
1 Bee, Ebin	NAMED	22	M	Full	1897	Tishomingo	34
2 " ~~Lina~~	~~Wife~~	~~25~~	F	"	~~1897~~	"	~~34~~

TRIBAL ENROLLMENT OF PARENTS

	NAME OF FATHER	YEAR	COUNTY	NAME OF MOTHER	YEAR	COUNTY
1	As-pika-hick-o-by	Dead	Chick Roll	Ho-loh-cha	Dead	Chick Roll
2	~~Silar Subatunta~~	~~1897~~	~~Chick resid'g in Choc. Nation~~	~~Sukey Quincy~~	"	~~Pickens~~

(NOTES)
No. 2 Died Nov. 1901; Proof of death filed Nov. 7, 1902.
11/4/02 No. 1 now husband of Eddie Hunnatubby, Chick 829.

                                                                              Oct. 1, 1898.

RESIDENCE: Tishomingo COUNTY   **CARD NO.**
POST OFFICE: Emet, I.T.   **FIELD NO.**

NAME	RELATION-SHIP TO PERSON FIRST NAMED	AGE	SEX	BLOOD	TRIBAL ENROLLMENT		
					YEAR	COUNTY	PAGE
1 Thompson, Thomas Benj.	NAMED	33	M	1/4	1897	Tishomingo	35
2 " Bertie	Wife	28	F	I.W.	1897	Pickens	79
3 " Eugene Ross	Son	4	M	1/8	1897	Tishomingo	35
4 " Mary Francis	Dau	3	F	"	1897	"	35
5 " Gladys Tryphena	"	1	F	"	~~1897~~	"	~~88~~
6 " Thomas B.	Son	5mo	M	1/8			
7 " Iona	Dau	3mo	F	1/8			

TRIBAL ENROLLMENT OF PARENTS

	NAME OF FATHER	YEAR	COUNTY	NAME OF MOTHER	YEAR	COUNTY
1	T.J. Thompson	Dead	Chick Roll	Lena Thompson	Dead	Chick Roll
2	Daniel Freund	1897	Non Citizen	Mary Freund	1897	Non Citizen
3	No. 1			No. 2		
4	No. 1			No. 2		
5	No. 1			No. 2		

6	No. 1			No. 2		
7	No. 1			No. 2		

(NOTES)

No. 5 Proof of birth received and filed Sept. 25, 1902   *(No. 5 Dawes' Roll No. 4165)*
No. 1 on Chickasaw Roll as T.B. Thompson   *(No. 2 Dawes' Roll No. 139)*
No. 3 "   "   " " Eugene Thompson
No. 5 "   "   " " Tayphina G. Thompson
No. 4 "   "   " " Mary Thompson
No. 6 died in January 1900
No. 7 enrolled March 5, 1901
No. 6 Died January 11, 1900. Evidence of death filed May 16, 1901.
No. 6 Enrolled Nov. 4, 1899.

Oct. 1, 1898.

RESIDENCE: Tishomingo, COUNTY   CARD NO.
POST OFFICE: Emet, I.T.   FIELD NO.

NAME	RELATION-SHIP TO PERSON FIRST NAMED	AGE	SEX	BLOOD	TRIBAL ENROLLMENT		
					YEAR	COUNTY	PAGE
1 Bradley, Edwin	NAMED	22	M	1/4	1897	Pontotoc	63
2 " William M.	Father	57	"	I.W.	1897	"	P.R.#2 ?

TRIBAL ENROLLMENT OF PARENTS

	NAME OF FATHER	YEAR	COUNTY	NAME OF MOTHER	YEAR	COUNTY
1	William Bradley	1897	Pontotoc	Elizabeth Bradley	Dead	Pontotoc
2	George W. Bradley	Dead	Non citizen	Elizabeth Bradley	Dead	Non citizen

(NOTES)

On June 15, 1869, No. 2 was married to Elizabeth Bradley, a recognized and enrolled citizen by blood of the Chickasaw Nation. No. 2 wife died about the *(Illegible)*
No. 2 then successively married Tallie Barister and Mary Harrimon, both non-citizens while *(illegible)*
No. 2 originally listed for enrollment on Chickasaw card D.198, Oct. 21/98,
transferred to this card Feb. 5, 1905. See decision of Jan. 20, 1905.

Oct. 1, 1898

RESIDENCE: Tishomingo COUNTY   CARD NO.
POST OFFICE: Conner, I.T.   FIELD NO.

NAME	RELATION-SHIP TO PERSON FIRST NAMED	AGE	SEX	BLOOD	TRIBAL ENROLLMENT		
					YEAR	COUNTY	PAGE
1 James, Lawrence	NAMED	20	M	Full	1897	Tishomingo	35

TRIBAL ENROLLMENT OF PARENTS

	NAME OF FATHER	YEAR	COUNTY	NAME OF MOTHER	YEAR	COUNTY
1	Pucknatubby	Dead	Pontotoc	Elizabeth	Dead	Pontotoc

(NOTES)

Oct. 1, 1898

RESIDENCE: Pontotoc COUNTY

POST OFFICE: Chickasha, I.T.

CARD NO.

FIELD NO.

	NAME	RELATION-SHIP TO PERSON FIRST NAMED	AGE	SEX	BLOOD	TRIBAL ENROLLMENT		
						YEAR	COUNTY	PAGE
1	Fletcher, Thomas B.	NAMED	48	M	1/8	1897	Pontotoc	66
2	" John Henry	Son	23	M	1/16	1897	"	66
3	" Katie May	Dau	10	F	1/16	1897	"	66
4	" Virgie	"	8	"	1/16	1897	"	66
5	" Abner Brown	Son	6	M	1/16	1897	"	66
6	" Sally V.		20	F	I.W.			

TRIBAL ENROLLMENT OF PARENTS

	NAME OF FATHER	YEAR	COUNTY	NAME OF MOTHER	YEAR	COUNTY
1	P.M. Fletcher	Dead	Pickens	Easter Jane Fletcher	Dead	Non Citizen
2	No. 1			Mary F. Fletcher	"	" "
3	No. 1			Carrie Fletcher	"	" "
4	No. 1		" "	"	"	" "
5	No. 1		" "	"	"	" "
6	John C. Guerry		Non Citizen	Louisa D. Guerry		" "

(NOTES)

No. 1 on Chickasaw Roll as T.B. Fletcher
No. 2 "   "   "   " John   "
No. 3 "   "   "   " K.M.   "
No. 5 "   "   "   " A.B.   "
No. 6 is wife of No. 2. Enrolled May 24, 1899, by order of Commissioner McKinnon.   *(No. 6 Dawes' Roll No. 138)*
See Card D.261.
No. 6 was also listed for enrollment on Chickasaw Card #D.266 but same was cancelled December 7, 1901.

No. 2 P.O. Hickory, I.T.

Oct. 1, 1898.

RESIDENCE: Pontotoc   COUNTY

POST OFFICE: Waupaunucka, I.T.

CARD NO.

FIELD NO.

	NAME	RELATION-SHIP TO PERSON FIRST NAMED	AGE	SEX	BLOOD	TRIBAL ENROLLMENT		
						YEAR	COUNTY	PAGE
1	Greenwood, Isaac	NAMED	30	M	Full	1897	Pontotoc	75
2	" Nellie	Wife	26	F	"	1897	"	75
3	" Hicks	Son	10	M	"	1897	"	75
4	" Ermina	Dau	7	F	"	1897	"	75
5	" Jimmy	Son	6	M	"	1897	"	75
6	" Josie Ann	Dau	4	F	"	1897	"	75
7	" Ebin	Son	1	M	"			
8	" Myrtle	Dau	2	F	"			

TRIBAL ENROLLMENT OF PARENTS

	NAME OF FATHER	YEAR	COUNTY	NAME OF MOTHER	YEAR	COUNTY
1	Hagan Greenwood	1897	Pontotoc	Iley Greenwood	Dead	Pontotoc
2	Madison Brown	Dead	"	Jane Brown	"	Panola
3	No. 1			No. 2		
4	No. 1			No. 2		
5	No. 1			No. 2		
6	No. 1			No. 2		
7	No. 1			No. 2		
8	No. 1			No. 2		

(NOTES)

No. 6 on Chickasaw Roll as Lela Greenwood
No. 4 "   "   "   " Ema   "
No. 7 died in November 1898. Proof of death received Aug. 2 1901, and
returned for correction. Received and filed Aug. 8, 1901.
No. 8 Born May 1900; Enrolled Nov. 7, 1902

(No. 8 Dawes' Roll No. 4464)

Oct. 1, 1898

RESIDENCE: Tishomingo   COUNTY

POST OFFICE: Ravia, I.T.

CARD NO.

FIELD NO.

	NAME	RELATION-SHIP TO PERSON FIRST NAMED	AGE	SEX	BLOOD	TRIBAL ENROLLMENT		
						YEAR	COUNTY	PAGE
1	Lavers, Overton	NAMED	40	M	1/2	1897	Tishomingo	32
2	" Eliza	Wife	30	F	Full	1897	"	32
3	" Ervin	Son	14	M	3/4	1897	"	32
4	" Isaac	"	11	"	3/4	1897	"	32

	Name	Relation	Age	Sex	Blood	Year	County	Page
5	" Bennett	"	7	"	3/4	1897	"	32
6	" Ella	Dau	4	F	3/4	1897	"	32
7	" Dawes	Son	1	M	3/4			
8	Hawkins, Josie	Neice[sic]	11	F	Full	1897	Pickens	11
9	" Molsie	"	7	"	"	1897	"	11
10	Mattahoya	Mother in Law	70	"	"	1893	Tishomingo	126
11	Lavers, Allice	Dau	9mo	"	3/4			

TRIBAL ENROLLMENT OF PARENTS

	NAME OF FATHER	YEAR	COUNTY	NAME OF MOTHER	YEAR	COUNTY
1	George Lavers	Dead	Non Citizen	Sally Lavers	Dead	Chick Roll
2	(Name Illegible)	"	Chick Roll	Mattahoya	1897	Tishomingo Roll
3	No. 1			No. 2		
4	No. 1			No. 2		
5	No. 1			No. 2		
6	No. 1			No. 2		
7	No. 1			No. 2		
8	Jimpson Hawkins	1897	Tishomingo	Lizzie Hawkins	Dead	Pickens
9	" "	"	"	" "	"	"
10	(Name Illegible)	Dead	Chick Roll	(Name Illegible)	"	Chick Roll
11	No. 1			No. 2		

(NOTES)

No. 10 on Chickasaw Roll as Matthoya
  Surname on Chickasaw Roll Lavis
No. 10 also on 1896 Chickasaw Roll, Tishomingo Co, Page 92.
No. 11 enrolled January 18, 1900.

Oct. 1, 1898.

RESIDENCE: Tishomingo	COUNTY				CARD NO.			
POST OFFICE: Regan, I.T.					FIELD NO.			

	NAME	RELATION-SHIP TO PERSON FIRST NAMED	AGE	SEX	BLOOD	TRIBAL ENROLLMENT		
						YEAR	COUNTY	PAGE
1	Hawkins, George		25	M	Full	1893	Pickens	101

TRIBAL ENROLLMENT OF PARENTS

	NAME OF FATHER	YEAR	COUNTY	NAME OF MOTHER	YEAR	COUNTY
1	Willis Hawkins	Dead	Tishomingo	Phens Hawkins	Dead	Pickens

(NOTES)

No. 1 also on 1896 Chickasaw Roll, Pickens Co., Page 94.

Oct. 1, '98

Chickasaw Enrollment Cards 1898-1914
Chickasaw by Blood   Volume IV

RESIDENCE: Choctaw Nation   ~~COUNTY~~   CARD NO.
POST OFFICE: Atoka, I.T.   FIELD NO.

NAME	RELATION-SHIP TO PERSON FIRST NAMED	AGE	SEX	BLOOD	TRIBAL ENROLLMENT		
					YEAR	COUNTY	PAGE
1 Porter, Angeline		29	F	1/4	1893	Pickens	P.R.#2 180
2 Pytchlyn, Jeff	Son	12	M	5/8	1893	"	"
3 " Isabella	Dau	10	F	5/8	1893	"	"
4 " Maulsey	"	8	"	5/8	1893	"	"
5 Porter, Carl Richard	Son	2	M	1/8			
6 " Andrew	Son	11/2	"	1/8			
7 " Lilie	Dau	11mo	F	1/8			

TRIBAL ENROLLMENT OF PARENTS

	NAME OF FATHER	YEAR	COUNTY	NAME OF MOTHER	YEAR	COUNTY
1	Richard Kimble		Chick Freedman	Maulsie Kimble	Dead	Pickens
2	George Pytchlyn	1897	Tishomingo	No. 1		
3	" "	"	"	No. 1		
4	" "	"	"	No. 1		
5	Teviner (or Twiner) Porter		Col. Non Citizen	No. 1		
6	" " "		" " "	No. 1		
7	" " "		" " "	No. 1		

(NOTES)

No. 1   on Chickasaw Roll as Angeline Pitchlynn   *(No. 1 Dawes' Roll No. 4933)*
Nos. 2, 3 & 4 "   "   " Surname as   "   *(No. 2 Dawes' Roll No. 4934)*
(No. 3 Dawes' Roll No. 4935)   *(No. 4 Dawes' Roll No. 4936)*   *(No. 5 Dawes' Roll No. 4937)*
No. 6 enrolled Dec. 8, 1900.   *(No. 6 Dawes' Roll No. 4938)*
No. 7 Born Dec. 17, 1901; enrolled April 23, 1902.   *(No. 7 Dawes' Roll No. 4939)*
7/24/02   Sister of No. 1 on Chickasaw *(remainder illegible)*

Oct. 1, 1898.

RESIDENCE: Tishomingo   COUNTY   CARD NO.
POST OFFICE: Tishomingo, I.T.   FIELD NO.

NAME	RELATION-SHIP TO PERSON FIRST NAMED	AGE	SEX	BLOOD	TRIBAL ENROLLMENT		
					YEAR	COUNTY	PAGE
1 Scoby, Lola		32	F	1/4	1897	Tishomingo	38
2 Garrett, Lula	Dau	18	"	1/8	1897	"	38
3 McGeehee, William	Son	16	M	1/8	1897	"	38
4 " Josie	Dau	12	F	1/8	1897	"	38

69

5	" Bessie	"	7	"	1/8	1897	"	38
6	Scoby, William Arthur	Son	5	M	1/8	1897	"	38
7	Garrett, Jessie Lynn	Gr.Son	3mo	"	1/16			

TRIBAL ENROLLMENT OF PARENTS

	NAME OF FATHER	YEAR	COUNTY	NAME OF MOTHER	YEAR	COUNTY
1	Henry Colbert	Dead	Chick Roll	Louisa Patterson	1897	Tishomingo
2	Robert McGeehee	"	Non Citizen	No. 1		
3	" "	"	" "	No. 1		
4	" "	"	" "	No. 1		
5	" "	"	" "	No. 1		
6	Arthur E. Scoby		White man	No. 1		
7	J.A. Garrett		Non Citizen	No. 2		

(NOTES)

No. 6 on Chickasaw Roll a W.A. Scoby
No. 2 is the wife of J.A. Garrett, a non Citizen. Evidence of marriage filed Dec. 16, 1901.
No. 7 Born Aug. 28, 1901; Enrolled Dec. 16, 1901.

P.O. of No. 3 is Wayne, I.T. 10/20/02

Oct. 1, 1898.

RESIDENCE: Tishomingo COUNTY						CARD NO.		
POST OFFICE: Emmet, I.T.						FIELD NO.		

	NAME	RELATION-SHIP TO PERSON FIRST NAMED	AGE	SEX	BLOOD	TRIBAL ENROLLMENT		
						YEAR	COUNTY	PAGE
1	McCoy, Joe	NAMED	21	M	1/2	1897	Tishomingo	34
2	Sharp, Lillie	Cousin	17	F	1/2	1897	Panola	4
3	McCoy, Jake	"	15	M	1/2	1897	"	4
4	" Bettie	"	13	F	1/2	1897	"	4
5	" Zena	"	11	F	1/2	1897	"	4
6	" Tommie	"	9	"	1/2	1897	"	4
7	Harris, Martha	Maternal Gr.Mother	68	"	3/4	1897	Tishomingo	34
8	Sharp, Ruby	Dau of No. 2	1	"	1/4			

TRIBAL ENROLLMENT OF PARENTS

	NAME OF FATHER	YEAR	COUNTY	NAME OF MOTHER	YEAR	COUNTY
1	Jim McCoy	Dead	Chick Roll	Ada McCoy	Dead	Tishomingo
2	Tom "	"	Panola	Ida McCoy	"	Panola
3	" "	"	"	" "	"	"
4	" "	"	"	" "	"	"

5	" "	"	"	" "	"	"
6	" "	"	"	" "	"	"
7	John B. Moore	"	Chick Roll	Deliney	"	Chick Roll
8	J.M. Sharp		Non Citizen	No. 2		

(NOTES)

No. 5 on Chickasaw Roll as Zena McCoy

June 19, 1900, Husband of Ida McCoy, Mother of Nos. 2 to 6 on Chick R. 62.

No. 2 is now the wife of J.M. Sharp, a non Citizen white man; Nov. 25, 1901.

12/2/02 P.O. Robbers Roost I T

Oct. 1, 1898,

RESIDENCE: Tishomingo ***COUNTY*** ***CARD NO.***

POST OFFICE: Tishomingo, I.T. ***FIELD NO.***

	NAME	RELATION-SHIP TO PERSON FIRST NAMED	AGE	SEX	BLOOD	TRIBAL ENROLLMENT		
						YEAR	COUNTY	PAGE
1	McGill, Noah		50	M	Full	1897	Tishomingo	37
2	" Eliza	Wife	37	F	1/2	1897	"	37
3	" Henry	Son	13	M	3/4	1897	"	37
4	" Rose	Dau	11	F	3/4	1897	"	37
5	" Ella	"	9	"	3/4	1897	"	37
6	" Sallie	"	6	"	3/4	1897	"	37
7	" Mack	Son	4	M	3/4	1897	"	37
8	" Selsie	Dau	3mo	F	3/4	DIED	PRIOR TO SEPTEMBER 25 1902	
9	" Ida May	Dau	9mo	F	3/4	New Born		

TRIBAL ENROLLMENT OF PARENTS

	NAME OF FATHER	YEAR	COUNTY	NAME OF MOTHER	YEAR	COUNTY
1	Mach McGill	Dead	Chick Roll	Eliza McGill	Dead	Chick Roll
2	George Bryna	"	Non Citizen	Catherine Fulsome	1897	Tishomingo
3	No. 1			No. 2		
4	No. 1			No. 2		
5	No. 1			No. 2		
6	No. 1			No. 2		
7	No. 1			No. 2		
8	No. 1			No. 2		
9	No. 1			No. 2		

(NOTES)

No. 8 Died Oct. 3. 1898. Enrollment cancelled *(remainder illegible)*

No. 4 on Chickasaw Roll as Roscoe McGill

No. 9 Enrolled June 8, 1900

No. 4 is a male and the correct given name is Roscoe.
See sworn statement of No. 1 relative thereto taken May 11, 1903.

Oct. 1, 1898.

RESIDENCE: Tishomingo COUNTY					CARD NO.			
POST OFFICE: Tishomingo, I.T.					FIELD NO.			

	NAME	RELATION-SHIP TO PERSON FIRST NAMED	AGE	SEX	BLOOD	TRIBAL ENROLLMENT		
						YEAR	COUNTY	PAGE
1	Bynum, Joseph	NAMED	43	M	1/8	1897	Tishomingo	34
2	" Gertrude	Wife	23	F	I.W.	1897	Pickens	79
3	" Joseph, Jr.	Son	1	M	1/16	~~1897~~	Tishomingo	~~88~~
4	" Lulu	Dau	15	F	5/16	1897	"	34
5	" Remonia	"	12	"	5/16	1897	"	35
6	" Lucy	"	9	"	5/16	1897	"	35
7	" Charley	Son	6	M	5/16	1897	"	35
8	" Nitterville R.	"	6mo	M	5/16			
9	" Julius Colbert	"	6mo	"	5/16			

TRIBAL ENROLLMENT OF PARENTS

	NAME OF FATHER	YEAR	COUNTY	NAME OF MOTHER	YEAR	COUNTY
1	Turner Bynum	Dead	Choc Roll	Lucy Bynum	Dead	Chick Roll
2	S.P. Elkins		Non Citizen	Maggie Elkins		Non Citizen
3	No. 1			No. 2		
4	No. 1			Alice Bynum	Dead	Tishomingo
5	No. 1			" "	"	"
6	No. 1			" "	"	"
7	No. 1			" "	"	"
8	No. 1			No. 2		
9	No. 1			No. 2		

(NOTES)

No. 9 enrolled Aug. 30, 1901.
No. 3 Proof of birth received and filed Sept. 23, 1902.
No. 4 is now the wife of William Franklin Bourland on Chickasaw Card #1636.
Evidence of marriage filed Nov. 12, 1902
No. 8 enrolled Nov. 3, 1899.

(No. 2 Dawes' Roll No. 137)
(No. 3 Dawes' Roll No. 4163)

Oct. 1, 1899[sic],

Chickasaw Enrollment Cards 1898-1914
Chickasaw by Blood   Volume IV

RESIDENCE: Tishomingo   COUNTY

POST OFFICE: Sulphur, I.T.

CARD NO.

FIELD NO.

	NAME	RELATION-SHIP TO PERSON FIRST NAMED	AGE	SEX	BLOOD	TRIBAL ENROLLMENT		
						YEAR	COUNTY	PAGE
1	Colbert, Dixie H.	NAMED	25	M	1/4	1897	Tishomingo	29
2	" Bulah	Dau	7	F	1/8	1897	"	29
3	" Mamie	"	5	"	1/8	1897	"	29
4	" Holmes	Son	3	M	1/8	1897	"	29
5	" Effie	Dau	19days	F	1/8			
6	" Elmer	Son	19days	M	1/8			
7	" Nettie	Wife	34	F	I.W.	1897	Pickens	79

TRIBAL ENROLLMENT OF PARENTS

	NAME OF FATHER	YEAR	COUNTY	NAME OF MOTHER	YEAR	COUNTY
1	Henry Colbert	Dead	Pickens	Louisa Patterson	1897	Tishomingo
2	No. 1			Nettie Colbert		White woman
3	No. 1			" "		" "
4	No. 1			" "		" "
5	No. 1			" "		" "
6	No. 1			" "		" "
7	Martin	Dead	non citz	M.L. Cannon		non-citizen

(NOTES)

No. 1 on Chickasaw Roll as Dixei Colbert

No. 3 "   "   " " Minnie   "

No. 5 & 6 Affidavits of attending physician to be supplied. Nos. 5 & 6 are twins.

No. 5 Evidence of birth received and filed March 18, 1902.

No. 6 Evidence of birth received and filed March 18, 1902.

No. 1 is husband of Nettie Colbert on Chickasaw Card #D.106.

No. 7 transferred from Chickasaw card #D.106, April 1, 1903.   *(No. 7 Dawes' Roll No. 42)*

See decision of March 16, 1903.

Oct. 1, 1898.

RESIDENCE: Tishomingo   COUNTY

POST OFFICE: Mill Creek, I.T.

CARD NO.

FIELD NO.

	NAME	RELATION-SHIP TO PERSON FIRST NAMED	AGE	SEX	BLOOD	TRIBAL ENROLLMENT		
						YEAR	COUNTY	PAGE
1	Van Zandt, Eva May	NAMED	10	F	3/8	1897	Chick resid'g in Choc. N. 1st Dist.	70
2	" Isaac N.	Father	33	M	I.W.	1897	Chick Residing in Choctaw N. 1st Dist.	82

73

	TRIBAL ENROLLMENT OF PARENTS					
NAME OF FATHER	YEAR	COUNTY	NAME OF MOTHER	YEAR	COUNTY
1	Isaac N. Van Zandt		White man	Martha Van Zandt	Dead	Tishomingo
2	Isaac N. Van Zandt	Dead	Non Citizen	Martha Van Zandt	Dead	non citizen

(NOTES)

On Chickasaw Roll as Van Zant

No. 1 is daughter of Isaac N. Van Zandt, on Chickasaw Card #D.105.

No. 2 also on 1896 Chickasaw Census roll, page 82 as Isaac N. Vansant

No. 2 transferred from Chickasaw Card #D105. See decision of August 17, 1904.

Oct. 1, 1898.

RESIDENCE: Tishomingo *COUNTY*			*CARD NO.*		
POST OFFICE: Tishomingo, I.T.			*FIELD NO.*		

	NAME	RELATION-SHIP TO PERSON FIRST NAMED	AGE	SEX	BLOOD	TRIBAL ENROLLMENT		
						YEAR	COUNTY	PAGE
1	Coss, Jimma	NAMED	26	M	Full	1897	Tishomingo	37
2	" Emma	Wife	20	F	"	1897	"	37
3	Maytubby, Sena	Mother	65	"	"	1897	"	37
4	Kickentubby, Lucy	Neice[sic]	14	"	"	1897	"	36
5	Pitchlyn, Eli	Nephew	19	M	"	1897	"	31

	TRIBAL ENROLLMENT OF PARENTS					
NAME OF FATHER	YEAR	COUNTY	NAME OF MOTHER	YEAR	COUNTY
1	Joe Coss	Dead	Tishomingo	Sena Maytubby	1897	Tishomingo
2	⟨Illegitimate⟩			Nicy Greenwood	1897	"
3	*(Name Illegible)*	Dead	Chick Roll	*(Name Illegible)*	Dead	Chick Roll
4	Ellie Kickentubby	"	Tishomingo	Den-hey Kickentubby	"	Tishomingo
5	Jack Pitchlyn	"	"	Julie Pitchlyn	"	"

(NOTES)

No. 1 on Chick. Roll as Jim Coss

No. 5 "   "   " " Edi Pitchlyn; is in the "Regular" Army

No. 4 "   "   " " Lucy Kickentubby

No. 1 also on 1893 Chickasaw Roll, Page 92 as Jimmie Cock.

Oct. 1, '98.

Chickasaw Enrollment Cards 1898-1914
Chickasaw by Blood   Volume IV

RESIDENCE: Pontotoc   COUNTY   CARD NO.
POST OFFICE: Waupaunuka, I.T.   FIELD NO.

NAME	RELATION-SHIP TO PERSON FIRST NAMED	AGE	SEX	BLOOD	TRIBAL ENROLLMENT		
					YEAR	COUNTY	PAGE
1 Cohee, Johnson	NAMED	49	M	1/2	1897	Pontotoc	58
2 " Emeline	Wife	40	F	Full	1897	"	58
3 Brown, Andrew L.	Ward	15	M	"	1897	"	58

TRIBAL ENROLLMENT OF PARENTS

NAME OF FATHER	YEAR	COUNTY	NAME OF MOTHER	YEAR	COUNTY
1 Charley Cohee	Dead	Chick. Freedman	Sho ni he	1897	Pontotoc
2 Cha lu ley	"	Chick Roll	Jonnie Cha lu ley	Dead	"
3 Edward Brown	"	Pontotoc	Sukey Brown	1897	"

(NOTES)

P.O. Fillmore, I.T.   Oct. 1, 1898.

RESIDENCE: Pontotoc   COUNTY   CARD NO.
POST OFFICE: Stonewall, I.T.   FIELD NO.

NAME	RELATION-SHIP TO PERSON FIRST NAMED	AGE	SEX	BLOOD	TRIBAL ENROLLMENT		
					YEAR	COUNTY	PAGE
1 Koey, Billie	NAMED	30	M	Full	1897	Pontotoc	45

TRIBAL ENROLLMENT OF PARENTS

NAME OF FATHER	YEAR	COUNTY	NAME OF MOTHER	YEAR	COUNTY
1 John Koey	Dead	Pontotoc	Li-o-key	Dead	Pontotoc

(NOTES)

Oct. 1, 1898.

RESIDENCE: Tishomingo   COUNTY   CARD NO.
POST OFFICE: Tishomingo, I.T.   FIELD NO.

NAME	RELATION-SHIP TO PERSON FIRST NAMED	AGE	SEX	BLOOD	TRIBAL ENROLLMENT		
					YEAR	COUNTY	PAGE
1 Kemp, Benjamin Franklin	NAMED	65	M	1/4	1897	Tishomingo	37
2 " Penelope Catherine	Wife	54	F	I.W.	1897	"	79
3 " Elsie	G.Dau	12	"	3/4	1897	"	37

TRIBAL ENROLLMENT OF PARENTS

NAME OF FATHER	YEAR	COUNTY	NAME OF MOTHER	YEAR	COUNTY
1 Jackson Kemp	Dead	Chick Roll	Eliza Kemp	Dead	Chick Roll

2	Jim Palmer	"	Non Citizen	*(Illegible)* Palmer	"	Non Citizen
3	Rem. Kemp	"	Pontotoc	Mattie Kemp	"	Pontotoc

(NOTES)

No. 1 on Chickasaw Roll as Ben F. Kemp
No. 2 "   "   " " P.C. Kemp.   *(No. 2 Dawes' Roll No. 328)*
11/7/02 No. 1 is guardian of Rhoda Kemp, Chickasaw card *(illegible)*
See statement of Zac Farmer relative to divorce between P.C. and Joseph Price filed April 4, 1900.

Oct. 1, 1898.

RESIDENCE: Tishomingo	*COUNTY*					*CARD NO.*		
POST OFFICE: Davis, I.T.						*FIELD NO.*		
NAME	**RELATION-SHIP TO PERSON FIRST NAMED**	**AGE**	**SEX**	**BLOOD**	**TRIBAL ENROLLMENT**			
					YEAR	**COUNTY**	**PAGE**	
1 Petigrew, Joe		19	M	Full	1897	Tishomingo	31	

TRIBAL ENROLLMENT OF PARENTS

NAME OF FATHER	**YEAR**	**COUNTY**	**NAME OF MOTHER**	**YEAR**	**COUNTY**
1 Foster Petigrew	Dead	Tishomingo	Fannie Petigrew	Dead	Tishomingo

(NOTES)

P.O. Doyle, I.T. 1/2/03   Oct. 1, 1898.

RESIDENCE: Tishomingo	*COUNTY*					*CARD NO.*		
POST OFFICE: Regan, I.T.						*FIELD NO.*		
NAME	**RELATION-SHIP TO PERSON FIRST NAMED**	**AGE**	**SEX**	**BLOOD**	**TRIBAL ENROLLMENT**			
					YEAR	**COUNTY**	**PAGE**	
1 Hart, Jackson		30	M	Full	1897	Tishomingo	36	

TRIBAL ENROLLMENT OF PARENTS

NAME OF FATHER	**YEAR**	**COUNTY**	**NAME OF MOTHER**	**YEAR**	**COUNTY**
1 E. Hart	Dead	Chick Roll	Martha Brown	1897	Tishomingo

(NOTES)

No. 1 is husband of Sallie Hart on Chickasaw Card #838.
and father of Johnslin Hart thereon.

Oct. 1, 1898.

RESIDENCE: Tishomingo COUNTY   CARD NO.

POST OFFICE: Tishomingo, I.T.   FIELD NO.

	NAME	RELATION-SHIP TO PERSON FIRST NAMED	AGE	SEX	BLOOD	TRIBAL ENROLLMENT		
						YEAR	COUNTY	PAGE
1	Cheadle, Martin Van Buren	NAMED	42	M	1/2	1897	Tishomingo	35
2	" Mary V.	Wife	29	F	3/4	1897	"	35
3	" Tommie	Son	10	M	5/8	1897	"	35
4	" Overton	"	7	"	5/8	1897	"	35
5	" Lurena	Dau	4	F	5/8	1897	"	35
6	" Ellis	Son	10mo	M	5/8			
7	Thompson, Mattie	Neice[sic]	19	F	3/4	1897	Tishomingo	35
8	Thompson, Ina	Gr.Niece	2mo	"	3/8			
9	Cheadle, Mary V.	Dau	2mo	"	5/8			
~~10~~	~~Thompson, Frankie M.~~	~~Gr. Niece~~	~~6wks~~	~~"~~	~~3/8~~	DIED PRIOR TO SEPTEMBER 25 1902		

TRIBAL ENROLLMENT OF PARENTS

	NAME OF FATHER	YEAR	COUNTY	NAME OF MOTHER	YEAR	COUNTY
1	Thos. F. Cheadle	Dead	Tishomingo	Rebecca Cheadle	Dead	Tishomingo
2	Ben Ellis	"	Pickens	Susan Ellis	"	Pickens
3	No. 1			No. 2		
4	No. 1			No. 2		
5	No. 1			No. 2		
6	No. 1			No. 2		
7	Jas. R. Cheadle	Dead	Tishomingo	Mrs. Betsy Meyers	1897	Pickens
8	Jacob L. Thompson		Choc. Roll	No. 7		
9	No. 1			No. 2		
10	Jacob L. Thompson	" "		No. 7		

(NOTES)

No. 10 Died Sept. 8, 1902

No. 1 on Chickasaw Roll as M.V. Cheadle

No. 5 " " " " Lorena "

No. 10 born Nov. 1st 1901; Enrolled Dec. 23, 1901

See sworn statement of Margaret (illegible) hereto attached.

No. 7 is now the wife of Jacob L. Thompson on Choctaw Card #327, Apl. 6, 1900.

No. 8 Enrolled May 24, 1900

No. 9 enrolled May 20, 1900

No. 9 Died Oct. 17, 1900; evidence of death filed July 14, 1902

No. 10 Died Sept. 8, 1902; proof of Death filed Nov. 11, 1902.

Oct. 1, 1898.

RESIDENCE: Tishomingo COUNTY					CARD NO.			
POST OFFICE: Regan, I.T.					FIELD NO.			
NAME	RELATION-SHIP TO PERSON FIRST NAMED	AGE	SEX	BLOOD	TRIBAL ENROLLMENT			
					YEAR	COUNTY	PAGE	
1 Underwood, Elonzo	NAMED	20	M	Full	1897	Tishomingo	34	

TRIBAL ENROLLMENT OF PARENTS						
NAME OF FATHER	YEAR	COUNTY	NAME OF MOTHER	YEAR	COUNTY	
1 Houston Underwood	Dead	Tishomingo	Zila Greenwood	Dead	Tishomingo	

(NOTES)
No. 1 is now the husband of Salina Lewis on Chickasaw Card #947. June 4, 1901.

Sept. 30, 1898.

RESIDENCE: Tishomingo COUNTY					CARD NO.			
POST OFFICE: Regan, I.T.					FIELD NO.			
NAME	RELATION-SHIP TO PERSON FIRST NAMED	AGE	SEX	BLOOD	TRIBAL ENROLLMENT			
					YEAR	COUNTY	PAGE	
1 Moore, Charles	NAMED	24	M	Full	1897	Tishomingo	29	
2 " William *(Illegible)*	Son	3	M	1/2				
3 " Viola Myrtle	Dau	1	F	1/2				

TRIBAL ENROLLMENT OF PARENTS						
NAME OF FATHER	YEAR	COUNTY	NAME OF MOTHER	YEAR	COUNTY	
1 Osborn Moore	Dead	Tishomingo	Matilda Moore	Dead	Tishomingo	
2 No. 1			Pearl Moore		Non Citizen	
3 No. 1			" "		" "	

(NOTES)
No. 1 is the husband of Pearl Moore, non Citizen, evidence of marriage filed Nov. 12, 1902.
No. 2 Born July 20, 1899; enrolled Nov. 11, 1902   *(No. 2 Dawes' Roll No. 4161)*
No. 3 Born Oct. 31, 1901; enrolled Nov. 11, 1902   *(No. 3 Dawes' Roll No. 4162)*

Sept. 30, 1898.

RESIDENCE: Pontotoc COUNTY					CARD NO.			
POST OFFICE: Ada. I.T.					FIELD NO.			
NAME	RELATION-SHIP TO PERSON FIRST NAMED	AGE	SEX	BLOOD	TRIBAL ENROLLMENT			
					YEAR	COUNTY	PAGE	
1 McGee, Reubin	NAMED	23	M	Full	1897	Pontotoc	48	

TRIBAL ENROLLMENT OF PARENTS						
NAME OF FATHER	YEAR	COUNTY	NAME OF MOTHER	YEAR	COUNTY	
1 Noah McGee	1897	Tishomingo	Nancy McGee	Dead	Pontotoc	

(NOTES)

No. 1 is now husband of Lucy Greenwood on Chickasaw Card #297.
See letter of Reubin McGee filed this day with records in #297. April 27, 1901.

Sept. 30 '98.

RESIDENCE: Tishomingo   **COUNTY**   **CARD NO.**
POST OFFICE: Reagan, I.T.   **FIELD NO.**

NAME	RELATION-SHIP TO PERSON FIRST NAMED	AGE	SEX	BLOOD	TRIBAL ENROLLMENT		
					YEAR	COUNTY	PAGE
1 McKinney, Lubon	NAMED	22	M	Full	1897	Tishomingo	32
2 Mike, Killissy **DEAD**	Sister	36	F	"	1893	"	P.R. #1 124

TRIBAL ENROLLMENT OF PARENTS						
NAME OF FATHER	YEAR	COUNTY	NAME OF MOTHER	YEAR	COUNTY	
1 Howolinchtubbee	Dead	Tishomingo	Ilbey	Dead	Tishomingo	
2 "	"	"	"	"	"	

(NOTES)

No. 2 on Chickasaw Roll as Killissy McKinney
No. 2 died Dec. 26, 1901; Proof of death filed June 11, 1902.

Sept. 30, 1898.

RESIDENCE: Tishomingo   **COUNTY**   **CARD NO.**
POST OFFICE: Mill Creek, I.T.   **FIELD NO.**

NAME	RELATION-SHIP TO PERSON FIRST NAMED	AGE	SEX	BLOOD	TRIBAL ENROLLMENT		
					YEAR	COUNTY	PAGE
1 Wilson, Newton G.	NAMED	27	M	1/2	1897	Tishomingo	29
2 " Willie	Son	3	"	1/4	1897	"	29

TRIBAL ENROLLMENT OF PARENTS						
NAME OF FATHER	YEAR	COUNTY	NAME OF MOTHER	YEAR	COUNTY	
1 Willie Wilson	Dead	Cherokee Citz.	Fena Lewis	1897	Tishomingo	
2 No. 1			Ollie Wilson	1897	Non Citizen	

(NOTES)

No. 1 is now husband of Icy Brown on Chickasaw Card #985, 9/10, '01
Full name of No. 1 is Newton Galoway Wilson. See letter filed Sept. 17, 1901.

Sept. 30, '98.

RESIDENCE: Tishomingo	COUNTY				CARD NO.			
POST OFFICE: Mill Creek, I.T.					FIELD NO.			

NAME	RELATION-SHIP TO PERSON FIRST NAMED	AGE	SEX	BLOOD	TRIBAL ENROLLMENT		
					YEAR	COUNTY	PAGE
1 Brown, Hobert	NAMED	26	M	Full	1897	Tishomingo	28

TRIBAL ENROLLMENT OF PARENTS

NAME OF FATHER	YEAR	COUNTY	NAME OF MOTHER	YEAR	COUNTY
1 Pinkie Brown	Dead	Tishomingo	Hepey Brown	1897	Tishomingo

(NOTES)

No. 1 also on Chickasaw Roll, Pickens County, Page 273, as Brown Hobert.

Sept. 30, '98.

RESIDENCE: Tishomingo	COUNTY				CARD NO.			
POST OFFICE: Regan, I.T.					FIELD NO.			

NAME	RELATION-SHIP TO PERSON FIRST NAMED	AGE	SEX	BLOOD	TRIBAL ENROLLMENT		
					YEAR	COUNTY	PAGE
1 Pickens, Hiram	NAMED	31	M	Full	1897	Tishomingo	38

TRIBAL ENROLLMENT OF PARENTS

NAME OF FATHER	YEAR	COUNTY	NAME OF MOTHER	YEAR	COUNTY
1 Edmund Pickens		Pickens	Peggie	Dead	Pickens

(NOTES)

No. 1 died April 10, 1901; Evidence of death filed Sept. 6, 1901.

Sept. 30, '98.

CANCELLED Stamped across card

RESIDENCE: Pontotoc	COUNTY				CARD NO.			
POST OFFICE: Ada, I.T.					FIELD NO.			

NAME	RELATION-SHIP TO PERSON FIRST NAMED	AGE	SEX	BLOOD	TRIBAL ENROLLMENT		
					YEAR	COUNTY	PAGE
1 Porter, Sebena	NAMED	44	F	Full	1893	Pontotoc	PR #2 182
2 " Susie	Dau	15	"	"	1893	"	183
3 " Elvina	"	9	"	"			

TRIBAL ENROLLMENT OF PARENTS

NAME OF FATHER	YEAR	COUNTY	NAME OF MOTHER	YEAR	COUNTY
1 Aaron Newberry	1897	Panola	Lila *(Illegible)*	Dead	Pontotoc
2 Ashway Porter	1897	"	No. 1		

3	" "	"	"	No. 1		

(NOTES)

No. 1 also on 1897 Roll, Page 99, Pontotoc Co., as Sibily Johnson
No. 2 also on 1896 Chickasaw Roll, Pontotoc Co., Page 96.

Sept. 30, '98.

RESIDENCE: Pontotoc   **COUNTY**   **CARD NO.**
POST OFFICE: Wiley, I.T.   **FIELD NO.**

	NAME	RELATION-SHIP TO PERSON FIRST NAMED	AGE	SEX	BLOOD	TRIBAL ENROLLMENT		
						YEAR	COUNTY	PAGE
1	Ensharkey, C.A.	NAMED	38	M	Full	1897	Pontotoc	56
2	" Serena	Dau	14	F	"	1897	"	56
3	" Ada	"	7	"	"	1897	"	56
4	" Sampson	Son	3	M	"	1897	"	56

TRIBAL ENROLLMENT OF PARENTS

	NAME OF FATHER	YEAR	COUNTY	NAME OF MOTHER	YEAR	COUNTY
1	Jim Sinshakey	Dead	Tishomingo	Ho le hona	Dead	Tishomingo
2	No. 1			Cordelia	"	Pontotoc
3	No. 1			Selina	"	"
4	No. 1			"	"	"

(NOTES)

No. 1 on Roll as C.A. Sharkey
No. 2 "   "   " Serena Sharkey
No. 3 "   "   " Ada   "
No. 4 "   "   " Sampson   "

Sept. 30 '98.

RESIDENCE: Tishomingo   **COUNTY**   **CARD NO.**
POST OFFICE: Tishomingo, I.T.   **FIELD NO.**

	NAME	RELATION-SHIP TO PERSON FIRST NAMED	AGE	SEX	BLOOD	TRIBAL ENROLLMENT		
						YEAR	COUNTY	PAGE
1	Dunigan, Lola	NAMED	23	F	Full	1897	Tishomingo	12
2	Byfield, Elsie	Dau	3	"	1/2	1897	"	12
3	~~Dunigan, Anna M.~~	"	~~7mo~~	"	~~1/2~~	DIED PRIOR TO SEPTEMBER 25 1902		
4	" Ethel Jermie Bell	Dau	6wks	F	1/2			

TRIBAL ENROLLMENT OF PARENTS

	NAME OF FATHER	YEAR	COUNTY	NAME OF MOTHER	YEAR	COUNTY
1	Noah McGill	1897	Tishomingo	Elsie McGill	Dead	Tishomingo

2	John Byfield	1897	Non Citizen	No. 1		
3	~~C.C. Dunigan~~		" "	~~No. 1~~		
4	" " "		" "	No. 1		

(NOTES)

No. 1 on Chickasaw Roll as Lela Byfield
No. 2 "   "   "   " Elsie "
No. 4 Born June 27, 1902; enrolled Aug. 9, 1902.
No. 3 Enrolled Dec. 14, 1899.

P.O. Maxwell, I.T. 12/32/02

Sept. 30 '98.

RESIDENCE: Pontotoc COUNTY						CARD NO.			
POST OFFICE: Victor, I.T.						FIELD NO.			
	NAME	RELATION-SHIP TO PERSON FIRST	AGE	SEX	BLOOD	TRIBAL ENROLLMENT			
						YEAR	COUNTY		PAGE
1	Victor, Emmet L.	NAMED	23	M	1/8	1897	Pontotoc		26
2	" Lee	Wife	19	F	I.W.				
3	" Wilson L.	Son	2mo	M	1/16				
4	" Julious Thomas	"	2wks	M	1/16				

TRIBAL ENROLLMENT OF PARENTS

	NAME OF FATHER	YEAR	COUNTY	NAME OF MOTHER	YEAR	COUNTY
1	Alfred Victor	1897	Choc. Roll	Lucy Victor	Dead	Pontotoc
2	J.L. Desmond	"	Non Citizen	Martha Desmond	"	Non Citizen
3	No. 1			No. 2		
4	No. 1			No. 2		

(NOTES)

No. 2 See decision of June 13 '04.   *(No. 2 Dawes' Roll No. 393)*
No. 1 on Chickasaw Roll as Emet L. Victor
No. 4 enrolled Dec. 4, 1900
No. 3 "   Nov. 3, 1899

P.O. is Dibble, I.T. 10/20/02

RESIDENCE: Tishomingo COUNTY						CARD NO.			
POST OFFICE: Regan, I.T.						FIELD NO.			
	NAME	RELATION-SHIP TO PERSON FIRST	AGE	SEX	BLOOD	TRIBAL ENROLLMENT			
						YEAR	COUNTY		PAGE
1	Maytubby, Sam	NAMED	32	M	Full	1893	Tishomingo		124

2	" Mary	Wife	323	F	Full	1893	"	124
3	" Polly	Dau	12	"	Full	1893	"	124
4	" Simeon	Son	9	M	Full	1893	"	124
5	" Peter P.	"	6	"	Full	1893	"	124
6	" Lyman	"	4	"	Full	1897	"	87
7	" Silas	"	1	"	Full	1897	"	88

TRIBAL ENROLLMENT OF PARENTS

	NAME OF FATHER	YEAR	COUNTY	NAME OF MOTHER	YEAR	COUNTY
1	Hogan Maytubby	Dead	Tishomingo	Catherine Maytubby	Dead	Tishomingo
2	Peter Allen	"	Panola	Lucy Allen	"	Panola
3	No. 1			No. 2		
4	No. 1			No. 2		
5	No. 1			No. 2		
6	No. 1			No. 2		
7	No. 1			No. 2		

(NOTES)

No. 4 on Chickasaw Roll as Simeion Maytubby
No. 5 "   "   " "   Peter   "
Nos. 1, 2, 3, 4 also on 1896 Chickasaw Roll, Tishomingo Co., Page 87.
No. 5 also on 1896 Chickasaw Roll, Tishomingo Co., Page 88
No. 6 Born Aug. 30, 1894. Proof of birth filed Oct. 5, 1903.
No. 2 is a full-blood Chickasaw Indian.
    See affidavit of No. 1 filed July 2, 1903.
No. 7 Born March 15, 1897. Proof of birth filed Oct. 5, '03.

Sept. 30, '98.

| RESIDENCE: Tishomingo COUNTY | | | | | CARD NO. | | | |
| POST OFFICE: Buckhorn, I.T. | | | | | FIELD NO. | | | |

	NAME	RELATION-SHIP TO PERSON FIRST NAMED	AGE	SEX	BLOOD	TRIBAL ENROLLMENT		
						YEAR	COUNTY	PAGE
1	Nail, Dixon	NAMED	62	M	Full	1897	Tishomingo	31
2	Hamilton, Jency	Wife	31	F	"	1897	"	31
3	Nail, Webster	Son	12	M	"	1897	"	31
4	" Selina	Dau	11	F	"	1897	"	31
5	" Alfred	Son	10	M	"	1897	"	31
6	" Malisey	Dau	5	F	"	1897	"	31
7	" Bitsie	"	2	"	"	1897	"	31
8	Cumley, Irvan	S.Son	11	M	"	1897	"	31
9	Pettigrew, Francis	S.Dau	12	F	Full	1897	"	31

10	Lowmer, Emely	S.Dau	14	"	"	1897	"	31
11	Bond, Lizzie	S.Gr.Dau	1	"	"			
~~12~~	~~Thomas, Rutha~~	~~Mother in Law~~	~~80~~	~~"~~	~~"~~	DIED PRIOR TO SEPTEMBER 25 1902 ~~1893~~ ~~Pontotoc~~		~~132~~
13	Lowmer, Mulsie	Dau of No. 10	15mo	"	"			
14	Nail, Buckie	Dau	3	"	"			

TRIBAL ENROLLMENT OF PARENTS

	NAME OF FATHER	YEAR	COUNTY	NAME OF MOTHER	YEAR	COUNTY
1	Ahpahisaha	Dead	Chick Roll	Iw-wah-hay	Dead	Chick Roll
2	Ben Thomas	"	Tishomingo	Rutha Thomas	1897	Tishomingo
3	No. 1			Minerva	Dead	"
4	No. 1			"	"	"
5	No. 1			"	"	"
6	No. 1			No. 2		
7	No. 1			No. 2		
8	George Cumley	Dead	Non Citizen	No. 2		
9	George Pettigrew	"	Tishomingo	No. 2		
10	" "	"	"	No. 2		
11	Jerome Bond	1897	"	No. 10		
~~12~~	~~Hi-o-cha-tubby~~	~~Dead~~	~~Chick Roll~~	~~Jeminey~~	~~Dead~~	~~Chick Roll~~
13	Adam Lowmer	1897	Pickens	No. 10		
14	No. 1			No. 2		

(NOTES)

No. 12 Died July 15, 1901; Enrollment cancelled by Dept. July 2, 1904.

No. 11 Affidavit of mother as to birth to be supplied. Received March 9, 1899,

Surname on Chickasaw Roll of first 8 names is Nail.

No. 8 on " " as Aivan Nail

No. 9 " " " " Francies Pettegold

No. 10 " " " " Emely Brown

No. 13 Born Jan. 24, 1901, enrolled April 17, 1902.

No. 10 is now the wife of Adam Lowmer, on Chickasaw Card #968. See his affidavit filed April 17, 1902.

No. 12 died July 15, 1901; Proof of death filed November 10, 1902.

Nos. 1 to 7 inclusive also on Chickasaw index Surname Nail

No. 1 is father of Jessie Nail on Chickasaw card #740

No. 1 died Dec. 25, 1900. Evidence of death filed Sept. 5, 1901.

No. 14 Born April 1, 1899. Enrolled April 22, 1902.

No. 2 is now the wife of Anderson Hamilton; See affidavit of Anderson Hamilton filed April 22, 1902.

Sept. 30, 1898.

Chickasaw Enrollment Cards 1898-1914
Chickasaw by Blood   Volume IV

RESIDENCE: Pontotoc   COUNTY   CARD NO.
POST OFFICE: Wiley, I.T.   FIELD NO.

NAME	RELATION-SHIP TO PERSON FIRST	AGE	SEX	BLOOD	TRIBAL ENROLLMENT		
					YEAR	COUNTY	PAGE
1 Brown, Willis P.	NAMED	35	M	Full	1897	Pontotoc	57
2 " Gincy	Wife	31	F	"	1897	"	57
3 " Betsey	Dau	13	"	"	1897	"	57
4 " Agnes	"	10	"	"	1897	"	57
5 " Esias	Son	8	M	"	1897	"	57
6 " Susan	Dau	5	F	"	1897	"	57
7 " Aaron DEAD	Son	6wks	M	"			

TRIBAL ENROLLMENT OF PARENTS

	NAME OF FATHER	YEAR	COUNTY	NAME OF MOTHER	YEAR	COUNTY
1	I-she-tubby	Dead	Pontotoc	Is-te-ho-che	Dead	Pontotoc
2	John Pucknatubby	"	"	Lucy Pucknatubby	"	"
3	No. 1			No. 2		
4	No. 1			No. 2		
5	No. 1			No. 2		
6	No. 1			No. 2		
7	No. 1			No. 2		

(NOTES)

No. 1 on Chickasaw Roll as Willis Brown
No. 7 died October 13, 1899. Evidence of death filed March 26, 1901.

Sept. 30, '98.

RESIDENCE: Pontotoc   COUNTY   CARD NO.
POST OFFICE: Center, I.T.   FIELD NO.

NAME	RELATION-SHIP TO PERSON FIRST	AGE	SEX	BLOOD	TRIBAL ENROLLMENT		
					YEAR	COUNTY	PAGE
1 Lanham, Susie Virginia	NAMED	31	F	1/16	1897	Pontotoc	47
2 Johnson, Malissa	Dau	9	"	1/32	1897	"	47
3 Lanham, Scott W.	Husb	55	M	I.W.			

TRIBAL ENROLLMENT OF PARENTS

	NAME OF FATHER	YEAR	COUNTY	NAME OF MOTHER	YEAR	COUNTY
1	Jim Taylor	Dead	Non Citizen	Margaret Taylor	Dead	Tishomingo
2	Jim Johnson		" "	No. 1		
3	P.G. Lanham	Dead	" "	Amanda Lanham		non citizen

85

Chickasaw Enrollment Cards 1898-1914
Chickasaw by Blood   Volume IV

(NOTES)

No. 1 on Chickasaw Roll as S.V. Lanham
No. 2 "   "   " " Malissa "
No. 2 also on "   "   "   " Johnson, Page 89 Pontotoc Co.
No. 1 is wife of Scott Lanham on Chickasaw Card #D.104.
No. 3 transferred from Chickasaw Card #D.104.   *(No. 3 Dawes' Roll No. 236)*
   See decision of March 5, 1904. Mar. 23, 1904.

Sept. 30, 1898.

RESIDENCE: Tishomingo **COUNTY**						**CARD NO.**		
POST OFFICE: Tishomingo, I.T.						**FIELD NO.**		

	NAME	RELATION-SHIP TO PERSON FIRST NAMED	AGE	SEX	BLOOD	TRIBAL ENROLLMENT		
						YEAR	COUNTY	PAGE
1	Harris, Benjamin Franklin	NAMED	24	M	Full	1897	Tishomingo	36
2	" Hindman H.	Son	2mo	"	1/2			
3	" Loren Thomas	Son	5mo	M	1/2			

TRIBAL ENROLLMENT OF PARENTS

	NAME OF FATHER	YEAR	COUNTY	NAME OF MOTHER	YEAR	COUNTY
1	Ben Harris	Dead	Chick Roll	Betsey Harris, now Myers	1897	Pickens
2	No. 1			Ella Harris		Non Citizen
3	No. 1			" "		" "

(NOTES)

No. 1 on Chickasaw Roll as Ben Buck Harris
No. 2 enrolled Dec. 14, 1899, subject to receipt of evidence of marriage of parents. Same requested. Received
   and filed Jan. 9, 1900.
No. 3 born July 31, 1901; Enrolled Dec. 23, 1901.

Sept. 30, 1898

RESIDENCE: Pontotoc **COUNTY**						**CARD NO.**		
POST OFFICE: Wiley, I.T.						**FIELD NO.**		

	NAME	RELATION-SHIP TO PERSON FIRST NAMED	AGE	SEX	BLOOD	TRIBAL ENROLLMENT		
						YEAR	COUNTY	PAGE
1	Fillmore, Epsie	NAMED	35	F	Full	1897	Pontotoc	59
2	Benton, Thomas	Son	20	M	"	1897	"	59
3	Fillmore, Jennette	Dau	13	F	1/2	1897	"	59
4	" Hannah	S.Son?	15	"	1/2	1897	"	59

TRIBAL ENROLLMENT OF PARENTS					
NAME OF FATHER	YEAR	COUNTY	NAME OF MOTHER	YEAR	COUNTY
1 Peter Burris	Dead	Chick Roll	Eliza Burris	1897	Pontotoc
2 Eastman Benton	"	Pontotoc	No. 1		
3 Elias Fillmore		Choc Roll	No. 1		
4 " "		" "	Winnie Fillmore	Dead	Pontotoc

(NOTES)

No. 1 wife of Elias Fillmore, Choctaw roll, Card No. 324
No. 1 on Chickasaw Roll as Epsie B. Fillmore
No. 3 "   "   "   " Jennet   "
No. 4 "   "   "   " Hanna   "
No. 2 Also on Page 36, Tishomingo Co.

Sept. 30, '98.

RESIDENCE: Tishomingo   COUNTY   CARD NO.
POST OFFICE: Mill Creek, I.T.   FIELD NO.

NAME	RELATION-SHIP TO PERSON FIRST NAMED	AGE	SEX	BLOOD	TRIBAL ENROLLMENT		
					YEAR	COUNTY	PAGE
1 Underwood, Thomas	NAMED	41	M	Full	1897	Tishomingo	29
2 " Proobe	Wife	42	F	"	1897	"	29
3 " Humphreys	Son	21	M	"	1897	"	29

TRIBAL ENROLLMENT OF PARENTS					
NAME OF FATHER	YEAR	COUNTY	NAME OF MOTHER	YEAR	COUNTY
1 Cornelius Underwood	Dead	Chick Roll	Lydia Underwood	Dead	Chick Roll
2 Don-ne-o-tubby	"	" "	Chil-le-lith	"	" "
3 No. 1			Susie Brown	"	Tishomingo

(NOTES)

No. 2 on Chickasaw Roll as Theba
No. 3 died Feby 15, 1901; Proof of death filed April 5, 1902.

Sept. 30, '98.

RESIDENCE: Pontotoc   COUNTY   CARD NO.
POST OFFICE: Wiley, I.T.   FIELD NO.

NAME	RELATION-SHIP TO PERSON FIRST NAMED	AGE	SEX	BLOOD	TRIBAL ENROLLMENT		
					YEAR	COUNTY	PAGE
1 John. Stephen	NAMED	30	M	Full	1897	Pontotoc	57
2 Keel, Willie	Ward	8	M	1/2	1897	"	95
3 " Freeman	"	6	"	1/2	1897	"	95

TRIBAL ENROLLMENT OF PARENTS						
	NAME OF FATHER	YEAR	COUNTY	NAME OF MOTHER	YEAR	COUNTY
1	John Pucknatubby	Dead	Pontotoc	Lucy Pucknatubby	Dead	Pontotoc
2	Easmon Keel	1897	Pontotoc	Sophie Keel	"	"
3	" "	1897	"	" "	"	"

(NOTES)

No. 3 on Chickasaw Roll as Aphrious Keel
No. 2 also on Page 58, Pontotoc Co, as Jack Keel
No. 3 " " " 58, " " " Fico "

Sept. 30, 1898.

CANCELLED Stamped across card
Cancelled Dec. 7, 1900, and transferred to Chickasaw card #1580.
(Signature Illegible)
Acting Chairman

RESIDENCE: Pontotoc *COUNTY*									*CARD NO.*
POST OFFICE: McGee, I.T.									*FIELD NO.*
	NAME	RELATION-SHIP TO PERSON FIRST NAMED	AGE	SEX	BLOOD	TRIBAL ENROLLMENT			
						YEAR	COUNTY	PAG	
1	Colbert, Ida O.		7	F	1/2	1893	Pontotoc	P.R. 57	
2	~~" Bessie Lee~~	~~Sister~~	~~5~~	"	~~1/2~~	DIED ~~1893~~	PRIOR TO SEPTEMBER 25 1902 "	"	

TRIBAL ENROLLMENT OF PARENTS						
	NAME OF FATHER	YEAR	COUNTY	NAME OF MOTHER	YEAR	COUNTY
1	Albert Colbert	Dead	Panola	Laura Colbert now McAfee		White woman
2	" "	"	"	" "		" "

(NOTES)

No. 2 Died Oct. 26, 1901. *(Remainder illegible)*
No. 2 on 1893 Chickasaw Roll as Jimmie
Laura McAfee, mother of Nos 1 and 2 on Chickasaw D.114.
No. 2 Died Oct. 26, 1901; Proof of death filed Oct. 25, 1902.

P.O. Walker, I.T. 10/22/02

Sept. 30, 1898.

RESIDENCE: Pontotoc   COUNTY

POST OFFICE: Wiley, I.T.

CARD NO.

FIELD NO.

NAME	RELATION-SHIP TO PERSON FIRST NAMED	AGE	SEX	BLOOD	TRIBAL ENROLLMENT		
					YEAR	COUNTY	PAGE
1 Wilson, Stephen	FIRST NAMED	50	M	Full	1893	Pontotoc	PR #1 140

TRIBAL ENROLLMENT OF PARENTS

NAME OF FATHER	YEAR	COUNTY	NAME OF MOTHER	YEAR	COUNTY
1 James Wilson	Dead	Chick Roll	Fannie Wilson	Dead	Chick Roll

(NOTES)

P.O. Mill Creek, I.T. 5/13-04

Sept. 30, '98.

RESIDENCE: Pontotoc   COUNTY

POST OFFICE: Waupaunuka, I.T.

CARD NO.

FIELD NO.

NAME	RELATION-SHIP TO PERSON FIRST NAMED	AGE	SEX	BLOOD	TRIBAL ENROLLMENT		
					YEAR	COUNTY	PAGE
1 Fillmore, Mary Ann	NAMED	40	F	Full	1897	Pontotoc	58
2 Holden, Annie	Neice[sic]	22	"	"	1897	"	58
3 Ensharkey, Carrie	Ward	10mo	"	"			

TRIBAL ENROLLMENT OF PARENTS

NAME OF FATHER	YEAR	COUNTY	NAME OF MOTHER	YEAR	COUNTY
1 Pe-can-stubby	Dead	Chick Roll	Tah-wy-ho-ho	Dead	Chick Roll
2 Edmen Holden	1897	Pontotoc	Susan Holden	"	Pontotoc
3 C.A. Ensharkey	1897	"	Salina Ensharkey	"	"

(NOTES)

No. 1 wife of Silas Fillmore, Choctaw Roll, Cardf No. 323.

Sept. 30, '98.

RESIDENCE: Tishomingo   COUNTY

POST OFFICE: Ravia, I.T.

CARD NO.

FIELD NO.

NAME	RELATION-SHIP TO PERSON FIRST NAMED	AGE	SEX	BLOOD	TRIBAL ENROLLMENT		
					YEAR	COUNTY	PAGE
1 Alberson, Wisey	FIRST NAMED	19	F	Full	1893	Tishomingo	P.R. #1 107

TRIBAL ENROLLMENT OF PARENTS

NAME OF FATHER	YEAR	COUNTY	NAME OF MOTHER	YEAR	COUNTY
1 Jason Alberson	Dead	Tishomingo	Nellie Alberson	Dead	Tishomingo

(NOTES)

Widow of No. 4 on Chick card 621. Evidence of marriage requested Nov. 13, 1902. Now spells her name Vicia.

Sept. 30, 98.

RESIDENCE: Tishomingo **COUNTY**   **CARD NO.**

POST OFFICE: Tishomingo, I.T.   **FIELD NO.**

	NAME	RELATION-SHIP TO PERSON FIRST NAMED	AGE	SEX	BLOOD	TRIBAL ENROLLMENT		
						YEAR	COUNTY	PAGE
1	Burris, Hindman H.	NAMED	36	M	Full	1897	Tishomingo	35
2	" Viola J.	Wife	23	F	1/2	1897	Pontotoc	52
3	" Hinmon Harrison	Son	2 1/2 mo	M	3/4			

TRIBAL ENROLLMENT OF PARENTS

	NAME OF FATHER	YEAR	COUNTY	NAME OF MOTHER	YEAR	COUNTY
1	Colbert A. Burris	1897	Pontotoc	An-ho-ye	Dead	Chick Roll
2	Wm H. Jackson	1897	Pontotoc	Anne D. Jackson	1897	
3	No. 1			No. 2		

(NOTES)

On Chickasaw Roll as H.H. Burris

No. 2 transferred from Chickasaw Card No. 202 to this card with her husband, Dec. 21, 1900. As to her identity see letter of Wolfer Maytubby Dec. 10, 1900.

Copy filed this day, Dec. 21, 1900

No. 3 enrolled December 21, 1900

Evidence of marriage of Nos. 1 and 2 to be supplied. Filed January 17, 1901.

No. 2 on Chickasaw Roll as Viola Jackson.

Sept. 30, '98.

RESIDENCE: Tishomingo **COUNTY**   **CARD NO.**

POST OFFICE: Ravia, I.T.   **FIELD NO.**

	NAME	RELATION-SHIP TO PERSON FIRST NAMED	AGE	SEX	BLOOD	TRIBAL ENROLLMENT		
						YEAR	COUNTY	PAGE
1	Jimmy, William	NAMED	50	M	Full	1897	Tishomingo	31
2	" Loman	Son	8	"	"	1897	"	31

TRIBAL ENROLLMENT OF PARENTS

	NAME OF FATHER	YEAR	COUNTY	NAME OF MOTHER	YEAR	COUNTY
1	Billy Jimmy	Dead	Chick Roll	Siney Jimmy	Dead	Chick Roll
2	No. 1			Sicey Jimmy	1897	Pickens

(NOTES)

No. 2 living with his mother, Sicey Jimmy.

Sept. 30, '98.

Chickasaw Enrollment Cards 1898-1914
Chickasaw by Blood   Volume IV

RESIDENCE: Tishomingo   COUNTY   CARD NO.
POST OFFICE: Davis, I.T.   FIELD NO.

	NAME	RELATIONSHIP TO PERSON FIRST NAMED	AGE	SEX	BLOOD	TRIBAL ENROLLMENT		
						YEAR	COUNTY	PAGE
1	James, Thomas		26	M	Full	1897	Tishomingo	30
2	" Mollie	Wife	28	F	"	DIED PRIOR TO SEPTEMBER 25 1902 1893	"	107
3	Cravatt, Imogene	S.Dau	10	"	"	1893	"	P.R.#1 117
4	" Albert	" Son	9	.	"	1893	"	"
5	Walker, Ida	" Dau	3	F	1/2			
6	Colbert, Maud	Wife	18	F	I.W.			

TRIBAL ENROLLMENT OF PARENTS

	NAME OF FATHER	YEAR	COUNTY	NAME OF MOTHER	YEAR	COUNTY
1	Simon James	Dead	Tishomingo	Missey James	Dead	Tishomingo
2	Chilly Alexander	1897	"	Caroline Alexander	"	"
3	Henderson Cravatt	Dead	Pontotoc	No. 2		
4	" "	"	"	No. 2		
5	Jim Walker		Non-Citizen	No. 2		
6	Duet Harris	Dead	Non-Citizen	Mag Harris		Non-Citizen

(NOTES)
No. 2 Died Oct. *(remainder illegible)*
No. 2 on Chickasaw Roll as Mollie Alberson
No. 3 "   "   " " Emma J. Cravatt
No. 4 " 1897 Roll, Page 92, Tishomingo Co.
No. 5 Died Jan. 17, 1899. Enrollment *(remainder illegible)*

(No. 5 Dawes' Roll No. 4160)
Sept. 30, '98.

RESIDENCE: Tishomingo   COUNTY   CARD NO.
POST OFFICE: Tishomingo, I.T.   FIELD NO.

	NAME	RELATIONSHIP TO PERSON FIRST NAMED	AGE	SEX	BLOOD	TRIBAL ENROLLMENT		
						YEAR	COUNTY	PAGE
1	Cooney, Alpha		20	F	1/2	1893	Pickens	P.R.#2 170
2	" Myrtle Lee	Dau	4mo	"	1/4	1897	"	87
3	" Neita Corine	"	2mo	"	1/4			
4	" Wallace Franklin	Son	7mo	"	1/4			
5	" Frank	husband	28	M	I.W.			

91

	TRIBAL ENROLLMENT OF PARENTS						
	NAME OF FATHER	YEAR	COUNTY	NAME OF MOTHER	YEAR	COUNTY
1	Oravior Ouroderigo	Dead	Mexican	Jane Ouroderigo	Dead	Chick Roll
2	Frank Cooney		White man	No. 1		
3	" "		" "	No. 1		
4	" "		" "	No. 1		
5	Pat Cooney		Non Citizen	Sarah Cooney		Non Citizen

(NOTES)

No. 2 on Chick Roll as Myrtle E. Cooney   *(No. 2 Dawes' Roll No. 4159)*
No. 1   "   "   "   "   " Alphy Osavior
No. 1 is wife of Frank Carney, Chickasaw D.102.
No. 4 Born Nov. 7, 1901; enrolled June 10, 1902.
No. 2 Proof of birth received and filed Oct. 10, 1902
No. 3 Enrolled June 1, 1899.
No. 5 transferred from Chickasaw Card #D102.   *(No. 5 Dawes' Roll No. 192)*
   See decision of May 5, 1902.

P.O. Ardmore, I.T. 6/10/02   Sept. 30, '98.

RESIDENCE: Tishomingo	COUNTY				CARD NO.			
POST OFFICE: Emmet, I.T.					FIELD NO.			

	NAME	RELATION-SHIP TO PERSON FIRST NAMED	AGE	SEX	BLOOD	TRIBAL ENROLLMENT		
						YEAR	COUNTY	PAGE
1	Johnston, Douglas Henry	NAMED	42	M	1/8	1897	Panola	2
2	" Bettie L.	Wife	33	F	1/2	1897	"	2
3	" Llewellyn	Son	16	M	1/8	1897	"	2
4	" Juanita	Dau	8	F	3/16	1897	"	2
5	" Douglas Harper	Son	3	M	3/16	1897	"	2
6	Davenport, Julia A.	Ward	20	F	1/8	1897	"	2
7	" Albert E.	husband of No. 6	29	M	I.W.			

	TRIBAL ENROLLMENT OF PARENTS						
	NAME OF FATHER	YEAR	COUNTY	NAME OF MOTHER	YEAR	COUNTY
1	John Johnston	Dead	Non Citizen	Mary Johnston	Dead	Chick resid'g in Choc N. 1st Dist.
2	Josh Harper	"	" "	Sirena Harper nee Factor	1897	Panola
3	No. 1			Nellie Johnston	Dead	"
4	No. 1			Bettie " (No. 2)		
5	No. 1			No. 2		
6	Wm Chisholm	Dead	Creek Citizen	Julia Chisholm	Dead	Pontotoc

| 7 | W.H.C. Davenport | | non citizen | Julia P. Davenport | | non citizen |

(NOTES)

No. I on Chickasaw Roll as D.H. Johnston
No. 3 "   "   "   " Ludie   "
No. 4 "   "   "   " Neta   "
No. 5 "   "   "   " Douglas "
No. 6 "   "   "   " Julia Chisolm
No. 6 is now wife of Albert E. Davenport on Chickasaw Card #D.282.
No. 7 transferred from Chickasaw card #D.282 March 29, 1903.   *(No. 7 Dawes' Roll No. 41)*
    See decision of March 13, 1903.

Sept. 30, '98.

RESIDENCE: Tishomingo   COUNTY   CARD NO.
POST OFFICE: Regan, I.T.   FIELD NO.

	NAME	RELATION-SHIP TO PERSON FIRST NAMED	AGE	SEX	BLOOD	TRIBAL ENROLLMENT		
						YEAR	COUNTY	PAGE
~~1~~	~~Brown, Charley~~		~~38~~	~~M~~	~~Full~~	DIED PRIOR TO SEPTEMBER 25 1902 ~~1897~~	~~Tishomingo~~	~~37~~
2	" Emely	Wife	23	F	"	1897	"	37
3	" Marial	Dau	10mo	F	"			

TRIBAL ENROLLMENT OF PARENTS

	NAME OF FATHER	YEAR	COUNTY	NAME OF MOTHER	YEAR	COUNTY
~~1~~	~~Ta-ha-tub-by~~	~~Dead~~	~~Chick Roll~~	~~Ah-to-hi-chey~~	~~Dead~~	~~Chick Roll~~
2	Ab-a-tish-she	"	Tishomingo	Malecha	"	Tishomingo
3	No. I			No. 2		

(NOTES)

No. 3 Enrolled Aug. 19, 1901.

Sept. 30, '98.

RESIDENCE: Pickens   COUNTY   CARD NO.
POST OFFICE: Kingston, I.T.   FIELD NO.

	NAME	RELATION-SHIP TO PERSON FIRST NAMED	AGE	SEX	BLOOD	TRIBAL ENROLLMENT		
						YEAR	COUNTY	PAGE
1	Opeasubby		66	M	Full	1897	Pickens	23
2	" Pheby	Wife	48	F	"	DIED PRIOR TO SEPTEMBER 25 1902 1897	"	23
3	Roberson, Emeline	Gr.Dau	9	"	"	1897	"	23
4	Seeney, Nellie	Ward	9	"	1/2	1897	"	23

TRIBAL ENROLLMENT OF PARENTS

	NAME OF FATHER	YEAR	COUNTY	NAME OF MOTHER	YEAR	COUNTY
1	Tos-e-ki-ah	Dead	Chick Roll	Ok-lick-e	Dead	Chick Roll
2	Num-pul-ley	"	" "	Sha-p?-o-ke	"	" "
3	Simon Roberson	1897	Pickens	Mahsey Roberson	1897	Pickens
4	Bill Seenet		Non Citizen	Nancy Seeney	Dead	"

(NOTES)

No. 4 on Chickasaw Roll as Nellie Sealy
No. 2 died July 4, 1900; Proof of death filed Nov. 8, 1902.

Sept. 30, '98

RESIDENCE: Tishomingo   COUNTY   CARD NO.
POST OFFICE: Davis, I.T.   FIELD NO.

	NAME	RELATION-SHIP TO PERSON FIRST NAMED	AGE	SEX	BLOOD	TRIBAL ENROLLMENT		
						YEAR	COUNTY	PAGE
1	Stewart, Minnie	NAMED	20	F	7/8	1897	Tishomingo	28
2	Stewart, Georgia	Dau	8mo	"	7/16			
3	" Lettie Bell	Dau	1mo	F	7.16			
4	" William	Son	1mo	M	7/16			

TRIBAL ENROLLMENT OF PARENTS

	NAME OF FATHER	YEAR	COUNTY	NAME OF MOTHER	YEAR	COUNTY
1	Billy Thomas	Dead	Tishomingo	Ziley Colbert or Thomas	Dead	Chick Roll
2	Revie Stewart		Non Citizen	No. 1		
3	" "		" "	No. 1		
4	" "		" "	No. 1		

(NOTES)

See reference to name of No. 1 on inclosed[sic] affidavit
No. 3 Enrolled Nov. 12, 1900
No. 4 Born Sept. 11, 1902. Enrolled Oct. 13, 1902.   (No. 4 Dawes' Roll No. 4138)
No. 2 enrolled March 1, 1899.

Sept. 28, '98.

RESIDENCE: Tishomingo   COUNTY   CARD NO.
POST OFFICE: Davis, Ind. Ter.   FIELD NO.

	NAME	RELATION-SHIP TO PERSON FIRST NAMED	AGE	SEX	BLOOD	TRIBAL ENROLLMENT		
						YEAR	COUNTY	PAGE
1	Colbert, Annie	NAMED	17	F	3/8	1893	Pickens	PR 2 57

TRIBAL ENROLLMENT OF PARENTS

	NAME OF FATHER	YEAR	COUNTY	NAME OF MOTHER	YEAR	COUNTY
1	Albert Colbert		Choctaw Roll	Ziley Colbert	dead	Chickasaw and Delaware

(NOTES)

See affidavit filed April 13, 1904, relinquishing any claims she may have in any other than Chickasaw Nation.

(No. 1 Dawes' Roll No. 4796)

Sept. 1898.

RESIDENCE: Pontotoc   COUNTY   CARD NO.

POST OFFICE: Wiley, I.T.   FIELD NO.

	NAME	RELATION-SHIP TO PERSON FIRST NAMED	AGE	SEX	BLOOD	TRIBAL ENROLLMENT		
						YEAR	COUNTY	PAGE
1	Underwood, Jimpson	NAMED	45	M	Full	1897	Pontotoc	59
2	" Sarah	Wife	30	F	"	1897	"	59
3	" Lena	Dau	14	"	"	1897	"	59
4	" Daniel	Father	80	M	"	1897	"	56
5	~~" Willie Bond~~	~~Gr. Son~~	~~3mo~~	"	"			

TRIBAL ENROLLMENT OF PARENTS

	NAME OF FATHER	YEAR	COUNTY	NAME OF MOTHER	YEAR	COUNTY
1	Daniel Underwood	1897	Pontotoc	Shunako yah	Dead	Chick Roll
2	Wallace "	Dead	Chick Roll	Lyn Underwood	"	Pontotoc
3	No. 1			No. 2		
4	Billy Underwood	Dead	Chick Roll	*(Name Illegible)*	Dead	Chick Roll
5	~~Burney Underwood~~	~~1897~~	~~Pontotoc~~	~~No. 3~~		

(NOTES)

No. 4 also on Page 56, Pontotoc County

No. 3 is now wife of Burney Underwood on Chickasaw Card #117, Jan 20, '02.

No. 5 born Oct. 18, 1901; Enrolled Jan. 25, 1902.

(Notation illegible)

The above notation as to Nos. 3 & 5 is in error. No. 3 is now wife of Jesse *(Illegible)*, Chick card 193

See his test. and that of Gibson T. Grayson of May 1/03.

No. 5 transferred to Chick card 290 Aug. 22/03.

Sept. 30, '98.

RESIDENCE: Tishomingo   COUNTY   CARD NO.
POST OFFICE: Ravia, I.T.   FIELD NO.

	NAME	RELATION-SHIP TO PERSON FIRST NAMED	AGE	SEX	BLOOD	TRIBAL ENROLLMENT		
						YEAR	COUNTY	PAGE
1	Carhee, Julia	NAMED	19	F	Full	1897	Tishomingo	30
2	" Florence	Dau	3	"	"	1897	"	30
3	" Alice	Dau	6mo	"	"			

TRIBAL ENROLLMENT OF PARENTS

	NAME OF FATHER	YEAR	COUNTY	NAME OF MOTHER	YEAR	COUNTY
1	Charley Carhee	Dead	Chick Roll	Serena Carhee	Dead	Tishomingo
2	Ben Lewis	1897	Tishomingo	No. 1		
3	Willie Gaddis			No. 1		

(NOTES)

No. 1 on Chickasaw Roll as Julia Carhee
No. 2 "   "   " " Florence Lewis
No. 3 " Enrolled February 26, 1900.

Sept. 30, 1898.

RESIDENCE: Tishomingo   COUNTY   CARD NO.
POST OFFICE: Ravia, I.T.   FIELD NO.

	NAME	RELATION-SHIP TO PERSON FIRST NAMED	AGE	SEX	BLOOD	TRIBAL ENROLLMENT		
						YEAR	COUNTY	PAGE
1	Crummey, Tennie	NAMED	23	F	Full	1897	Tishomingo	36
2	Jimmy, Johnson	S.Son	3	M	"	1897	"	36
3	" Robert DEAD	Son	1	M		1897	"	87
4	Crummey, Clarence	Son	6mo	"	1/2			
5	" George	Husband	28	M	I.W.			

TRIBAL ENROLLMENT OF PARENTS

	NAME OF FATHER	YEAR	COUNTY	NAME OF MOTHER	YEAR	COUNTY
1	Lovison John	Dead	Tishomingo	(Name Illegible)	Dead	Tishomingo
2	Wilson Jimmy	"	"	Sophie Jimmy	"	"
3	" "	"	"	No. 1		
4	George Crummey		Non Citizen	No. 1		
5	(Name Illegible)			(Name Illegible)		

(NOTES)

No. 1 on Chickasaw Roll as Tennie John   (No. 1 Dawes' Roll No. 4156)
No. 1 is now the wife of George Crummey, non Citizen -   (No. 2 Dawes' Roll No. 4597)
    Evidence of marriage requested Nov. 4, 1902.
No. 4 Born May 6, 1902. Enrolled Nov. 4, 1902.   (No. 4 Dawes' Roll No. 4157)

No. 3 Died in April 1899; Proof of death filed Nov. 14, 1902.
No. 5 placed on this card June 22nd 1905, in accordance with decision of Commission of that date holding application was made within prescribed by act of Congress approved July 1, 1902 (32 Stat. 64?) Sept. 30, 1905 - Granted - No. 5.

Sept. 30, 1898.

	NAME	RELATION-SHIP TO PERSON FIRST NAMED	AGE	SEX	BLOOD	TRIBAL ENROLLMENT		
						YEAR	COUNTY	PAGE
1	Burch, Charles E.		11	M	9/16	1893	Pickens	PR#2 40

RESIDENCE: Pickens   *COUNTY*   *CARD NO.*
POST OFFICE: Wynnewood, I.T.   *FIELD NO.*

TRIBAL ENROLLMENT OF PARENTS

	NAME OF FATHER	YEAR	COUNTY	NAME OF MOTHER	YEAR	COUNTY
1	James Burch		Non Citizen	Annie Burch	Dead	Pickens

(NOTES)
No. 1 on Chickasaw Roll as Chas. E. Burch.

Sept. 30, '98.

RESIDENCE: Tishomingo   *COUNTY*   *CARD NO.*
POST OFFICE: Regan, I.T.   *FIELD NO.*

	NAME	RELATION-SHIP TO PERSON FIRST NAMED	AGE	SEX	BLOOD	TRIBAL ENROLLMENT		
						YEAR	COUNTY	PAGE
1	Colbert, Mary		26	F	Full	1897	Tishomingo	32
2	Hickentubby, Mina	Ward	15	"	"	1897	"	32
3	Brown, Francis	Dau	14	"	"	1893	"	P.R. #1 108

TRIBAL ENROLLMENT OF PARENTS

	NAME OF FATHER	YEAR	COUNTY	NAME OF MOTHER	YEAR	COUNTY
1	Sesune Greenwood	Dead	Chick Roll	Jemima Greenwood	Dead	Tishomingo
2	Ellis Hickentubby	"	Tishomingo	Jincy	"	"
3	Willie Brown	"	"	No. 1		

(NOTES)
No. 3 on Chickasaw Roll as Francis Brown
No. 1   "   "   " " Maryan Colbert
No. 2   "   "   " " Mina Ellis, Pickens County, Page 19.

Sept. 30, '98.

RESIDENCE: Pickens   COUNTY   CARD NO.

POST OFFICE: Burneyville, I.T.   FIELD NO.

	NAME	RELATION-SHIP TO PERSON FIRST	AGE	SEX	BLOOD	TRIBAL ENROLLMENT		
						YEAR	COUNTY	PAGE
1	Roberson, Simon	NAMED	35	M	Full	1897	Pickens	22
2	" Martha	Wife	27	F	"	1897	"	22
3	" Lila	Dau	17	"	"	1897	"	22
4	" Benjamin	Son	7	M	"	1897	"	22
5	" Easter	Dau	5	F	"	1897	"	22
6	" Tilman	Son	2	M	"	1897	"	22
7	" Logan	"	2mo	"	"			
8	" Caroline	Dau	9mo	F	"			
9	" Davison	Gr.Son	3	M	"			
10	" Hattie Mary	Gr.Dau	1	F	"			

TRIBAL ENROLLMENT OF PARENTS

	NAME OF FATHER	YEAR	COUNTY	NAME OF MOTHER	YEAR	COUNTY
1	Kiffey Roberson	Dead	Chick Roll	Sho-pi-o-ke	Dead	Chick Roll
2	Tomoley	"	" "	Mamdey	"	" "
3	No. 1			Un-lah-ho-ye	"	Pickens
4	No. 1			No. 2		
5	No. 1			No. 2		
6	No. 1			No. 2		
7	No. 1			No. 2		
8	No. 1			No. 2		
9	Unknown			No. 3		
10	"			No. 3		

(NOTES)

No. 9 born April 2, 1899; Enrolled April 23, 1902.
No. 10 "   " 19, 1901;   "   " 23, 1902.
Nos. 9 and 10 have been legally adopted by James C. McCurtain on Chickasaw Card #822. Act of Chickasaw National Legislative of Oct. 23, 1901 disapproved by President on June 6, 1902.

Sept. 30, '98.

RESIDENCE: Pickens   COUNTY   CARD NO.

POST OFFICE: Oakland, I.T.   FIELD NO.

	NAME	RELATION-SHIP TO PERSON FIRST	AGE	SEX	BLOOD	TRIBAL ENROLLMENT		
						YEAR	COUNTY	PAGE
1	Brown, Chicklin	NAMED	37	M	Full	1897	Pickens	25

2	" Linda	Wife	33	F	"	1897	"	25
3	" Levi	Son	14	M	"	1897	"	25
4	~~" Rena~~	~~Dau~~	~~11~~	~~F~~	~~"~~	~~1897~~	~~"~~	~~25~~
5	" Holmes	Son	7	M	"	1897	"	25
6	" Laura	Dau	1	F	"			
7	" Lucy	"	3mo	"	"			

TRIBAL ENROLLMENT OF PARENTS

	NAME OF FATHER	YEAR	COUNTY	NAME OF MOTHER	YEAR	COUNTY
1	By loy oh tubby	Dead	Chick Roll	Ollichey	Dead	Chick Roll
2	Jon Hamden	"	" "	Polly Hamden	1897	Pickens
3	No. 1			No. 2		
4	~~No. 1~~			~~No. 2~~		
5	No. 1			No. 2		
6	No. 1			No. 2		
7	No. 1			No. 2		

(NOTES)

No. 1 also known as "Byhoyoh"
No. 2 on Chickasaw Roll as Lincy Brown
No. 4 "   "   " " Roner   "
No. 4 died Sept. 21, 1902; Proof of death filed Nov. 8, 1902
No. 7 enrolled Dec. 16, 1899.
No. 4 Died Sept. 21, 1902; Enrollment cancelled by Dept. July *(remainder illegible)*

Sept. 30, 1898.

RESIDENCE: Pickens **COUNTY**   **CARD NO.**
POST OFFICE: Mansville, I.T.   **FIELD NO.**

	NAME	RELATION-SHIP TO PERSON FIRST NAMED	AGE	SEX	BLOOD	TRIBAL ENROLLMENT		
						YEAR	COUNTY	PAGE
1	Courtney, Tyson		35	M	Full	1897	Pickens	11
2	" Sophia	Wife	30	F	"	1897	"	11
3	" Sammie	Son	10	M	"	1897	"	11
4	" Betsie	Dau	12	F	"	1897	"	11
5	" Elsie Sena	"	2 1/2	"	"	1897	"	11
6	" Adeline	"	2mo	"	"			
7	" Emma	"	1	"	"			

TRIBAL ENROLLMENT OF PARENTS

	NAME OF FATHER	YEAR	COUNTY	NAME OF MOTHER	YEAR	COUNTY
1	Peter Courtney	Dead	Chick Roll	Lena Courtney	Dead	Chick Roll
2	*(Name Illegible)*	"	" "	Siley	"	" "

99

3	No. 1			No. 2		
4	No. 1			No. 2		
5	No. 1			No. 2		
6	No. 1			No. 2		
7	No. 1			No. 2		

(NOTES)

No. 5 on Chickasaw Roll as Elsie
No. 6 enrolled Nov. 3, 1899.
No. 7 was born Sept. 15, 1902; application received Nov. 6, 1902

P.O. Norton, I.T.   Sept. 30, '98.

RESIDENCE: Tishomingo COUNTY						CARD NO.		
POST OFFICE: Tishomingo, I.T.						FIELD NO.		

	NAME	RELATION-SHIP TO PERSON FIRST NAMED	AGE	SEX	BLOOD	TRIBAL ENROLLMENT		
						YEAR	COUNTY	PAGE
1	Courtney, Ben		48	M	Full	1897	Tishomingo	32
2	" Ellen	Wife	28	F	"	1893	"	P.R.#1 III
3	Carney, Johnson	S.Son	10	M	"	1893	"	"
4	Courtney, Ben, Jr.	Son	6	"	"	1893	"	"
5	" Willie	"	2	"	"	1897	"	88
6	" Adelaide	Dau	2	F	"	1897	"	88
7	" Sally	"	3mo	"	"			

TRIBAL ENROLLMENT OF PARENTS

	NAME OF FATHER	YEAR	COUNTY	NAME OF MOTHER	YEAR	COUNTY
1	Peter Courtney	Dead	Chick Roll	Lena Courtney	Dead	Chick Roll
2	John Johnson	"	" "	Sena Johnson	1897	Pontotoc
3	Sampson Carney	1897	Pontotoc	No. 2		
4	No. 1			No. 2		
5	No. 1			No. 2		
6	No. 1			No. 2		
7	No. 1			No. 2		

(NOTES)

No. 3 on Chickasaw Roll as Johnson Courtney
No. 6 "   "   " " Adlet "
No. 7 enrolled Nov. 3, 1899.

Sept. 30, '98.

RESIDENCE: Pontotoc COUNTY					CARD NO.		
POST OFFICE: Waupaunucka, I.T.					FIELD NO.		

	NAME	RELATION-SHIP TO PERSON FIRST NAMED	AGE	SEX	BLOOD	TRIBAL ENROLLMENT		
						YEAR	COUNTY	PAGE
1	Ream, Robert Lee		26	M	1/8	1897	Pontotoc	49
2	" Leona	Dau	3mo	F	1/16			
3	" Robert Lee, Jr.	Son	2wks	M	1/16			
4	" Ona O'Neal	Wife	23	F	I.W.			

TRIBAL ENROLLMENT OF PARENTS							
	NAME OF FATHER	YEAR	COUNTY	NAME OF MOTHER	YEAR	COUNTY	
1	Robert Lee Ream	Dead	Non-Citizen	Annie Guy Addington	1897	Pontotoc	
2	No. 1			Ona Ream		White woman	
3	No. 1			Ona B. Ream		" "	
4	Benj. O'Neal		non citizen	Martha O'Neal		non citizen	

(NOTES)

Husband of Ona O'Neal Ream, Chickasaw Card No. D.101.
On Chickasaw Roll as R.L. Ream
Correct name of Mother of Nos. 2 and 3 is Ona Beatrice Ream.
Evidence of marriage filed in Chickasaw Case #D.101, July 10, 1901.
January 4, 1900. Evidence of marriage of parents of No. 2 attached to Card No. D.101.
No. 3 Enrolled July 15, 1901.
No. 2   "   Nov. 4, 1899
No. 4 transferred from Chickasaw card #D.101.   *(No. 4 Dawes' Roll No. 285)*
   See decision of March 5, 1904, Mar. 23, 1904.

Sept. 30, 1898.

RESIDENCE: Pontotoc COUNTY					CARD NO.		
POST OFFICE: Waupaunuka, I.T.					FIELD NO.		

	NAME	RELATION-SHIP TO PERSON FIRST NAMED	AGE	SEX	BLOOD	TRIBAL ENROLLMENT		
						YEAR	COUNTY	PAGE
1	Addington, Andrew Jackson		46	M	I.W.			
2	" Annie Guy	Wife	46	F	1/4	1897	Pontotoc	49
3	Ream, James Boudinot	S.Son	24	M	1/8	1897	"	49
4	" Mary	Dau of No. 3	3mo	F	1/16			
5	" Mattie	Wife of No. 3	24	F	I.W.			

TRIBAL ENROLLMENT OF PARENTS						
NAME OF FATHER	YEAR	COUNTY	NAME OF MOTHER	YEAR	COUNTY	
1 Jerry Addington	Dead	Non Citizen	Lucinda Addington	Dead	Non Citizen	
2 William Guy	"	" "	Jane McGee Guy	"	Chickasaw	
3 Robert Lee Ream	"	" "	No. 2			
4 No. 3			Mattie Ream		White woman	
5 A.A. Taylor		non citizen	Elizabeth Taylor		non citizen	

(NOTES)

No. 2 on Chickasaw Roll as A.G. Brown   *(No. I Dawes' Roll No. 136)*
No. 3 member of Ist Tennessee Infantry, Gone to Manilla
No. 3 on Chickasaw Roll as J.B. Ream
No. 3 is now the husband of Mattie Ream on Chickasaw Card #D.345 = 4/24, '01
No. 4 Born Feby 15, 1902; Enrolled May 23, 1902.
No. 5 transferred from Chickasaw card #D.345 April 7, 1904   *(No. 5 Dawes' Roll No. 327)*
    See decision of March 15, 1904.

Sept. 30, 1898.

RESIDENCE: Tishomingo COUNTY						CARD NO.		
POST OFFICE: Regan, I.T.						FIELD NO.		

NAME	RELATION-SHIP TO PERSON FIRST NAMED	AGE	SEX	BLOOD	TRIBAL ENROLLMENT		
					YEAR	COUNTY	PAGE
1 Henderson, Sissum		35	M	Full	1893	Tishomingo	119

TRIBAL ENROLLMENT OF PARENTS						
NAME OF FATHER	YEAR	COUNTY	NAME OF MOTHER	YEAR	COUNTY	
1 Jim Henderson	Dead	Tishomingo	Susie Henderson	Dead	Tishomingo	

(NOTES)

No. I on Chickasaw Roll as Sesum Henderson
No. I also on 1896 Chickasaw Roll, Tishomingo Co., Page 92.

Sept. 30, 1898

RESIDENCE: Tishomingo COUNTY						CARD NO.		
POST OFFICE: Emmet, I.T.						FIELD NO.		

NAME	RELATION-SHIP TO PERSON FIRST NAMED	AGE	SEX	BLOOD	TRIBAL ENROLLMENT		
					YEAR	COUNTY	PAGE
1 Keel, Mollie		39	F	Full	1893	Tishomingo	P.R.#1 124
2 Maytubby, Hagan	Son	17	M	"	1897	"	37
3 " Ben	"	7	"	"	1897	"	37

102

	NAME	RELATIONSHIP	AGE	SEX	BLOOD	YEAR		PAGE
4	" ~~Lena~~	~~Dau~~	5	F	"	~~1897~~	"	~~36~~
5	Keel, Noah	Son	9mo	M	"			
6	" Phoebe	Dau	9mo	F	"			
7	" Eastman	Husband of No. 1	41	M	"	1893		P.R. #2 Page 2 No. 132

TRIBAL ENROLLMENT OF PARENTS

	NAME OF FATHER	YEAR	COUNTY	NAME OF MOTHER	YEAR	COUNTY
1	Jimpson Eschochey	Dead	Chick Roll	Rachael	Dead	Chick Roll
2	Hogan Maytubby	"	Tishomingo	No. 1		
3	" "	"	"	No. 1		
4	~~" "~~	~~"~~	~~"~~	~~No. 1~~		
5	Eastman Keel		Chickasaw	No. 1		
6	" "		"			
7	Cay-nom-tom-by	Dead	Choctaw Roll	(Name Illegible)		

(NOTES)

No. 4 died January 28, 1902; Enrollment cancelled by Department Dec. 24, 1904.
No. 1 on Chickasaw Roll as Mollie Maytubby
No. 2 "   "   "   " Hogan   "
No. 1 wife of Easmon Keel, Choctaw Roll Card No. 322
No. 2 died Sept. 1899. Evidence of death filed Nov. 26, 1902
No. 4 "   Sept. 1901;   "   "   "   "   "   " 1902
No. 6 born February 7, 1902; Enrolled Nov. 28, 1902   *(No. 6 Dawes' Roll No. 4455)*
No. 5 enrolled Nov. 3, 1899
No. 7 on Chickasaw Roll, Pontotoc Co, Page 95
No. 7 transferred from Choctaw Card #322. See decision of July 21, 1903.

Sept. 30, 1898.

RESIDENCE: Panola COUNTY					CARD NO.			
POST OFFICE: Meade, I.T.					FIELD NO.			

	NAME	RELATION-SHIP TO PERSON FIRST NAMED	AGE	SEX	BLOOD	TRIBAL ENROLLMENT		
						YEAR	COUNTY	PAGE
1	Underwood, Joe		28	M	Full	1897	Panola	1

TRIBAL ENROLLMENT OF PARENTS

	NAME OF FATHER	YEAR	COUNTY	NAME OF MOTHER	YEAR	COUNTY
1	Allen Underwood	Dead	Chick Roll	Jemima Underwood	1897	Tishomingo

(NOTES)

Children of No. 1 on Chickasaw #1077.

Sept. 30, 1898

RESIDENCE: Tishomingo	COUNTY				CARD NO.			
POST OFFICE: Ravia, I.T.					FIELD NO.			

NAME	RELATION-SHIP TO PERSON FIRST	AGE	SEX	BLOOD	TRIBAL ENROLLMENT		
					YEAR	COUNTY	PAGE
1 McLish, Lottie	NAMED	65	F	Full	1897	Tishomingo	36
2 Taylor, Annie	Gr.Dau	10	"	"	"	"	36

TRIBAL ENROLLMENT OF PARENTS							
NAME OF FATHER	YEAR	COUNTY	NAME OF MOTHER		YEAR	COUNTY	
1 Sha-ha-tah-pe	Dead	Chick Roll	Sho-shak-ne		Dead	Chick Roll	
2 Frank Taylor	1897	Tishomingo	Ellen Taylor		"	Tishomingo	

(NOTES)

PO. Troy, I.T. 1/25-04

Sept. 30, '98.

RESIDENCE: Tishomingo	COUNTY				CARD NO.			
POST OFFICE: Ravia, I.T.					FIELD NO.			

NAME	RELATION-SHIP TO PERSON FIRST	AGE	SEX	BLOOD	TRIBAL ENROLLMENT		
					YEAR	COUNTY	PAGE
1 Hawkins, Jimpson	NAMED	35	M	Full	1897	Tishomingo	11
2 " Lila	Wife	21	F	"	1897	"	36
3 " Betsey	Dau	4	"	"	1897	"	36
4 " Sarah	"	19days	"	"			

TRIBAL ENROLLMENT OF PARENTS							
NAME OF FATHER	YEAR	COUNTY	NAME OF MOTHER		YEAR	COUNTY	
1 William Hawkins	Dead	Pickens	Pah-ni-cy		Dead	Pickens	
2 Shelton McLish	"	Tishomingo	Lottie McLish		1897	Tishomingo	
3 No. 1			No. 2				
4 No. 1			No. 2				

(NOTES)

No. 2 on Chickasaw Roll as Lila McLish
No. 1 died Aug. 24, 1899; Proof of death filed Aug. 13, 1901.

Sept. 30, 1898.

RESIDENCE: Tishomingo	COUNTY				CARD NO.			
POST OFFICE: Belton, I.T.					FIELD NO.			

NAME	RELATION-SHIP TO PERSON FIRST	AGE	SEX	BLOOD	TRIBAL ENROLLMENT		
					YEAR	COUNTY	PAGE
1 Greenwood, Frank	NAMED	26	M	Full	1897	Tishomingo	33

2	" Nicy	Wife	40	F	"	1897	"	36
3	Frazier, Victoria	S.Dau	16	"	"	1897	"	36
4	" Minnie	" "	13	"	"	1897	"	36
5	" Fletcher	" Son	4	M	"	1897	"	36
6	Greenwood, Jeff	Son	6	"	"	1897	"	36
7	" Barney	"	4	"	"	1897	"	36
8	" Ruby Condon	Dau	3mo	F	"			
9	Johnson, Rosa Lee	Dau of No. 4	1	F	"			

TRIBAL ENROLLMENT OF PARENTS

	NAME OF FATHER	YEAR	COUNTY	NAME OF MOTHER	YEAR	COUNTY
1	Jefferson Greenwood	Dead	Tishomingo	Louisa Greenwood	Dead	Tishomingo
2	Wilson Wolfe	"	"	Sealy Wolfe	"	"
3	Willie Frazier	"	"	No. 2		
4	" "	"	"	No. 2		
5	" "	"	"	No. 2		
6	No. 1			Julia Greenwood	Dead	Tishomingo
7	No. 1			" "	"	"
8	No. 1			No. 2		
9	Eastman M. Johnson	1896	Tishomingo	No. 4		

(NOTES)

No. 8 died June 10, 1902; Enrollment cancelled by Department Dec. 28, 1904

No. 2 on Chickasaw Roll as Nicy Frazier

No. 8 Enrolled January 10, 1901.

No. 2 died Dec. 27. 1900. Proof of death filed March 11, 1901

No. 4 now wife of Eastman Johnson, Chick 860

No. 9 was born Aug. 7, 1902; application received and name placed on this card March 25, 1905. Under provision of Act of Congress approved March 3, 1905.   *(No. 9 Dawes' Roll No. 4979)*

P.O. of Nos. 3 and 4 Milburn, I.T.   Sept. 30, '98.

RESIDENCE: Tishomingo COUNTY						CARD NO.		
POST OFFICE: Regan, I.T.						FIELD NO.		
NAME	RELATION-SHIP TO PERSON FIRST NAMED	AGE	SEX	BLOOD	TRIBAL ENROLLMENT			
					YEAR	COUNTY	PAGE	
1	Keel, Gipson	NAMED	50	M	Full	1897	Tishomingo	37
2	" Pearilee	Wife	25	F	"	1897	"	37
3	" Lizzie	Dau	9	"	"	1897	"	37
4	" Hattie	"	5	"	"	1897	"	37

	NAME	RELATION	AGE	SEX	BLOOD	YEAR	COUNTY	PAGE
5	" Archison	Son	3	M	"	1897	"	37
6	" Bertha	Dau	I	F	"	~~1897~~	"	~~37~~
7	Johnson, Eastman	Bro in Law	30	M	"	1897	Tishomingo	38
8	Brown, Overton	"	17	"	"	1897	"	37
9	Tyson, Elonzo	"	11	"	"	1897	"	18
10	Keel, Thomas	Son	7mo	"	"			

TRIBAL ENROLLMENT OF PARENTS

	NAME OF FATHER	YEAR	COUNTY	NAME OF MOTHER	YEAR	COUNTY
1	George Keel	Dead	Chick Roll	Betsey Keel	Dead	Chick Roll
2	Tecumseh Cohe	"	Pontotoc	Sally Cohe	"	Tishomingo
3	No. 1			No. 2		
4	No. 1			No. 2		
5	No. 1			No. 2		
6	No. 1			No. 2		
7	Martin Johnson	Dead	Chick Roll	Sally Cohe	Dead	Tishomingo
8	Ponkey Brown	"	Tishomingo	" "	"	"
9	Tyson Cubbush	"	"	" "	"	"
10			*(This line left blank on microfilm)*			

(NOTES)

No. 2 on Chickasaw Roll as Polly   *(No. 6 Dawes' Roll No. 4154)*   *(No. 7 Dawes' Roll No. 2541)*
No. 5 "   "   " " Artson   *(No. 8 Dawes' Roll No. 2542)*
Father of No. 10 is No. 1 - Mother of No. 10 is No. 2   *(No. 9 Dawes' Roll No. 2543)*
No. 10 Enrolled May 25, 1900.   *(No. 10 Dawes' Roll No. 2540)*
No. 6 = Proof of birth received and filed Oct. 15, 1902.
No. 7 now husband of Minnie Frazier, Chick 861
Affidavit of No. 2 as to her divorce from James Daniels, filed May 20, 1903.

P.O. No. 7 Milburn, I.T.   Sept. 30, '98.

RESIDENCE: Pontotoc COUNTY				CARD NO.			
POST OFFICE: Stonewall, I.T.				FIELD NO.			

	NAME	RELATION-SHIP TO PERSON FIRST NAMED	AGE	SEX	BLOOD	TRIBAL ENROLLMENT		
						YEAR	COUNTY	PAGE
1	Pershica, Millie	NAMED	37	F	Full	1897	Tishomingo	32
2	~~Lewis, Molliean~~	~~Dau~~	14	"	"	~~1897~~	"	~~32~~

TRIBAL ENROLLMENT OF PARENTS

	NAME OF FATHER	YEAR	COUNTY	NAME OF MOTHER	YEAR	COUNTY
1	Pershica	Dead	Chickasaw Roll	Siley	Dead	Panola
2	~~Dixon Lewis~~	"	~~Pontotoc~~	~~No. 1~~		

(NOTES)

No. 1 on Chickasaw Roll as Willie Pershica
No. 2 "   "   "   " Millean Lewis
No. 2 Died April, 1899 *(remainder illegible)*

P.O. Ragen, I.T. 1/28-03   Sept. 30, '98.

RESIDENCE: Pickens   COUNTY   CARD NO.
POST OFFICE: Oakland, I.T.   FIELD NO.

NAME	RELATION-SHIP TO PERSON FIRST NAMED	AGE	SEX	BLOOD	TRIBAL ENROLLMENT		
					YEAR	COUNTY	PAGE
1	Russell, Silas	NAMED	32	M	Full	1897	Tishomingo	32
2	" Margerette	Wife	19	F	"	1897	"	32
3	Lacher, Hix	Bro in Law	16	M	"	1897	Pickens	18
4	Russell, Pearl DEAD	Dau	5mo	F	Full			
5	" Richard	Son	2mo	M	"			

TRIBAL ENROLLMENT OF PARENTS

	NAME OF FATHER	YEAR	COUNTY	NAME OF MOTHER	YEAR	COUNTY
1	A-ma-non-tubby	Dead	Chick Roll	Siley	Dead	Panola
2	Sto-e-he-aha	"	Tishomingo	Masey	"	Tishomingo
3	Noah Lacher	"	"	"	"	"
4	No. 1			No. 2		
5	No. 1			No. 2		

(NOTES)

No. 4 died Nov. 5, 1900; Proof of death filed Aug. 13, 1901.
No. 3 is the husband of Annie Brown on Chickasaw Card #848.
    See affidavit of Hicks Lacher filed with papers in that case. Aug. 19, 1901.
No. 5 Born Sept. 4, 1901; enrolled Nov. 16, 1901.
No. 5 Died Aug. 15, 1902; Proof of death filed Nov. 11, 1902.
No. 4 enrolled June 8, 1899.
No. 5 Correct date of death is Dec. 20/02. See test Silas Russell of Oct. 15/03.

No. 3 P.O. Russet, I.T. 2/2/04   Sept. 30, '98.

RESIDENCE: Tishomingo   COUNTY   CARD NO.
POST OFFICE: Tishomingo, I.T.   FIELD NO.

NAME	RELATION-SHIP TO PERSON FIRST NAMED	AGE	SEX	BLOOD	TRIBAL ENROLLMENT		
					YEAR	COUNTY	PAGE
1	Alowatubbee, Susanna	NAMED	25	F	Full	1897	Tishomingo	35

2	" Adeline	Dau	1	"	"			
3	Pickens, Hiram	Son	2mo	M	"			

TRIBAL ENROLLMENT OF PARENTS

	NAME OF FATHER	YEAR	COUNTY	NAME OF MOTHER	YEAR	COUNTY
1	Amos Alowatubbee	Dead	Chick Roll	*(Name Illegible)*	Dead	Chick Roll
2	Hiram Pickens	1897	Tishomingo	No. 1		
3	" "	"	"	No. 1		

(NOTES)

No. 1 on Chickasaw Roll as Susan Nelson
No. 1 is mother of Elonzo Shico on Chickasaw Card #261 Nov. 12, 1902.
No. 3 enrolled Aug. 17, 1899.
No. 1 is mother of Nos. 3 and 4 on Chickasaw Card #820.
No. 2 is same as Hallit Condon on Chickasaw Card #820.
   See letters of G.D. Rodgers of Nov. 5 and 6, 1902, filed with Chickasaw #820. Feby 21, 1903.

P.O. Regan I.T. 2/3-04   Sept. 30, '98.

RESIDENCE: Pickens COUNTY					CARD NO.			
POST OFFICE: Russell					FIELD NO.			

	NAME	RELATION-SHIP TO PERSON FIRST NAMED	AGE	SEX	BLOOD	TRIBAL ENROLLMENT		
						YEAR	COUNTY	PAGE
1	Porter, Edmon	NAMED	26	M	Full	1897	Pickens	11
2	" Harriet	Wife	25	F	1/2	1897	"	11
3	" Robert	Son	10	M	3/4	1897	"	11
4	" Jody	"	6	"	3/4	1897	"	11
5	" Emeline	Dau	2mo	F	3/4			

TRIBAL ENROLLMENT OF PARENTS

	NAME OF FATHER	YEAR	COUNTY	NAME OF MOTHER	YEAR	COUNTY
1	No?. Porter	Dead	Pickens	Cha-?e-cha	Dead	Pickens
2	Im-ma-ha-bee	"	Choctaw Roll	Sally	"	"
3	No. 1			No. 2		
4	No. 1			No. 2		
5	No. 1			No. 2		

(NOTES)

No. 4 on Chickasaw Roll as Julia
No. 2 died in Oct. 1899; Proof of death filed Aug. 13, 1901
No. 5 died Aug. 12, 1899; Proof of death filed Aug. 12, 1901.

                                                                Sept. 30, '98.

RESIDENCE: Tishomingo **COUNTY** **CARD NO.**
POST OFFICE: Regan, I.T. **FIELD NO.**

	NAME	RELATIONSHIP TO PERSON FIRST NAMED	AGE	SEX	BLOOD	TRIBAL ENROLLMENT YEAR	COUNTY	PAGE
1	Keel, Nannie		21	F	Full	1897	Tishomingo	34
~~2~~	~~" Liney~~	~~Dau~~	~~5mo~~	~~"~~	~~"~~	DIED PRIOR TO SEPTEMBER 25 1902		

TRIBAL ENROLLMENT OF PARENTS

	NAME OF FATHER	YEAR	COUNTY	NAME OF MOTHER	YEAR	COUNTY
1	Henry Keel	Dead	Pontotoc	Sibbie Keel	Dead	Pontotoc
~~2~~	~~Charley Brown~~	~~1897~~	~~Tishomingo~~	~~No. 1~~		

(NOTES)

No. 1 Died June 27, 1902; Proof of death filed Sept. 4, 1902.
No. 1 was at the time of her death, the wife of Eli Loman on Chickasaw Card # *(illegible)*.
See affidavit of Gene Wisdom, filed with proof of death Sept. 4, 1902.
No. 2 died in August 1901; Enrollment cancelled by Department Dec. 28, 1904.

Sept. 30. '98.

RESIDENCE: Choctaw Nation ~~**COUNTY**~~ **CARD NO.**
POST OFFICE: Wilburton, I.T. **FIELD NO.**

	NAME	RELATIONSHIP TO PERSON FIRST NAMED	AGE	SEX	BLOOD	TRIBAL ENROLLMENT YEAR	COUNTY	PAGE
1	McCann, Mary		27	F	1/2	1897	Chick resid'g in Choc. N. 1st Dist.	71

TRIBAL ENROLLMENT OF PARENTS

	NAME OF FATHER	YEAR	COUNTY	NAME OF MOTHER	YEAR	COUNTY
1	Alex McCann	Dead	Choctaw Roll	Lucy McCann	Dead	Chick Roll

(NOTES)

Now wife of No. 1 on Choctaw card 402. Evidence of marriage requested Dec. 20/02.

Sept. 30, '98.

RESIDENCE: Panola **COUNTY** **CARD NO.**
POST OFFICE: Mead, I.T. **FIELD NO.**

	NAME	RELATIONSHIP TO PERSON FIRST NAMED	AGE	SEX	BLOOD	TRIBAL ENROLLMENT YEAR	COUNTY	PAGE
1	Kemp, George		52	M	Full	1897	Panola	1
2	" Jemima	Wife	46	F	"	1897	"	1
3	Factor, Henry	Ward	13	M	"	1897	"	1

Chickasaw Enrollment Cards 1898-1914
Chickasaw by Blood   Volume IV

	TRIBAL ENROLLMENT OF PARENTS						
	NAME OF FATHER	YEAR	COUNTY	NAME OF MOTHER	YEAR	COUNTY	
1	Reuben Kemp	Dead	Chick Roll	Kalsie Kemp	Dead	Chick Roll	
2	(Name Illegible)	"	" "	Polly	"	" "	
3	Aaron Factor	"	Panola	Jennie Factor	"	Tishomingo	

(NOTES)

Sept. 30, '98.

RESIDENCE: Tishomingo   *COUNTY*   *CARD NO.*

POST OFFICE: Tishomingo. I.T.   *FIELD NO.*

NAME	RELATION-SHIP TO PERSON FIRST NAMED	AGE	SEX	BLOOD	TRIBAL ENROLLMENT		
					YEAR	COUNTY	PAGE
1 Moore, Thomas	NAMED	6	M	1/2	1897	Tishomingo	32
2 Howard, Ella	Mother	29	F	I.W.	1893	Chick Payroll #1	124

	TRIBAL ENROLLMENT OF PARENTS						
	NAME OF FATHER	YEAR	COUNTY	NAME OF MOTHER	YEAR	COUNTY	
1	Thomas Moore	Dead	Tishomingo	Ella Moore now Howard		White woman	
2	Cook McGee		non citizen	Minerva McGee		non citizen	

(NOTES)

No. 1 is the son of Ella Howard on Chickasaw Card #0.100

No. 2 married Thomas Moore, Chickasaw Indian in 1891, married F.D. Howard non citz in 1894.

No. 2 transferred from Chickasaw Card #0100. See decision of August 17, 1904.

Sept. 30, 1898.

RESIDENCE: Tishomingo   *COUNTY*   *CARD NO.*

POST OFFICE: Mill Creek, I.T.   *FIELD NO.*

NAME	RELATION-SHIP TO PERSON FIRST NAMED	AGE	SEX	BLOOD	TRIBAL ENROLLMENT		
					YEAR	COUNTY	PAGE
1 Sealy, Charley	NAMED	40	M	Full	1897	Tishomingo	35
2 " Frances	Wife	32	F	"	1897	"	35
3 " Thompson	Son	11	M	"	1897	"	36
4 " Gilbert	"	9	"	"	1897	"	36
5 " Lela	Dau	3	F	"	1897	"	36
6 " Susan	"	1mo	"	"			

	TRIBAL ENROLLMENT OF PARENTS						
	NAME OF FATHER	YEAR	COUNTY	NAME OF MOTHER	YEAR	COUNTY	
1	O-te-con-nin-tubby	Dead	Chick Roll	Patsey	1897	Tishomingo	
2	Justin Brown	"	Tishomingo	Jincy Brown	Dead	"	

3	No. 1			No. 2		
4	No. 1			No. 2		
5	No. 1			No. 2		
6	No. 1			No. 2		

(NOTES)

No. 2 on Chickasaw Roll as Francis Sealy
No. 5   "   "   "   " Lillie   "
No. 2 Died Aug. 2, 1902; Proof of death filed Nov. 11, 1902.
No. 6 Enrolled Mar. 18, 1899.

P.O. 11/7/02, Troy, I.T.   Sept. 30, '98.

RESIDENCE: Tishomingo	COUNTY				CARD NO.		
POST OFFICE:	Mill Creek, I.T.				FIELD NO.		

	NAME	RELATION-SHIP TO PERSON FIRST NAMED	AGE	SEX	BLOOD	TRIBAL ENROLLMENT		
						YEAR	COUNTY	PAGE
1	Lewis, Dina	NAMED	35	F	Full	1897	Tishomingo	29
2	Frazier, Thompson	Son	6	M	"	1897	"	29
3	" Elsie	Dau	10mo	F	"			

TRIBAL ENROLLMENT OF PARENTS

	NAME OF FATHER	YEAR	COUNTY	NAME OF MOTHER	YEAR	COUNTY	
1	Bi-ok-lo-na	Dead	Chick Roll	A-lum-ka	Dead	Chick Roll	
2	Jim Frazier	1897	Pickens	No. 1			
3	" "	"	"	No. 1			

(NOTES)

No. 1 on Chickasaw Roll as Tina Frazier

Sept. 30, '98.

RESIDENCE: Tishomingo	COUNTY				CARD NO.		
POST OFFICE:	Regan, I.T.				FIELD NO.		

	NAME	RELATION-SHIP TO PERSON FIRST NAMED	AGE	SEX	BLOOD	TRIBAL ENROLLMENT		
						YEAR	COUNTY	PAGE
1	Lewis, Kellon	NAMED	32	M	Full	1897	Tishomingo	37
2	" Ruthie	Wife	38	F	3/4	1897	"	37
3	Mike, Morina	Ward	7	"	Full	1893	"	P.R.#1 124

111

Chickasaw Enrollment Cards 1898-1914
Chickasaw by Blood   Volume IV

TRIBAL ENROLLMENT OF PARENTS

	NAME OF FATHER	YEAR	COUNTY	NAME OF MOTHER	YEAR	COUNTY
1	Ib-ba-lish-ey	Dead	Chick Roll	Ok-ha-ho-na	Dead	Chick Roll
2	Arch McGee	"	" "	Lucy McGee	"	" "
3	Forbus Mike	"	Tishomingo	Malisa Mike	1897	Tishomingo

(NOTES)

No. 3 on 1893 Chickasaw Pay Roll No. 1 Page 124 as Morina McKinney.
Louis Seely on Chick #836 is now guardian of No. 3.

Sept. 30, '98.

RESIDENCE: Pickens   COUNTY   CARD NO.

POST OFFICE: Russett, I.T.   FIELD NO.

	NAME	RELATION-SHIP TO PERSON FIRST NAMED	AGE	SEX	BLOOD	TRIBAL ENROLLMENT		
						YEAR	COUNTY	PAGE
1	~~Lacher, Annie~~	NAMED	~~26~~	F	~~Full~~	~~1897~~	~~Pickens~~	~~25~~
2	Fulsome, Edmon	Son	5	M	"	1897	"	25
3	Lacher, Myrtle	Dau	2mo	F	"			
4	" Florance	Dau	3wks	"	"			

TRIBAL ENROLLMENT OF PARENTS

	NAME OF FATHER	YEAR	COUNTY	NAME OF MOTHER	YEAR	COUNTY
1	~~Jim Johnson~~	~~Dead~~	~~Chick Roll~~	~~Polly Johnson~~	~~Dead~~	~~Chick Roll~~
2	Dixon Fulsome	"	Pickens	No. 1		
3	Hicks Lacher	1897	"	No. 1		
4	" "	"	"	No. 1		

(NOTES)

No. 1 Died Aug. 23, 1902; Enrollment cancelled by Dept. July *(remainder illegible)*
No. 1 is wife of Hix Lacher on Chickasaw Card #858. See affidavit on file herein.
No. 4 enrolled Aug. 19, 1901.
No. 1 died Aug. 23, 1901; Proof of death filed Nov. 7, 1902.

Sept. 30, '98,

RESIDENCE: Tishomingo   COUNTY   CARD NO.

POST OFFICE: Mill Creek, I.T.   FIELD NO.

	NAME	RELATION-SHIP TO PERSON FIRST NAMED	AGE	SEX	BLOOD	TRIBAL ENROLLMENT		
						YEAR	COUNTY	PAGE
1	Lewis, Wall	NAMED	47	M	Full	1897	Tishomingo	33
2	" Mary	Wife	43	F	"	1897	"	33
3	" Lula Belle	Dau	3	"	"	1897	"	33

112

4	Greenwood, Lizzie	S.Dau	9	"	"	1897	"	33
5	Hamilton, Aaron	S.Neph.	12	M	"	1893	"	P.R. #I 119
6	" Simeon	S.Son	15	"	"	1893	"	P.R.#I 119

TRIBAL ENROLLMENT OF PARENTS

	NAME OF FATHER	YEAR	COUNTY	NAME OF MOTHER	YEAR	COUNTY
1	Isum Sheappee	Dead	Chickasaw Roll	Sophie Sheappee	Dead	Chick Roll
2	" "	"	" "	Gilse Brown	"	" "
3	No. 1			No. 2		
4	Frank Greenwood	1897	Tishomingo	No. 2		
5	Carmon Hamilton	Dead	"	Minerva Hamilton	Dead	Tishomingo
6	William "	"	"	No. 2		

(NOTES)

No. 3 on Chickasaw Roll as Lula Lewis
No. 6   "   "   "   " Simon Hamilton
No. 5 also on 1896 Chickasaw Roll, Tishomingo County, Page 92

P.O. Regan, I.T.   Sept. 30, '98.

RESIDENCE: Pickens   *COUNTY*   *CARD NO.*
POST OFFICE: Berroin, I.T.   *FIELD NO.*

	NAME	RELATION- SHIP TO PERSON FIRST NAMED	AGE	SEX	BLOOD	TRIBAL ENROLLMENT		
						YEAR	COUNTY	PAGE
1	Massey, John W.	NAMED	27	M	I.W.			
2	" Juel	Wife	18	F	1/8	1897	Tishomingo	37
3	" Bennie W.	Son	2mo	M	1/16			

TRIBAL ENROLLMENT OF PARENTS

	NAME OF FATHER	YEAR	COUNTY	NAME OF MOTHER	YEAR	COUNTY
1	Jas. L. Massey		Non Citizen	Rachel Massey		Non Citizen
2	B.F. Boyd	Dead	Pickens	Louisa J. Poyner (I.W.)	1897	Tishomingo
3	No. 1			No. 2		

(NOTES)

No. 2 on 1896 Roll as Jewell Boyd
     As to marriage of parents of No. 2, see testimony of E.S. Barney
No. 2 is daughter of Louisa J. Poyner on Chickasaw ~~Roll~~ Card #D.99.
No. 1 enrolled Aug. 15, 1899.   *(No. 1 Dawes' Roll No. 135)*
No. 2   "   Sept. 30, 1899
No. 3   "   Nov. 3, 1899

RESIDENCE: Pickens   COUNTY   CARD NO.
POST OFFICE: Woodville, I.T.   FIELD NO.

NAME	RELATION-SHIP TO PERSON FIRST NAMED	AGE	SEX	BLOOD	TRIBAL ENROLLMENT		
					YEAR	COUNTY	PAGE
1 Cain, Lottie	NAMED	44	F	Full	1897	Pickens	8
2 Bowlin, Maggie	Dau	19	"	1/2	1897	"	8
3 Durham, Stella	Gr.Dau	1	"	1/2	~~1897~~	"	~~86~~
4 " John	Son	16	M	1/2	1897	"	8
5 " Arthur	"	14	"	1/2	1897	"	8
6 " Sudie	Dau	12	F	1/2	1897	"	8
7 " Berry	Son	8	M	1/2	1897	"	8
8 Bowlin, Tressa	Gr.Dau	2mo	F	1/4			
9 " Sudie	Gr.Dau	2wks	"	1/4			

TRIBAL ENROLLMENT OF PARENTS

	NAME OF FATHER	YEAR	COUNTY	NAME OF MOTHER	YEAR	COUNTY
1	Ben McLaughlin	Dead	Chick Roll	Amanda McLaughlin	Dead	Chick Roll
2	J.H. Durham	"	Non Citizen	No. 1		
3	Dan Ayers		" "	No. 2		
4	J.H. Durham	Dead	" "	No. 1		
5	" " "	"	" "	No. 1		
6	" " "	"	" "	No. 1		
7	" " "	"	" "	No. 1		
8	Charles Bowlin		" "	No. 2		
9	" "		" "	No. 2		

(NOTES)

No. 1 wife of M.A. Cain, U.S. Citizen from whom she has separated.   *(No. 3 Dawes' Roll No. 4153)*
No. 2 now the wife of Chas. Bowlin, a non citizen. Evidence of marriage filed February 18, 1901.
No. 8 enrolled February 18, 1901.
No. 9 born Aug. 26, 1902; enrolled Sept. 21, 1902.
No. 3 Proof of birth received and filed Oct. 10, 1902

Sept. 30, '98.

RESIDENCE: Pontotoc   COUNTY   CARD NO.
POST OFFICE: Stonewall, I.T.   FIELD NO.

NAME	RELATION-SHIP TO PERSON FIRST NAMED	AGE	SEX	BLOOD	TRIBAL ENROLLMENT		
					YEAR	COUNTY	PAGE
1 Collins, Serena	NAMED	24	F	Full	1893	Pontotoc	P.R.#2 54

Chickasaw Enrollment Cards 1898-1914
Chickasaw by Blood Volume IV

TRIBAL ENROLLMENT OF PARENTS						
NAME OF FATHER	YEAR	COUNTY	NAME OF MOTHER	YEAR	COUNTY	
1	J.D. Collins	1897	Pontotoc	Salina Collins	1897	Pontotoc

(NOTES)

Sept. 30, '98.

RESIDENCE: Pickens   COUNTY   CARD NO.

POST OFFICE: Cumberland, I.T.   FIELD NO.

	NAME	RELATION-SHIP TO PERSON FIRST NAMED	AGE	SEX	BLOOD	TRIBAL ENROLLMENT		
						YEAR	COUNTY	PAGE
1	Barney, Louisa	NAMED	52	F	Full	1897	Pickens	9
2	" Bennie Bennett	Son	17	M	"	1897	"	9
3	" Paul Earnest	"	13	"	"	1897	"	9
4	" Arvilla	Dau	10	F	"	1897	"	9
5	~~Colbert, Luella~~	~~G.Dau~~	5	~~F~~	~~"~~	DIED PRIOR TO SEPTEMBER 25 1902 ~~1897~~ ~~"~~		~~9~~
6	" Burney	" "	3	"	"	1897	"	9

TRIBAL ENROLLMENT OF PARENTS						
	NAME OF FATHER	YEAR	COUNTY	NAME OF MOTHER	YEAR	COUNTY
1	Isaac Alberson	Dead	Chick Roll	Lucy Gaines Alberson	Dead	Chick Roll
2	Ben Barney	"	Pickens	No. 1		
3	" "	"	"	No. 1		
4	" "	"	"	No. 1		
5	~~Amos Colbert~~	~~"~~	~~"~~	~~Ada Barney Colbert~~	~~Dead~~	~~Pickens~~
6	" "	"	"	" " "	"	"

(NOTES)

No. 5 Died Jan. 26, 1899. Enrollment *(remainder illegible)*

No. 2 on Chickasaw Roll as Bennie Barney

No. 5 died Jan. 26, 1899; Proof of death filed Nov. 10, 1902.

Sept. 30, '98.

RESIDENCE: Tishomingo   COUNTY   CARD NO.

POST OFFICE: Tishomingo, I.T.   FIELD NO.

	NAME	RELATION-SHIP TO PERSON FIRST NAMED	AGE	SEX	BLOOD	TRIBAL ENROLLMENT		
						YEAR	COUNTY	PAGE
1	Condon, Michael Jefferson	NAMED	23	M	1/2	1897	Tishomingo	37
2	Cravatt, Tom	Ward	17	"	1/2	1897	Pickens	18
3	" Ben	"	14	"	1/2	1897	"	18

115

4	~~Condon, E?a Loucille~~	~~Dau~~	~~3mo~~	~~F~~	~~1/4~~	DIED	PRIOR TO SEPTEMBER 25 1902	
5	~~" Willard Warrenton~~	~~Son~~	~~4mo~~	~~M~~	~~1/4~~	DIED	PRIOR TO SEPTEMBER 25 1902	
6	Cravatt, Ludocea D.	Dau of No. 2	2wks	F	1/4			

TRIBAL ENROLLMENT OF PARENTS

	NAME OF FATHER	YEAR	COUNTY	NAME OF MOTHER	YEAR	COUNTY
1	Michael Condon (I.W.)	1897	Tishomingo	Lizzie Condon	Dead	Tishomingo
2	Alex Cravatt	Dead	"	*(Illegible)* Cravatt	"	"
3	" "	"	"	" "	"	"
4	~~No. 1~~			~~Mattie Condon~~		~~Non Citizen~~
5	~~No. 1~~			" "		" "
6	No. 2			Bettie Cravatt		" "

(NOTES)

No. 4 Died July 27, 1899. Enrollment *(remainder illegible)*
No. 5 Died June 1, 1900. *(remainder illegible)*
No. 1 on Chickasaw Roll as M.J. Condon
No. 2 " " " " Thomas Cravatt
No. 5 enrolled May 25, 1900.
No. 2 is now the husband of Bettie Cravatt - a non citizen
Evidence of marriage filed Aug. 8, 1902.
No. 6 Born July 21, 1902; enrolled Aug. 8, 1902.
No. 4 Died July 27, 1899; Proof of death filed Nov. 8, 1902
No. 5 " June 1, 1900; " " " " Nov. 8, 1902.

Sept. 30, '98.

RESIDENCE: Pontotoc	COUNTY	CARD NO.	
POST OFFICE: Johnson, I.T.		FIELD NO.	

	NAME	RELATIONSHIP TO PERSON FIRST NAMED	AGE	SEX	BLOOD	TRIBAL ENROLLMENT YEAR	TRIBAL ENROLLMENT COUNTY	TRIBAL ENROLLMENT PAGE
1	Smith, Robert E.		30	M	I.W.	1897	Pontotoc	81
2	" Minnie D.	Wife	22	F	1/16	1893	"	P.R. #2 204

TRIBAL ENROLLMENT OF PARENTS

	NAME OF FATHER	YEAR	COUNTY	NAME OF MOTHER	YEAR	COUNTY
1	W.A. Smith		Non Citizen	M.J. Smith		Non Citizen
2	Marion Davis		" "	Catherine Davis	Dead	Panola

(NOTES)

No. 1 on Chickasaw Roll as R.E. Smith *(No. 1 Dawes' Roll No. 134)*
No. 2 " 1897 " " Page 64, as Minnie Smith

License and Cort Record destroyed. Rev. C.F. Roberts, of Ardmore, testified under oath that he performed the marriage ceremony and saw the license before doing so. He knows that Mr. Smith had a license.

Affidavit of H. Colbert as to marriage license and the marriage hereunder of No. I and No. 2 received and filed Nov. 13, 1902.

Sept. 30, '98.

	RESIDENCE: Pontotoc COUNTY				CARD NO.			
	POST OFFICE: Wiley, I.T.				FIELD NO.			
	NAME	RELATION-SHIP TO PERSON FIRST NAMED	AGE	SEX	BLOOD	TRIBAL ENROLLMENT		
						YEAR	COUNTY	PAGE
1	Craley, Cephus		23	M	Full			

	TRIBAL ENROLLMENT OF PARENTS						
	NAME OF FATHER	YEAR	COUNTY	NAME OF MOTHER	YEAR	COUNTY	
1	Sampson Craley	Dead	Chick Roll	Serena Sealey	Dead	Chick Roll	

(NOTES)

Husband of Susan Craley, Choctaw Roll, Card No. 398.
On Choctaw Census Record No. 2, Page 117, transferred to Chickasaw Roll by Dawes Commission
   On Choctaw Roll, 1896, Blue County, No. 2896.

Sept. 29, '98.

CANCELLED Stamped across card
Transferred to Choctaw Card No. 5??9
Oct. ??, 1902

	RESIDENCE: Tishomingo COUNTY				CARD NO.			
	POST OFFICE: Mill Creek, I.T.				FIELD NO.			
	NAME	RELATION-SHIP TO PERSON FIRST NAMED	AGE	SEX	BLOOD	TRIBAL ENROLLMENT		
						YEAR	COUNTY	PAGE
1	Newberry, Levi		35	M	Full	1897	Tishomingo	27
2	" Katie	Wife	28	F	"	1897	"	27
3	" Jane	Dau	18	"	"	1897	"	27

	TRIBAL ENROLLMENT OF PARENTS						
	NAME OF FATHER	YEAR	COUNTY	NAME OF MOTHER	YEAR	COUNTY	
1	I-o-da-te-cha	Dead	Tishomingo	Lucy	Dead	Tishomingo	
2	Wilson Lewis	"	Pontotoc	Ho-ye-cha	"	"	
3	No. I			Salena Newberry	"	"	

(NOTES)

No. I on Chickasaw Roll as Levi Newberry

Sept. 29, '98.

RESIDENCE: Tishomingo   COUNTY   CARD NO.

POST OFFICE: Regan, I.T.   FIELD NO.

NAME	RELATION-SHIP TO PERSON FIRST NAMED	AGE	SEX	BLOOD	TRIBAL ENROLLMENT		
					YEAR	COUNTY	PAGE
1 Hart, Sallie	NAMED	30	F	Full	1897	Tishomingo	36
2 Cass, Sam	Son	13	M	"	1897	"	36
3 Sealy, Annie	Dau	6	F	"	1897	"	36
4 Hart, Johnstin	Son	3	M	"	1897	"	36

TRIBAL ENROLLMENT OF PARENTS

	NAME OF FATHER	YEAR	COUNTY	NAME OF MOTHER	YEAR	COUNTY
1	Bon-low-by	Dead	Tishomingo	Kilsey	Dead	Pontotoc
2	Wall Cass	1897	Pontotoc	No. 1		
3	Dave Sealy	1897	Pickens	No. 1		
4	Jackson Hart	1897	Tishomingo	No. 1		

(NOTES)

Nos. 1 and 4 are wife and child of Jackson Hart, on Chickasaw Card #911.

Sept. 29, '98

RESIDENCE: Pontotoc   COUNTY   CARD NO.

POST OFFICE: Conner, I.T.   FIELD NO.

NAME	RELATION-SHIP TO PERSON FIRST NAMED	AGE	SEX	BLOOD	TRIBAL ENROLLMENT		
					YEAR	COUNTY	PAGE
1 Stephens, Agnes	NAMED	28	F	Full	1897	Pontotoc	55
2 Kowey, Isaac	Son	4mo	M	"			

TRIBAL ENROLLMENT OF PARENTS

	NAME OF FATHER	YEAR	COUNTY	NAME OF MOTHER	YEAR	COUNTY
1	Ollicke Williams	Dead	Chick Roll	Elizabeth Williams	Dead	Pontotoc
2	Billie Kowey		" "	No. 1		

(NOTES)

No. 1 died Oct. 6, 1902; Proof of death filed Nov. 24, 1902.

No. 2 enrolled March 28, 1899.

Sept. 29, 1898

118

RESIDENCE: Tishomingo *COUNTY* *CARD NO.*

POST OFFICE: Ravia, I.T. *FIELD NO.*

NAME	RELATION-SHIP TO PERSON FIRST NAMED	AGE	SEX	BLOOD	TRIBAL ENROLLMENT		
					YEAR	COUNTY	PAGE
1 Seely, Lewis	NAMED	39	M	Full	1897	Tishomingo	35
2 " Ellen	Wife	25	F	"	1897	"	35

TRIBAL ENROLLMENT OF PARENTS

	NAME OF FATHER	YEAR	COUNTY	NAME OF MOTHER	YEAR	COUNTY
1	A-bah-na-tubby	Dead	Tishomingo	Sophie	1897	Tishomingo
2	Ben Kunanntubbee	"	"	Sophia Kunanntubbey	1897	"

(NOTES)

Surname on Chickasaw Roll as Sealy.

P.O. Troy, I.T. 1/26-04   Sept. 29, 1898

RESIDENCE: Tishomingo *COUNTY* *CARD NO.*

POST OFFICE: Mill Creek, I.T. *FIELD NO.*

NAME	RELATION-SHIP TO PERSON FIRST NAMED	AGE	SEX	BLOOD	TRIBAL ENROLLMENT		
					YEAR	COUNTY	PAGE
1 Kunanntubbee, Sophia	NAMED	40	F	Full	1897	Tishomingo	29
2 " Elias	Son	17	M	"	1897	"	29
3 " Joseph	"	10	"	"	1897	"	29

TRIBAL ENROLLMENT OF PARENTS

	NAME OF FATHER	YEAR	COUNTY	NAME OF MOTHER	YEAR	COUNTY
1	Ma-sha	Dead	Chick Roll	Polly	Dead	Chick Roll
2	Ben Kunanntubbee	"	Tishomingo	No. 1		
3	" "	"	"	No. 1		

(NOTES)

No. 1 on Chick. Roll as Sophia Cunnentubby
No. 2 "   "   " " Lines   "
No. 3 "   "   " " Josiah   "

Sept. 29, '98.

RESIDENCE: Tishomingo COUNTY					CARD NO.			
POST OFFICE: Tishomingo, I.T.					FIELD NO.			

NAME	RELATION-SHIP TO PERSON FIRST NAMED	AGE	SEX	BLOOD	TRIBAL ENROLLMENT		
					YEAR	COUNTY	PAGE
1 Shuckey, Patsey	NAMED	70	F	Full	1897	Tishomingo	30

TRIBAL ENROLLMENT OF PARENTS

NAME OF FATHER	YEAR	COUNTY	NAME OF MOTHER	YEAR	COUNTY
1 Shuckey	Dead	Chick Roll	(Name Illegible)	Dead	Chick Roll

(NOTES)

No. 1 is the wife of No. 1 on Chickasaw Card #0.240

Sept. 29, '98.

RESIDENCE: Tishomingo COUNTY					CARD NO.			
POST OFFICE: Tishomingo, I.T.					FIELD NO.			

NAME	RELATION-SHIP TO PERSON FIRST NAMED	AGE	SEX	BLOOD	TRIBAL ENROLLMENT		
					YEAR	COUNTY	PAGE
1 Holoata	NAMED	67	M	Full	1897	Tishomingo	31
2 " Sier	Wife	60	F	"	1897	"	31

TRIBAL ENROLLMENT OF PARENTS

NAME OF FATHER	YEAR	COUNTY	NAME OF MOTHER	YEAR	COUNTY
1 Ti-yub-by	Dead	Chick Roll	Fin-no-ye	Dead	Chick Roll
2 Os-pah-tubby	"	" "	Pah-no-he	"	" "

(NOTES)

Sirname on Chickasaw Roll as Holoata

Sept. 29, '98.

RESIDENCE: Pontotoc COUNTY					CARD NO.			
POST OFFICE: Wiley, I.T.					FIELD NO.			

NAME	RELATION-SHIP TO PERSON FIRST NAMED	AGE	SEX	BLOOD	TRIBAL ENROLLMENT		
					YEAR	COUNTY	PAGE
1 Fillmore, Selan	NAMED	30	F	Full	1897	Pontotoc	59
2 " Mollie	Dau	17	"	3/4	1897	"	59
3 " Robert	Son	14	M	3/4	1897	"	59
4 " Maria	Dau	9	F	3/4	1897	"	59
5 " Nellie	"	5	"	3/4	1897	"	59
6 " Marcum	Son	3	M	3/4	1897	"	59
7 " ~~Tecumseh~~	"	7mo	"	3/4	DIED PRIOR TO SEPTEMBER 25 1902		

120

Chickasaw Enrollment Cards 1898-1914
Chickasaw by Blood   Volume IV

							DIED PRIOR TO SEPTEMBER 25 1902		
8	~~Burris, Eliza~~	~~Mother~~	~~80~~	F	~~Full~~	~~1897~~	~~"~~		~~59~~
9	Fillmore, Frances	Dau	11/2	"	3/4				

TRIBAL ENROLLMENT OF PARENTS

	NAME OF FATHER	YEAR	COUNTY	NAME OF MOTHER	YEAR	COUNTY
1	E-mul-a-tubby	Dead	Chick Roll	Liza Burris	1897	Pontotoc
2	Jacob Fillmore		Choc. resid'g in Chickasaw Dist.	No. 1		
3	" "		"	No. 1		
4	" "		"	No. 1		
5	" "		"	No. 1		
6	" "		"	No. 1		
7	" "		"	No. 1		
8	~~Mar-to-fe-cha~~	~~Dead~~	~~Chick Roll~~	~~Fah-kah-ke~~	~~Dead~~	~~Chick Roll~~
9	" "		"	No. 1		

(NOTES)

No. 7 Died *(remainder illegible)*
No. 1 wife of Jacob Fillmore, Choctaw roll, Card No. 317.
No. 7 died May 28, 1900; Proof of death filed Nov. 8, 1902.
No. 8 died Jan. 11, 1901; Proof of death filed Nov. 8, 1902.
No. 9 Born May 10, 1901; Enrolled Nov. 8, 1902.

(No. 9 Dawes' Roll No. 4152)
Sept. 29, '98.

RESIDENCE: Pontotoc *COUNTY*   CARD NO.
POST OFFICE: Wiley, I.T.   FIELD NO.

	NAME	RELATION-SHIP TO PERSON FIRST NAMED	AGE	SEX	BLOOD	TRIBAL ENROLLMENT		
						YEAR	COUNTY	PAGE
1	Holden, Wemon	NAMED	48	M	Full	1897	Pontotoc	59
2	" Lucy	Wife	25	F	"	1897	"	59
3	" Johnie	Son	23	M	"	1897	"	59
4	" Siney	Dau	11	F	"	1897	"	59
5	" Emma	"	4	"	"	1897	"	59
6	" Elsie	"	9mo	"	"			
7	Carney, Katie	Niece	13	"	"	1897	"	59
8	Peter, Pitman	S.Son	6	M	"	1897	"	59
9	Holden, Walter	Son	4mo	"	"			

TRIBAL ENROLLMENT OF PARENTS

	NAME OF FATHER	YEAR	COUNTY	NAME OF MOTHER	YEAR	COUNTY
1	Abna??-tubby	Dead	Chick Roll	Shimioke	Dead	Chick Roll
2	Adam Lewis	"	" "	Amanda Lewis	"	" "

121

3	No. 1			Susie Holden	"	" "
4	No. 1			Jennie "	"	" "
5	No. 1			No. 2		
6	No. 1			No. 2		
7	Charley Cainey	Dead	Chick Roll	Salina Carney	Dead	Chick Roll
8	Harvey Peter	1897	Panola	No. 2		
9	No. 1			No. 2		

(NOTES)

No. 5 on Chickasaw Roll as Sina
No. 6 Affidavit as to birth to be supplied. received and filed Feby 24, 1900.
No. 9 Enrolled July 10, 1901.

Sept. 29, '98.

RESIDENCE: Tishomingo   **COUNTY**   **CARD NO.**
POST OFFICE: Tishomingo, I.T.   **FIELD NO.**

	NAME	RELATION-SHIP TO PERSON FIRST NAMED	AGE	SEX	BLOOD	TRIBAL ENROLLMENT		
						YEAR	COUNTY	PAGE
1	Gaddis, Sallie		23	F	Full	1897	Tishomingo	32
2	McKinney. Turner	Son	1	M	"	~~1897~~	"	~~88~~
3	Tushhatomby, Mamie	Dau	5	F	"	1897	"	32
4	Gaddis. Claud	Son	3mo	M	1/2			
5	" Lizzie	Dau	2mo	F	1/2			
6	" Will	Husb	28	M	1/2	1896	Tishomingo	38

TRIBAL ENROLLMENT OF PARENTS

	NAME OF FATHER	YEAR	COUNTY	NAME OF MOTHER	YEAR	COUNTY
1	Joe Benton	Dead	Tishomingo	Lizzie Benton	Dead	Tishomingo
2	Jonas McKinney	"	"	No. 1		
3	Willis Tushhatomby	"	"	No. 1		
4	Wm Gaddis	CCR#2 216	Choctaw residing in Chickasaw District	No. 1		
5	" "	"	"	No. 1		
6	Jack Gaddis	1897	Cherokee Citz	Melvina Johnson	1897	Choc residing in Chick Dist.

(NOTES)

No. 2 on Chickasaw Roll as Truer McKinney   *(No. 2 Dawes' Roll No. 4151)*
No. 3 "   "   " " Mamie Tushha
No. 1 is now the wife of Wm Gaddis on Choctaw Card #326
No. 4 enrolled June 25, 1900
No. 5 Born March 8, 1902; Enrolled May 24, 1902
No. 2 Proof of birth received and filed Nov. 16, 1902

No. 6 transferred from Choctaw card #326 March 19, 1904   *(No. 6 Dawes' Roll No. 4932)*

No. 6 on 1893 Choctaw Pay Roll, Chickasaw District, page 23, No. 222, as Wm Gaddis

No application was ever made to Commission for enrollment of No. 6 as a Cherokee, not is he listed on any Cherokee card.

P.O. Alhambra, I.T.   Sept. 29, '98.

RESIDENCE: Pontotoc *COUNTY*   *CARD NO.*

POST OFFICE: Emmet, I.T.   *FIELD NO.*

	NAME	RELATION-SHIP TO PERSON FIRST NAMED	AGE	SEX	BLOOD	TRIBAL ENROLLMENT		
						YEAR	COUNTY	PAGE
1	Hannatubby, Isaiah		50	M	Full	1897	Pontotoc	58
2	" Sarah	Wife	45	F	"	1897	"	58
3	" Eddie	Dau	16	"	"	1897	"	58
4	Colbert, *(Illegible)*	*(Illegible)*	9	M	"	1897	"	58

TRIBAL ENROLLMENT OF PARENTS

	NAME OF FATHER	YEAR	COUNTY	NAME OF MOTHER	YEAR	COUNTY
1	Hannatubby	Dead	Chick Roll	*(Name Illegible)*	Dead	Chick Roll
2	Tom Benton	"	" "	Minokey	"	" "
3	No. 1			No. 2		
4	Watson Colbert	Dead	Pontotoc	Elsie Colbert	Dead	Pontotoc

(NOTES)

No. 3 on Chickasaw Roll as Abbie

No. 2 died February 5, 1901; Proof of death filed Aug. 19, 1901.

No. 1 is now the husband of Delphia Watson on Chickasaw Card #985 11/8 '01

No. 3 now the wife of Ebin Bee, Chickasaw 931 11/4/02

Sept. 29, 1898.

RESIDENCE: Tishomingo *COUNTY*   *CARD NO.*

POST OFFICE: *(Illegible),* I.T.   *FIELD NO.*

	NAME	RELATION-SHIP TO PERSON FIRST NAMED	AGE	SEX	BLOOD	TRIBAL ENROLLMENT		
						YEAR	COUNTY	PAGE
1	Brown, John		56	M	Full	1897	Tishomingo	36
2	" Mollie	Wife	40	F	"	1897	"	36
3	" ~~Ella~~	~~S.Dau~~	~~12~~	~~"~~	~~1/2~~	DIED PRIOR TO SEPTEMBER 25 1902 ~~1897~~	"	~~36~~
4	" Milton	Son	6	M	Full	1897	"	36
5	Underwood, Ben	S.Son	14	"	"	1897	"	36
6	Brown, Frances	Niece	13	F	"	1897	"	36

123

| 7 | Seely, Odus | | Son of No. 3 | I | M | 1/2 | | | |

TRIBAL ENROLLMENT OF PARENTS

	NAME OF FATHER	YEAR	COUNTY	NAME OF MOTHER	YEAR	COUNTY
1	Con-neu-ya	Dead	Chick Roll	(Name Illegible)	Dead	Chickasaw Roll
2	Toney Maytubbee	"	" "	hoke	"	" "
3	William Case		Non-Citizen	No. 2		
4	No. I			No. 2		
5	Houston Underwood	Dead	Chickasaw	No. 2		
6	Mitchell Brown	"	Tishomingo	Sophie Maytubby	Dead	Tishomingo
7	Esau Sealy			No. 3		

(NOTES)

No. 3 Died Aug. 16, 1902. Enrollment (remainder illegible)

No. I also known as Onola tubbee

No. 6 on Chickasaw Roll as Francis

No. 3 died Aug. 16, 1902; Proof of death filed Nov. 8, 1902

No. 7 was born Aug. 16, 1902. Application received April 1, 1905 under Act of Congress approved March 3, 1905

Father of No. 7, Esau Sealy, No. 2 on Chick card #475

Sept. 29, 1898.

RESIDENCE: Tishomingo	COUNTY					CARD NO.			
POST OFFICE: Tishomingo, I.T.						FIELD NO.			

NAME	RELATION-SHIP TO PERSON FIRST NAMED	AGE	SEX	BLOOD	TRIBAL ENROLLMENT		
					YEAR	COUNTY	PAGE
1 Alexander, Sallie	NAMED	40	F	Full	1897	Tishomingo	39

TRIBAL ENROLLMENT OF PARENTS

	NAME OF FATHER	YEAR	COUNTY	NAME OF MOTHER	YEAR	COUNTY
1	(Name Illegible)	Dead	Tishomingo	(Name Illegible)	Dead	Tishomingo

(NOTES)

Sept. 29, '98.

RESIDENCE: Choctaw Nation	COUNTY					CARD NO.			
POST OFFICE: Waupaunuka, I.T.						FIELD NO.			

NAME	RELATION-SHIP TO PERSON FIRST NAMED	AGE	SEX	BLOOD	TRIBAL ENROLLMENT		
					YEAR	COUNTY	PAGE
1 Dick, Sampson	NAMED	22	M	1/2			
2 " Taylor	Bro	15	"	1/2			
3 " Malina	Sister	14	F	1/2			

Chickasaw Enrollment Cards 1898-1914
Chickasaw by Blood   Volume IV

	TRIBAL ENROLLMENT OF PARENTS					
	NAME OF FATHER	YEAR	COUNTY	NAME OF MOTHER	YEAR	COUNTY
1	Martin Dick		Atoka Co. Chick Roll	Jemima Dick	Dead	Chick residing in Choc N. 3rd Dist.
2	" "		"	" "	"	"
3	" "		"	" "	"	"

(NOTES)

All on Choctaw Census Record No. 2, Page 149, transferred to Chickasaw Roll by Dawes Commission
No. 1 on Choctaw Roll, 1896, Atoka County, No. 3616
No. 2 "   "   " 1896,   "   "   " 3617
No. 3 "   "   " 1896,   "   "   " 3619, as Melissa Dick
Father of above children as Martin Dick on Choctaw Card #4315

Sept. 29, 1898.

CANCELLED Stamped across card
Transferred to Choctaw Card #5566

RESIDENCE: Pontotoc   *COUNTY*   *CARD NO.*
POST OFFICE: Belton, I.T.   *FIELD NO.*

	NAME	RELATION-SHIP TO PERSON FIRST NAMED	AGE	SEX	BLOOD	TRIBAL ENROLLMENT		
						YEAR	COUNTY	PAGE
1	Columbus, Emely	NAMED	28	F	Full	1897	Pontotoc	59
2	" Byars	Son	12	M	"	1897	"	59
3	" Ephus	"	10	"	"	1897	"	59
4	" Dawes Tandy	"	8	"	"	1897	"	59
5	" Lizzie	Dau	4	F	"	1897	"	59

	TRIBAL ENROLLMENT OF PARENTS					
	NAME OF FATHER	YEAR	COUNTY	NAME OF MOTHER	YEAR	COUNTY
1	Bond Underwood	Dead	Chick Roll	Susie Patterson	Dead	Chick Roll
2	Walton Columbus	"	Pontotoc	No. 1		
3	" "	"	"	No. 1		
4	" "	"	"	No. 1		
5	" "	"	"	No. 1		

(NOTES)

No. 5 on Chickasaw Roll as Baby
No. 4 "   "   "   " Dawes Columbus
No. 1 died July 17, 1900; Proof of death filed Aug. 13, 1901.

Sept. 29, '98.

RESIDENCE: Pickens   COUNTY   CARD NO.

POST OFFICE: Lebanon, I.T.   FIELD NO.

| NAME | RELATION- SHIP TO PERSON FIRST NAMED | AGE | SEX | BLOOD | TRIBAL ENROLLMENT | | |
					YEAR	COUNTY	PAGE
1 McCurtain, James Cotton	NAMED	26	M	Full	1897	Pickens	23
2 " Tykie	Wife	21	F	"	1897	"	23

TRIBAL ENROLLMENT OF PARENTS

NAME OF FATHER	YEAR	COUNTY	NAME OF MOTHER	YEAR	COUNTY
1 Holmes McCurtain	Dead	Chick Roll	Adaline McCurtain	Dead	Chick Roll
2 Lone Nothintubby	"	" "	Elie Lone	1893	Pickens

(NOTES)

No. 1 on Chickasaw Roll as Jim Cotten

No. 2 "   "   "   " Fykie Cotten

Davison and Hattie Mary Roberson on Chickasaw Card #872 are the legally adopted wards of Nos. 1 and 2.

Sept. 29, '98.

RESIDENCE: Pickens   COUNTY   CARD NO.

POST OFFICE: Lebanon, I.T.   FIELD NO.

| NAME | RELATION- SHIP TO PERSON FIRST NAMED | AGE | SEX | BLOOD | TRIBAL ENROLLMENT | | |
					YEAR	COUNTY	PAGE
1 Lone, Elie	NAMED	38	F	Full	1893	Pickens	P.R. #2 141
2 Pickens, Aaron	Son	17	M	Full	1897	"	23
3 " Lizzie	Ward	12	F	"	1897	"	23

TRIBAL ENROLLMENT OF PARENTS

NAME OF FATHER	YEAR	COUNTY	NAME OF MOTHER	YEAR	COUNTY
1 Pis-to-chine	Dead	Chick Roll	Ish-to-pi-he	Dead	Chick Roll
2 Thompson Pickens	1897	Pickens	No. 1		
3 Tyson "	Dead	"	Sissy Pickens	Dead	Pickens

(NOTES)

No. 1 on Chickasaw Roll as Eli Lone   *(No. 2 Dawes' Roll No. 4150)*

No. 1 also on 1896 Chickasaw Roll as Eli Lone   *(No. 3 Dawes' Roll No. 4754)*

Affidavit of Elie Lone as to Chickasaw blood of No. 2 filed October 13, 1902

No. 3 now married to a man by the name of Courtney.

   See affidavit of Elie Lone as to degree of Chickasaw blood possessed by No. 3, filed Aug. 21, 1903

P.O. Raw. Ind. Ter. of No. 3 Mannsville, I.T.   Sept. 29, '98.

RESIDENCE: Tishomingo   COUNTY — CARD NO.

POST OFFICE: Tishomingo. I.T. — FIELD NO.

NAME	RELATIONSHIP TO PERSON FIRST NAMED	AGE	SEX	BLOOD	TRIBAL ENROLLMENT		
					YEAR	COUNTY	PAGE
1 Condon, Michael Charles	NAMED	54	M	I.W.	1897	Pickens	79
2 " Lucy	Wife	33	F	3/4	1897	Tishomingo	37
3 Alexander, Cora	Ward	3	F	Full	1897	"	35
4 ~~Condon, Hattie~~ Void	~~Ward~~	~~3~~	~~F~~	~~"~~			

TRIBAL ENROLLMENT OF PARENTS

	NAME OF FATHER	YEAR	COUNTY	NAME OF MOTHER	YEAR	COUNTY
1	John Condon	Died	Non Citizen	Mary Condon	Dead	Non Citizen
2	Gibson (Illegible)	1897	Pontotoc	Sarah Johnson	1897	Pontotoc
3	Robinson Alexander	Dead	Tishomingo	Rose Ann Alexander	1897	Tishomingo
4	~~Hiram Pickens~~			~~Susanna Alowatubbee~~	~~1897~~	~~"~~

(NOTES)

No. 1 See decision of June 13 '04   (No. 1 Dawes' Roll No. 392)

No. 1 on Chickasaw Roll as M.C. Condon

Mother of No. 4 is Susanna Alowatubbee on Chickasaw Card #857

No. 3 Proof of birth received and filed Nov. 12, 1902   (No. 3 Dawes' Roll No. 4753)

No. 4 Born in 1899, enrolled Nov. 12, 1902

Nos. 3 and 4 have been made legal wards of No's 1 and 2. See papers relativ hereto filed Nov. 12, 1902.

No. 4 is a duplication of Adeline Alowatubbee on Chickasaw card #857.

See letters of G.D. Rodgers Nov. 5 and 6, 1902 filed herein Feby 21, 1903.

P.O. Milburn, I.T.   Sept. 29, 1898.

RESIDENCE: Choctaw Nation   ~~COUNTY~~ — CARD NO.

POST OFFICE: Waupaunuka, I.T. — FIELD NO.

NAME	RELATIONSHIP TO PERSON FIRST NAMED	AGE	SEX	BLOOD	TRIBAL ENROLLMENT		
					YEAR	COUNTY	PAGE
1 Billis, Louvina	NAMED	42	F	Full			
2 Page, Lewis	Son	15	M	"			
3 " Benson	S.Son	10	M	1/2			
4 " Alive	" Dau	8	F	1/2			
5 Dick, Thomas	Son	11	M	1/2			

TRIBAL ENROLLMENT OF PARENTS

	NAME OF FATHER	YEAR	COUNTY	NAME OF MOTHER	YEAR	COUNTY
1	Pe-tish-tubby	Dead	Chick Roll	Sha-to-po-yo	Dead	Chick Roll
2	Wall Page	"	" "	No. 1		

127

3	Jackson Billis		Atoka Co. Choctaw Roll	Nancy Gillis	Dead	Chick resid'g in Choc. N. 3rd Dist.
4	" "		"	" "	"	"
5	Martin Dick		"	No.		

(NOTES)

No. 1 on Choctaw Roll as Lorina; wife of Jackson Billis, Choctaw Card No. 2316
No. 2 "   "   "   " Willis
Nos. 1,2,3 & 4 on Choctaw Census Record, No. 2, Page 74, transferred to Chick Roll by Dawes Com.
No. 5 on Choctaw Census Record No. 2, Page 149; transferred to Chick. Roll by Dawes Com.
No. 1 "   "   Roll, 1896, Atoka Co., No. 1820, as Lorina Billis
No. 2 "   "   " 1896, "   "   " 1821, " Willis   "
No. 3 "   "   " 1896, "   "   " 1822, " Benson   "
No. 4 "   "   " 1896, "   "   " 1223, " Allie   "
No. 5 "   "   " 1896, "   "   " 3597
Father of No. 5 is Martin Dick, Choctaqw Card #4315
No. 2 on 1896 ~~Roll~~ Choctaw Roll as Davis Peach, Page 269, #10548
No. 4 " 1896   "   " " Ada Peach,   " 269, #10549.

Sept. 29, 1898.

CANCELLED Stamped across card
Transferred to Choctaw Card No. 5496
Oct. 14, 1902

RESIDENCE: Tishomingo COUNTY						CARD NO.			
POST OFFICE: Ravia, I.T.						FIELD NO.			

NAME		RELATION-SHIP TO PERSON FIRST NAMED	AGE	SEX	BLOOD	TRIBAL ENROLLMENT		
						YEAR	COUNTY	PAGE
1	Brown, Julia		32	F	1/2	1893	Tishomingo	108
2	" Mamie	Dau	16	F	3/4	1893	"	108
3	" Reachel	G.Dau	2wks	F	7/8			

TRIBAL ENROLLMENT OF PARENTS

	NAME OF FATHER	YEAR	COUNTY	NAME OF MOTHER	YEAR	COUNTY
1	Dixon Brown	Dead	Chick Freedman	Jincy Cooper	Dead	Chick Roll
2	Gipson Keel	1897	Tishomingo	No. 1		
3	Martin Brown	1897	"	No. 2		

(NOTES)

No. 2 on Chickasaw Roll as Minnie - 1893 Pay Roll No. 1, Page 108
No. 2 is the wife of Martin Brown on Chickasaw Card #987.
        See affidavit of Martin Brown as to marriage filed Aug. 13, 1901.
No. 3 enrolled Aug. 13, 1901.
No's 1-2 also on 1896 Chickasaw Roll, Tishomingo Co, Page 92.

Sept. 29, 1898

RESIDENCE: Pontotoc COUNTY   CARD NO.
POST OFFICE: Viola, I.T.   FIELD NO.

NAME	RELATION-SHIP TO PERSON FIRST NAMED	AGE	SEX	BLOOD	TRIBAL ENROLLMENT		
					YEAR	COUNTY	PAGE
1 Lewis, Sallie	NAMED	30	F	Full	1897	Pontotoc	56
2 " Lula	Dau	7	"	"	1897	"	56
3 " ~~Cubb~~	~~Son~~	~~4mo~~	M	~~"~~	DIED PRIOR TO SEPTEMBER 25 1902		

TRIBAL ENROLLMENT OF PARENTS

	NAME OF FATHER	YEAR	COUNTY	NAME OF MOTHER	YEAR	COUNTY
1	Richard Deering	1897	Pontotoc	Aggie Patterson	1897	Pontotoc
2	Joe Lewis	Dead	"	No. 1		
3	" "	"	"	~~No. 1~~		

(NOTES)

No. 3 died Feby 1, 1899; Proof of death filed Nov. 8, 1902.

Sept. 29, 1898.

RESIDENCE: Pickens COUNTY   CARD NO.
POST OFFICE: Russell, I.T.   FIELD NO.

NAME	RELATION-SHIP TO PERSON FIRST NAMED	AGE	SEX	BLOOD	TRIBAL ENROLLMENT		
					YEAR	COUNTY	PAGE
1 Hawkins, Eliza	NAMED	49	F	Full	1893	Pickens	P.R. #2 102
2 Keel, Cabon	Ward	17	M	"	1897	"	18

TRIBAL ENROLLMENT OF PARENTS

	NAME OF FATHER	YEAR	COUNTY	NAME OF MOTHER	YEAR	COUNTY
1	I-a-pa-hub-by	1897	Pickens	(Name Illegible)	Dead	Chick Roll
2	Johnson Keel	Dead	"	Louisa Keel	"	Pickens

(NOTES)

(No. 2 Dawes' Roll No. 4680)

Sept. 29, 1898.

RESIDENCE: Choctaw Nation COUNTY   CARD NO.
POST OFFICE: Savanna, I.T.   FIELD NO.

NAME	RELATION-SHIP TO PERSON FIRST NAMED	AGE	SEX	BLOOD	TRIBAL ENROLLMENT		
					YEAR	COUNTY	PAGE
1 Johnson, William	NAMED	13	M	1/2	1897	Chick residing in Choc. N. 1st Dist.	71
2 " Samuel	Bro	7	"	1/2	1897	"	71

TRIBAL ENROLLMENT OF PARENTS

	NAME OF FATHER	YEAR	COUNTY	NAME OF MOTHER	YEAR	COUNTY
1	Geo. W. Johnson	Dead	Chick Roll	Mary Johnson	Dead	Non Citizen
2	" " "	"	" "	" "	"	" "

(NOTES)

Sept. 29, 1898.

RESIDENCE: Choctaw Nation ~~COUNTY~~   CARD NO.

POST OFFICE: Stewart, I.T.   FIELD NO.

	NAME	RELATION- SHIP TO PERSON FIRST NAMED	AGE	SEX	BLOOD	TRIBAL ENROLLMENT		
						YEAR	COUNTY	PAGE
1	Gates, Bennington	FIRST NAMED	49	M	Full	1897	Chick resid'g in Choc. Nation, 1st Dist.	67
2	" Catherine	Wife	55	F	I.W.	1897	"	82

TRIBAL ENROLLMENT OF PARENTS

	NAME OF FATHER	YEAR	COUNTY	NAME OF MOTHER	YEAR	COUNTY
1	La-fay-nah	Dead	Chick Roll	Liza	Dead	Chick Roll
2	William Garvin	"	Non Citizen	Bitsey Connor	"	Non Citizen

(NOTES)

No. 2 died Jan. 31, 1901; Proof of death filed Nov. 12, 1902.

Sept. 29, 1898

RESIDENCE: Pickens COUNTY   CARD NO.

POST OFFICE: Woodville, I.T.   FIELD NO.

	NAME	RELATION- SHIP TO PERSON FIRST NAMED	AGE	SEX	BLOOD	TRIBAL ENROLLMENT		
						YEAR	COUNTY	PAGE
1	Hume, Olena	FIRST NAMED	11	F	1/8	1897	Pickens	26
2	" Benjamin Alfred	Bro	9	M	1/8	1897	"	26
3	" Paul Earnest	"	7	"	1/8	1897	"	26
4	" William Robert	Father	33	M	I.W.			

TRIBAL ENROLLMENT OF PARENTS

	NAME OF FATHER	YEAR	COUNTY	NAME OF MOTHER	YEAR	COUNTY
1	Wm Robert Hume		White man	Lucy Hume	Dead	Pickens
2	" " "		" "	" "	"	"
3	" " "		" "	" "	"	"
4	Alfred Hume	Dead	Non Citz	Mary E. Hume		Non Citz

Chickasaw Enrollment Cards 1898-1914
Chickasaw by Blood   Volume IV

(NOTES)

No. 2 on Chickasaw Roll as Bennie Hume
No. 3 "   "   "   " Paul E. "
William Robert Hume, father of Nos 1, 2 and 3, on Chickasaw D.#131
No. 4 transferred from Chickasaw Card #D.131.   *(No. 4 Dawes' Roll No. 432)*
     See decision of August 17, 1904. Sept. 1, 1904.

Oct. 4, 1898

RESIDENCE: Choctaw Nation   ~~COUNTY~~   CARD NO.
POST OFFICE: Steward, I.T.   FIELD NO.

NAME	RELATION-SHIP TO PERSON	AGE	SEX	BLOOD	TRIBAL ENROLLMENT		
					YEAR	COUNTY	PAGE
1 Quincy. Herbert M.	FIRST NAMED	43	M	Full	1897	Chick resid'g in Choc. N. 1st Dist.	69

TRIBAL ENROLLMENT OF PARENTS

NAME OF FATHER	YEAR	COUNTY	NAME OF MOTHER	YEAR	COUNTY
1 Ho-yub-by	Dead	Chick Roll	Liza	Dead	Chick Roll

(NOTES)

Husband of Melvina Quincy, Choctaqw Roll, Card No. 314.

Sept. 29, '98.

RESIDENCE: Choctaw Nation   ~~COUNTY~~   CARD NO.
POST OFFICE: Stewart, I.T.   FIELD NO.

NAME	RELATION-SHIP TO PERSON	AGE	SEX	BLOOD	TRIBAL ENROLLMENT		
					YEAR	COUNTY	PAGE
1 Anoletubby, Ellis	FIRST NAMED	27	M	Full	1897	Chick residing in Choc N. 1st Dist.	69
2 " Annie	Wife	40	F	"	1897	"	69

TRIBAL ENROLLMENT OF PARENTS

NAME OF FATHER	YEAR	COUNTY	NAME OF MOTHER	YEAR	COUNTY
1 Jon Anoletubby	Dead	Chick Roll	Nicey Anoletubby	Dead	Chick Roll
2 A-o-cah-tubby	"	" "	Tah-ho-te	"	" "

(NOTES)

Sept. 29, 1898

131

RESIDENCE: Tishomingo COUNTY					CARD NO.			
POST OFFICE: Emmet, I.T.					FIELD NO.			
NAME	RELATION-SHIP TO PERSON FIRST NAMED	AGE	SEX	BLOOD	TRIBAL ENROLLMENT			
					YEAR	COUNTY		PAGE
1 Easton, Henry	NAMED	16	M		1897	Pickens		16

TRIBAL ENROLLMENT OF PARENTS

NAME OF FATHER	YEAR	COUNTY	NAME OF MOTHER	YEAR	COUNTY
1 James H. Easton		White woman[sic]	Margaret Easton	Dead	Tishomingo

(NOTES)

No. 1 is son of James H. Easton on Chickasaw Card #D.98.

Sept. 29, '98.

RESIDENCE: Pontotoc COUNTY					CARD NO.			
POST OFFICE: Conway, I.T.					FIELD NO.			
NAME	RELATION-SHIP TO PERSON FIRST NAMED	AGE	SEX	BLOOD	TRIBAL ENROLLMENT			
					YEAR	COUNTY		PAGE
1 Allison, Alice	NAMED	18	F	Full	1897	Pontotoc		11
2 Colbert, Judie	Dau	14mo	"	"	~~1897~~	"		~~87~~
3 Allison, Hilda	"	2mo	"	1/2				
4 " Alikchi May	"	2mo	"	1/2				
5 " Wade H.	Husband	35	M	I.W.				

TRIBAL ENROLLMENT OF PARENTS

NAME OF FATHER	YEAR	COUNTY	NAME OF MOTHER	YEAR	COUNTY
1 Hogan Keel	1897	Pontotoc	Malinda Walton	1897	Pontotoc
2 Jon Colbert	Dead	"	No. 1		
3 Wade H. Allison		Non Citizen	No. 1		
4 " " "		" "	No. 1		
5 A.S. Allison		Non Citizen	Jennie T. Allison		Non Citizen

(NOTES)

No. 1 on Chickasaw Roll as Alice Hawkins   *(No. 2 Dawes' Roll No. 4147)*

No. 4 enrolled May 23, 1901

Wade H. Allison, husband of No. 1 on Chickasaw D.97.

No. 2 Proof of birth received and filed Oct. 17, 1902.

No. 3 Enrolled November 3, 1899

No. 5 transferred from Chickasaw Card #D.97. See decision of May 1, 1902.   *(No. 5 Dawes' Roll No. 191)*

Sept. 29, '98

Chickasaw Enrollment Cards 1898-1914
Chickasaw by Blood   Volume IV

RESIDENCE: Choctaw Nation   ~~COUNTY~~   CARD NO.
POST OFFICE: South Canadian, I.T.   FIELD NO.

NAME	RELATION-SHIP TO PERSON FIRST NAMED	AGE	SEX	BLOOD	TRIBAL ENROLLMENT		
					YEAR	COUNTY	PAGE
1 Lee, Allen G.	NAMED	58	M	I.W.			
2 " Lucy	Wife	48	F	1/2			

TRIBAL ENROLLMENT OF PARENTS

	NAME OF FATHER	YEAR	COUNTY	NAME OF MOTHER	YEAR	COUNTY
1	(Name Illegible)	Dead	Non citizen	(Name Illegible)	Dead	Non Citizen
2	Wm Wade	"	Choc. Roll	Annie Wade	"	Chick Roll

(NOTES)

No. 1 on Choctaw Intermarried Roll, Page 64, transferred to Chickasaw Roll by Dawes Commission
No. 2 on Choctaw Census Record No. 2, Page 331, transferred to Chickasaw Roll by Dawes Commission
No. 1 on Choctaw Roll as Allen J. Lee
No. 1 on Choctaw Roll, 1896, Tobucksy County, No. 7862, as Lucy A. Lee
No. 2 died January 24, 1901; Proof of death filed July 9, 1901
No. 1 died Aug. 6, 1901; Proof of death filed Sept. 21, 1901

Sept. 29, '98

CANCELLED Stamped across card
Died prior to (remainder illegible)

RESIDENCE: Choctaw Nation   ~~COUNTY~~   CARD NO.
POST OFFICE: South Canadian, I.T.   FIELD NO.

NAME	RELATION-SHIP TO PERSON FIRST NAMED	AGE	SEX	BLOOD	TRIBAL ENROLLMENT		
					YEAR	COUNTY	PAGE
1 Morgan, Robert A.	NAMED	30	M	I.W.			
2 " Alice	Wife	30	F	1/4			
3 " Helen Lee	Dau	2mo	"	1/8			
4 " William Allen	So	1mo	M	1/8			

TRIBAL ENROLLMENT OF PARENTS

	NAME OF FATHER	YEAR	COUNTY	NAME OF MOTHER	YEAR	COUNTY
1	Wm Morgan		Non Citizen	Louisa Morgan		Non Citizen
2	Allen, A.L. (I.W.)		Choc. Roll	Lucy Lee		Choc. Roll
3	No. 1			No. 2		
4	No. 1			No. 2		

(NOTES)

No. 2 on Choctaw Census Record No. 2, Page 331, as Alice F. Lee
    Transferred to Chickasaw Roll by Dawes Commission. Her parents were transferred to Chickasaw Roll.
No. 2 on Choctaw Roll, 1896, Tobucksy County, No. 7863, as Alice F. Lee.

Chickasaw Enrollment Cards 1898-1914
Chickasaw by Blood   Volume IV

No. 4 enrolled Sept. 21, 1901.
No. 3 enrolled Nov, 3, 1899.

Sept. 29, 1898.

CANCELLED Stamped across card
Transferred to Choctaw Card No. 54?4
October 17, 1902

RESIDENCE: Tishomingo COUNTY					CARD NO.			
POST OFFICE: Tishomingo, I.T.					FIELD NO.			
NAME	RELATION-SHIP TO PERSON FIRST NAMED	AGE	SEX	BLOOD	TRIBAL ENROLLMENT			
					YEAR	COUNTY	PAGE	
1 Wooten, James Henry	NAMED	26	M	I.W.	1897	Tishomingo	89	
2 " Lillie	Wife	23	F	1/2	1897	"	37	
3 Turnbull, Estella	S.Day	6	"	1/2	1897	"	37	

TRIBAL ENROLLMENT OF PARENTS

NAME OF FATHER	YEAR	COUNTY	NAME OF MOTHER	YEAR	COUNTY
1 John Wooten		Non Citizen	Sally Wooten		Non Citizen
2 Calvin Moore	Dead	Chick Roll	Catherine Folsome	1897	Tishomingo
3 Alex Turnbull	"	Tishomingo	No. 2		

(NOTES)

No. 1 on Chickasaw Roll as "Wooton"   *(No. 1 Dawes' Roll No. 326)*
No. 2 "   "   "   " Lillie Turnbull
No. 3 "   "   "   " Estalla   "
Affidavit of No. 2 as to her divorce from James Daniels filed May 20, 1903.

P.O. Kingston, I.T.   Sept. 29, '98.

RESIDENCE: Tishomingo COUNTY					CARD NO.			
POST OFFICE: Tishomingo, I.T.					FIELD NO.			
NAME	RELATION-SHIP TO PERSON FIRST NAMED	AGE	SEX	BLOOD	TRIBAL ENROLLMENT			
					YEAR	COUNTY	PAGE	
1 Folsome, Catherine	NAMED	46	F	1/2	1897	Tishomingo	36	
2 McGee, Hiram	S.Son	10	M	3/4	1897	"	36	
3 " Cornelius	" Son	17	"	3/4	1897	"	36	
4 " Nellie	" Dau	16	F	3/4	1897	"	36	
5 " Hattie	" "	11	"	3/4	1897	"	36	
6 Lucas, Edward	Hus. of No. 4	28	M	I.W.				

	TRIBAL ENROLLMENT OF PARENTS					
	NAME OF FATHER	YEAR	COUNTY	NAME OF MOTHER	YEAR	COUNTY
1	Wall Folsome	Dead	Chick Roll	Liza Folsome	Dead	Non Citizen
2	Cornelius McGee	"	Tishomingo	No. 1		
3	" "	"	"	No. 1		
4	" "	"	"	No. 1		
5	" "	"	"	No. 1		
6	E.R. Lucas		non-citizen	N.B. Lucas	"	non citizen

(NOTES)

No. 1 wife of John Folsome, Choctaw Roll, Card No. 312.
No. 4 is now the wife of E.B. Lucas on Chickasaw Card #D.371, Sept. 23, 1902.
No. 6 transferred from Chick. Card D.371. *(remainder illegible)*
No. 4 is wife of *illegible)*

Sept. 29, 1898

RESIDENCE: Tishomingo COUNTY CARD NO.
POST OFFICE: Tishomingo, I.T. FIELD NO.

	NAME	RELATION-SHIP TO PERSON FIRST NAMED	AGE	SEX	BLOOD	TRIBAL ENROLLMENT		
						YEAR	COUNTY	PAGE
1	Duke, Lucy		62	F	Full	1897	Tishomingo	36

	TRIBAL ENROLLMENT OF PARENTS					
	NAME OF FATHER	YEAR	COUNTY	NAME OF MOTHER	YEAR	COUNTY
1	*(Name Illegible)*	Dead	Choc Roll	*(Name Illegible)*	Dead	Chick Roll

(NOTES)

Also knows as Okahoyah.

Sept. 29, '98.

RESIDENCE: Pontotoc COUNTY CARD NO.
POST OFFICE: Waupaunuka, I.T. FIELD NO.

	NAME	RELATION-SHIP TO PERSON FIRST NAMED	AGE	SEX	BLOOD	TRIBAL ENROLLMENT		
						YEAR	COUNTY	PAGE
~~1~~	~~Humes, Alfred~~		~~56~~	~~M~~	~~1/2~~	~~1897~~	~~Pontotoc~~	~~56~~
2	Perkins, Mary	Wife	35	F	Full	1897	"	56
3	Humes, Jesse	Son	14	M	3/4	1897	"	56
4	" Melton	"	12	"	3/4	1897	"	56
5	" Emma	Dau	8	F	3/4	1897	"	56
6	" Loomis	Son	4	M	3/4	1897	"	56
~~7~~	~~" John~~	~~"~~	~~3~~	~~"~~	~~3/4~~	~~1897~~	~~"~~	~~56~~

8	" ~~Sampson~~	"	~~2mo~~	~~"~~	~~3/4~~				
9	Perkins, Edward	Son of No. 2	4mo	"	Full				

TRIBAL ENROLLMENT OF PARENTS

	NAME OF FATHER	YEAR	COUNTY	NAME OF MOTHER	YEAR	COUNTY
1	~~Alfred Humes~~	~~Dead~~	~~Non-Citizen~~	~~Rhoda Humes~~	~~Dead~~	~~Chick Roll~~
2	*(Name Illegible)*	"	Chick Roll	Lucy Puknatubby	"	Pontotoc
3	No. 1			No. 2		
4	No. 1			No. 2		
5	No. 1			No. 2		
6	No. 1			No. 2		
7	~~No. 1~~			~~No. 2~~		
8			*(This line left blank on microfilm)*			
9	George G. Perkins		Choc Card #3804	No. 2		

(NOTES)

No. 3 on Chickasaw Roll as Jessie
No. 5   "   "   "   " Awa
No. 7 died in Sept, 1899; Evidence of death filed April 12, 1901
No. 8   "   "   1899;   "   "   "   "   12, 1901
No. 1   "   "   Dec. 1899;   "   "   "   "   May 1, 1901
No. 2 now the wife of George G. Perkins on Choc. Card #3804; Evidence of marriage requested June 25. 1902

Sept. 29, '98.

RESIDENCE: Tishomingo	COUNTY			CARD NO.		
POST OFFICE: Tishomingo, I.T.				FIELD NO.		

	NAME	RELATION-SHIP TO PERSON FIRST NAMED	AGE	SEX	BLOOD	TRIBAL ENROLLMENT		
						YEAR	COUNTY	PAGE
1	Ward, William Thomas	NAMED	28	M	1/4	1897	Tishomingo	35
2	" Estelle	Wife	23	F	1/8	1897	Panola	2
3	" Estwill	Son	9mo	M	3/16			
4	" Beatrix Theodosia	Dau	2mo	F	3/16			

TRIBAL ENROLLMENT OF PARENTS

	NAME OF FATHER	YEAR	COUNTY	NAME OF MOTHER	YEAR	COUNTY
1	William Ward	Dead	Non Citizen	Elizabeth Ward	Dead	Pontotoc
2	Wm Chisholm	"	Creek Citizen	Julia McLish	"	Chick Roll
3	No. 1			No. 2		
4	No. 1			No. 2		

(NOTES)

No. 1 on Chickasaw Roll as Willie Ward
No. 2   "   "   "   " Stella Chisholm
No. 4 Born Jany. 12, 1902; enrolled March 25, 1902.

Sept. 29, 1898.

RESIDENCE: Tishomingo COUNTY   CARD NO.

POST OFFICE: Emmet, I.T.   FIELD NO.

NAME	RELATION-SHIP TO PERSON FIRST NAMED	AGE	SEX	BLOOD	TRIBAL ENROLLMENT		
					YEAR	COUNTY	PAGE
1 Washington, Hugh	NAMED	24	M	1/2	1897	Tishomingo	34
2 " Mollie	Wife	17	F	I.W.			
3 " Isaac Monroe	Son	4mo	M	1/4			
4 " George Edwin	"	1mo	"	1/4			

TRIBAL ENROLLMENT OF PARENTS

	NAME OF FATHER	YEAR	COUNTY	NAME OF MOTHER	YEAR	COUNTY
1	Geo. Washington	Dead	Chick Roll	Serena Black		White woman
2	J.M. Collins		Non Citizen	Mary Collins		Non Citizen
3	No. 1			No. 2		
4	No. 1			No. 2		

(NOTES)

No. 1 Evidence of marriage of parents attached to card No. D.88

No. 3 Enrolled May 24, 1900

No. 4 Born May 2, 1902; enrolled June 3, 1902

No. 2 Enrolled Aug. 17, 1899.   *(No. 2 Dawes' Roll No. 133)*

Sept. 29, '98.

RESIDENCE: Pickens COUNTY   CARD NO.

POST OFFICE: Cumberland, I.T.   FIELD NO.

NAME	RELATION-SHIP TO PERSON FIRST NAMED	AGE	SEX	BLOOD	TRIBAL ENROLLMENT		
					YEAR	COUNTY	PAGE
1 Crockett, Major	NAMED	25	M	1/4	1897	Pickens	9
2 " Mack	Bro	17	"	1/4	1897	Pickens	2
3 " Elizabeth	Sister	14	F	1/4	1897	Pickens	9

TRIBAL ENROLLMENT OF PARENTS

	NAME OF FATHER	YEAR	COUNTY	NAME OF MOTHER	YEAR	COUNTY
1	Jan Crockett	Dead	Non Citizen	Amanda Crockett	Dead	Chick Roll
2	" "	"	" "	" "	"	" "
3	" "	"	" "	" "	"	" "

(NOTES)

No. 3 on Chickasaw Roll as Lizzie

No. 1 "   "   " " Maj. Crockett

Sept. 29, '98.

RESIDENCE: Tishomingo   COUNTY   CARD NO.

POST OFFICE: Tishomingo, I.T.   FIELD NO.

	NAME	RELATION-SHIP TO PERSON FIRST NAMED	AGE	SEX	BLOOD	TRIBAL ENROLLMENT		
						YEAR	COUNTY	PAGE
1	Kingsberry, William	NAMED	29	M	1/4	1897	Tishomingo	37
2	" Ruthie	Wife	25	F	1/4	1897	"	37
3	" Charley	Son	5	M	1/4	1897	"	37
4	" Joel	"	5mo	"	1/4			
5	" Jessie Corinne	Dau	3 1/2 mo	F	1/4			

TRIBAL ENROLLMENT OF PARENTS

	NAME OF FATHER	YEAR	COUNTY	NAME OF MOTHER	YEAR	COUNTY
1	Charley Kingsberry (I.W.)	Dead	Panola	Minnie Kingsberry now *(Illegible)*	1897	Panola
2	John Turnbull	"	Chick Roll	Lucy TurnBULL	Dead	Chick Roll
3	No. 1			No. 2		
4	No. 1			No. 2		
5	No. 1			No. 2		

(NOTES)

No. 4 Affidavit of Physician to be supplied. Rec'd Oct. 31, 1898.
No. 5 Enrolled January 2, 1901.

Sept. 29, '98.

RESIDENCE: Tishomingo   COUNTY   CARD NO.

POST OFFICE: Nebo, I.T.   FIELD NO.

	NAME	RELATION-SHIP TO PERSON FIRST NAMED	AGE	SEX	BLOOD	TRIBAL ENROLLMENT		
						YEAR	COUNTY	PAGE
1	Hawkins, Sam	NAMED	23	M	Full	1897	Tishomingo	28
2	" Lucy Belle	Wife	20	F	I.W.	1897	"	85
3	" William Lloyd	Son	6mo	M	1/2			

TRIBAL ENROLLMENT OF PARENTS

	NAME OF FATHER	YEAR	COUNTY	NAME OF MOTHER	YEAR	COUNTY
1	James Hawkins	Dead	Chick Roll	Patsey Hawkins	Dead	Chick Roll
2	Franklin Anders	"	Non Citizen	Rebecca Anders	"	Non Citizen
3	No. 1			No. 2		

(NOTES)

No. 2 on Chickasaw Roll as Lucy Hawkins
Evidence of marriage between Nos. 1 and 2 received and filed Nov. 13, 1902.

Sept. 29, '98.

Chickasaw Enrollment Cards 1898-1914
Chickasaw by Blood Volume IV

RESIDENCE: Tishomingo COUNTY					CARD NO.		
POST OFFICE: Berwyn, I.T.					FIELD NO.		

NAME	RELATION-SHIP TO PERSON FIRST NAMED	AGE	SEX	BLOOD	TRIBAL ENROLLMENT		
					YEAR	COUNTY	PAGE
1 Sealy, Joel	NAMED	21	M	Full	1897	Panola	2

TRIBAL ENROLLMENT OF PARENTS

NAME OF FATHER	YEAR	COUNTY	NAME OF MOTHER	YEAR	COUNTY
1 Simon Sealy	Dead	Chick Roll	Lucy Sealy	Dead	Chick Roll

(NOTES)

No. 1 also on Chickasaw Roll, Pickens County, Page 17.

P.O. Mead, I.T. Sept. 29, 1898.

RESIDENCE: Tishomingo COUNTY					CARD NO.		
POST OFFICE: Berwyn, I.T.					FIELD NO.		

NAME	RELATION-SHIP TO PERSON FIRST NAMED	AGE	SEX	BLOOD	TRIBAL ENROLLMENT		
					YEAR	COUNTY	PAGE
1 Strickland, Walter	NAMED	28	M	1/4	1897	Tishomingo	30
2 " John	Son	5	"	1/8	1897	"	30
3 " Granville	"	3	"	1/8	1897	"	30
4 " Homer	"	2	"	1/8	1897	"	88
5 " Joseph Bryan	"	6mo	"	1/8			
6 " Meda Ann	Dau	3mo	F	1/8			
7 " Ada May	"	1 1/2 mo	"	1/8			
8 " Carrie	Wife	29	F	I.W.			

TRIBAL ENROLLMENT OF PARENTS

NAME OF FATHER	YEAR	COUNTY	NAME OF MOTHER	YEAR	COUNTY
1 Chas Strickland	Dead	Chick Roll	Lucy Strickland	Dead	Chick Roll
2 No. 1			Carrie Strickland		White woman
3 No. 1			" "		" "
4 No. 1			" "		" "
5 No. 1			" "		" "
6 No. 1			" "		" "
7 No. 1			" "		" "
8 (Name Illegible)		Non Citizen	Annie (Illegible)		Non Citizen

(NOTES)

No. 3 on Chickasaw Roll as Greenville

139

Chickasaw Enrollment Cards 1898-1914
Chickasaw by Blood   Volume IV

January 4, 1900, Evidence of marriage of No. 1 and Carrie Strickland attached to card No. D.96
No. 7 Born Feby 19, 1902; enrolled April 4, 1902.
No. 4 Proof of birth filed Oct. 13, 1902.   *(No. 4 Dawes' Roll No. 4146)*
No. 6 enrolled June 5, 1900   *(No. 8 Dawes' Roll No. 190)*

McGee, I.T.   Sept. 29, 1898.

RESIDENCE: Tishomingo COUNTY					CARD NO.			
POST OFFICE: Emmet, I.T.					FIELD NO.			
NAME	RELATION-SHIP TO PERSON FIRST NAMED	AGE	SEX	BLOOD	TRIBAL ENROLLMENT			
					YEAR	COUNTY	PAGE	
1 Collins, Ben F.	NAMED	28	M	1/8	1897	Tishomingo	35	
2 " Mary Annetta	Dau	10mo	F	1/16				
3 " Benjamin F.	Son	1mo	M	1/16				

TRIBAL ENROLLMENT OF PARENTS

	NAME OF FATHER	YEAR	COUNTY	NAME OF MOTHER	YEAR	COUNTY
1	John Collins	Dead	Non Citizen	Mary Collins	Dead	Panola
2	No. 1			" "	"	"
3	No. 1			" "	"	"

(NOTES)

No. 1 on Chickasaw Roll as Ben Collins
No. 2 = Affidavit of attending Physician to be supplied. Received Oct. 11, 1898.
No. 3 enrolled 6/14, 1900.

Sept. 29, 1898.

RESIDENCE: Tishomingo COUNTY					CARD NO.			
POST OFFICE: Wiley, I.T.					FIELD NO.			
NAME	RELATION-SHIP TO PERSON FIRST NAMED	AGE	SEX	BLOOD	TRIBAL ENROLLMENT			
					YEAR	COUNTY	PAGE	
1 Davis, Daniel	NAMED	19	M	Full	1897	Pickens	14	

TRIBAL ENROLLMENT OF PARENTS

	NAME OF FATHER	YEAR	COUNTY	NAME OF MOTHER	YEAR	COUNTY
1	Bush Davis	Dead	Pickens	Easter Davis	Dead	Pickens

(NOTES)

Sept. 29, 1898.

RESIDENCE: Tishomingo   COUNTY   CARD NO.

POST OFFICE: Berwyn, I.T.   FIELD NO.

	NAME	RELATION-SHIP TO PERSON FIRST NAMED	AGE	SEX	BLOOD	TRIBAL ENROLLMENT		
						YEAR	COUNTY	PAGE
1	Hutchins, John	NAMED	25	M	I.W.	1897	Pickens	79
2	" Mamie	Wife	31	F	Full	1897	"	27
3	Cutchontubbee, Shimoheche	Mother in Law	75	"	"	1897	"	27
4	~~Hutchins, Stella~~	~~Dau~~	~~2mo~~	"	~~1/2~~	DIED PRIOR TO SEPTEMBER 25 1902		
5	" Lola Melissa	"	2mo	"	1/2			

TRIBAL ENROLLMENT OF PARENTS

	NAME OF FATHER	YEAR	COUNTY	NAME OF MOTHER	YEAR	COUNTY
1	John A. Hutchins		Non Citizen	C.V. Hutchins		Non Citizen
2	John Greenwood	Dead	Chick Roll	Shimoheche Cutchontubbee	1897	Tishomingo
3	(Name Illegible)	"	" "	(Name Illegible)	Dead	Chick Roll
4	~~No. 1~~			~~No. 2~~		
5	No. 1			No. 2		

(NOTES)

No. 1 on Chickasaw Roll as John Hujjings   (No. 1 Dawes' Roll No. 39)
No. 2 "   "   "   "   Mamie Hujjins
No. 3 "   "   "   "   Cretch Greenwood
No. 5 Enrolled January 22, 1901
No. 4 died Aug. 1900; Proof of death filed Nov. 3, 1902
No. 4 May 12, 1899

P.O. Sylvan, I.T. 11/5/02   Sept. 29, '98.

RESIDENCE: Pickens   COUNTY   CARD NO.

POST OFFICE: Cumberland, I.T.   FIELD NO.

	NAME	RELATION-SHIP TO PERSON FIRST NAMED	AGE	SEX	BLOOD	TRIBAL ENROLLMENT		
						YEAR	COUNTY	PAGE
1	Crockett, Hayes	NAMED	20	M	1/4	1897	Pickens	9
2	" Joseph D. McKinley	Son	1mo	"	1/8			

TRIBAL ENROLLMENT OF PARENTS

	NAME OF FATHER	YEAR	COUNTY	NAME OF MOTHER	YEAR	COUNTY
1	James Crockett	Dead	Non Citizen	Amanda Crockett	Dead	Pickens
2	No. 1			Lizzie Crockett		Non Citizen

(NOTES)

On Chickasaw Roll as Haze Crockett
No. 1 is married to Lizzie Crockett. Evidence of marriage filed Aug. 8, 1901.
No. 2 Enrolled August 8, 1901.

Sept. 29, '98

RESIDENCE: Tishomingo COUNTY						CARD NO.			
POST OFFICE: Emmet, I.T.						FIELD NO.			
NAME		RELATION-SHIP TO PERSON FIRST NAMED	AGE	SEX	BLOOD	TRIBAL ENROLLMENT			
						YEAR	COUNTY		PAGE
1	Creecy, Frank	NAMED	28	M	I.W.	1897	Pickens		79
2	" Gracie	Wife	24	F	1/8	1893	"		P.R.#1 115
3	" Clora Susie	Dau	2	"	1/16	1897	Tishomingo		88
4	" ~~Lira Nettie~~	"	~~3mo~~	"	~~1/16~~				
5	" Juel	"	1mo	"	1/16				

TRIBAL ENROLLMENT OF PARENTS

	NAME OF FATHER	YEAR	COUNTY	NAME OF MOTHER	YEAR	COUNTY
1	Jesse Creecy	Dead	Non Citizen	Sarah Creecy		Non Citizen
2	Jim Easton		" "	Margaret Easton	Dead	Tishomingo
3	No. 1			No. 2		
4	~~No. 1~~			~~No. 2~~		
5	No. 1			No. 2		

(NOTES)

No. 1 on Chickasaw Roll as Frank Creacy   *(No. 1 Dawes' Roll No. 325)*
No. 2 "   "   " " Gracie Easton
No. 3 "   "   " " Clora
No. 2 Also on 1897 Roll, Page 32, Tishomingo County as Gracy Creecy
No. 5 Enrolled August 22, 1900
No. 3 Proof of birth received and filed Sept. 29, 1902
No. 4 Died May 18, 1899; Proof of death filed Oct. 13, 1902.

P.O. Milburn, I.T. 6/29-04   Sept. 29, '98

RESIDENCE: Choctaw Nation   ~~COUNTY~~   CARD NO.

POST OFFICE: Oconee, I.T.   FIELD NO.

NAME	RELATIONSHIP TO PERSON FIRST NAMED	AGE	SEX	BLOOD	TRIBAL ENROLLMENT		
					YEAR	COUNTY	PAGE
4 ~~James Mack~~	FIRST NAMED	~~18~~	M	~~3/4~~	~~1897~~	~~Chick resid'g in Choc N. 3rd Dist.~~	~~75~~

TRIBAL ENROLLMENT OF PARENTS

NAME OF FATHER	YEAR	COUNTY	NAME OF MOTHER	YEAR	COUNTY
1 Marrin James	Dead	Chick Roll	Margaret James	1897	Pontotoc

(NOTES)

Sept. 29, 1898.

RESIDENCE: Pontotoc   COUNTY   CARD NO.

POST OFFICE: Conway, I.T.   FIELD NO.

NAME	RELATIONSHIP TO PERSON FIRST NAMED	AGE	SEX	BLOOD	TRIBAL ENROLLMENT		
					YEAR	COUNTY	PAGE
1 Shields, Henry	FIRST NAMED	21	M	1/2	1893	Pontoc[sic]	P.R.#2 203

TRIBAL ENROLLMENT OF PARENTS

NAME OF FATHER	YEAR	COUNTY	NAME OF MOTHER	YEAR	COUNTY
1 Willis Shields	Dead	Choc Roll	Epsey Shields	1897	Pontotoc

(NOTES)

Sept. 29, 1898.

RESIDENCE: Tishomingo   COUNTY   CARD NO.

POST OFFICE: Emmet, I.T.   FIELD NO.

NAME	RELATIONSHIP TO PERSON FIRST NAMED	AGE	SEX	BLOOD	TRIBAL ENROLLMENT		
					YEAR	COUNTY	PAGE
4 ~~Collins, Albert~~	FIRST NAMED	~~22~~	M	~~1/8~~	~~1897~~	~~Tishomingo~~	~~30~~
2 " Albert, Jr.	Son	8mo	"	1/16			
3 " Roy	"	3mo	"	1/16			
4 " Mary Etta	Dau	7wks	F	1/16			

TRIBAL ENROLLMENT OF PARENTS

NAME OF FATHER	YEAR	COUNTY	NAME OF MOTHER	YEAR	COUNTY
4 ~~John Collins~~	~~Dead~~	~~Non-Citizen~~	~~Etta Collins~~	~~1897~~	~~Pickens~~
2 No. 1			Ella "		Non Citizen
3 No. 1			" "		" "

143

4	No. 1			" "		" "

(NOTES)

No. 2 Affidavit of Physician to be supplied. Received Oct. 11, 1898.
No. 4 Born Nov. 16, 1901; enrolled Jan. 3, 1902
No. 3 Enrolled Nov. 3, 1899.

P.O. seems to be Lenox, I.T.   Sept. 29, '98.

RESIDENCE:	Tishomingo	COUNTY				CARD NO.		
POST OFFICE:	Emmett, Ind. Ter.					FIELD NO.		

	NAME	RELATION-SHIP TO PERSON FIRST NAMED	AGE	SEX	BLOOD	TRIBAL ENROLLMENT		
						YEAR	COUNTY	PAGE
1	Collins, Charles	NAMED	47	M	I.W.	1897	Tishomingo	79
2	" Jennie	Wife	30	F	1/8	1897	"	35
3	" Maggie	Dau	15	"	1/16	1897	"	35
4	" Allie	"	10	"	1/16	1897	"	35
5	" John	Son	8	M	1/16	1897	"	35
6	" Berry E.	"	4	"	1/16	1897	"	35
7	" Virgie	"	1	"	1/16			

TRIBAL ENROLLMENT OF PARENTS

	NAME OF FATHER	YEAR	COUNTY	NAME OF MOTHER	YEAR	COUNTY
1	George Collins	Dead	Non-citizen	Mildred Collins	Dead	Non-citizen
2	Joe Trenton	1897	Pickens	Mary Trenton	"	Chickasaw Roll
3	No. 1			Ada McCoy Collins	"	Tishomingo
4	No. 1			No. 2		
5	No. 1			No. 2		
6	No. 1			No. 2		
7	No.1			No. 2		

(NOTES)

No. 1 See decision of June 13, '04.   *(No. 1 Dawes' Roll No. 391)*
No. 7 Affidavit of Physician to be supplied. Received Oct. 21/98.
No. 3 is now the wife of Ricel Fenton Taylor on Choctaw card #310.
    Evidence of marriage filed Nov. *(remainder illegible)*
No. 1 and 2 are divorced and No. 2 is now the wife W.L. T??ilton
    Evidence of marriage filed Dec. 22, 1902
Evidence of divorce between Nos 1 and 2 filed Jan. 14, 1903
    "   "   "   "   Nos 1 and 2 filed Feby 18, 1903

P.O. Nida I.T.   Sept. 28, 98.

RESIDENCE: Choctaw Nation (3rd Dist.)   ~~COUNTY~~   CARD NO.

POST OFFICE: Oconee, I.T.   FIELD NO.

NAME	RELATION-SHIP TO PERSON FIRST NAMED	AGE	SEX	BLOOD	TRIBAL ENROLLMENT		
					YEAR	COUNTY	PAGE
1 Keel, Johnson	FIRST NAMED	29	M	Full	1897	Chick resid'g in Choc N. 3rd Dist.	75
2 " Alice	Wife	30	F	3/4	1897	"	75
3 " Eula	"[sic]	6	"	7/8	1897	"	75
4 " May	"[sic]	5	"	7/8	1897	"	75
5 " Dora	"[sic]	4	"	7/8	1897	"	75
6 " ~~Nancy~~	"~~[sic]~~	~~2~~	~~"~~	~~7/8~~	DIED PRIOR TO SEPTEMBER 25 1902 ~~1897~~ "	~~75~~
7 " Madelaine	"[sic]	8mo	"	7/8			
8 " Lewis, Jr	Son	1mo	M	7/8			
9 " Simon	"	1mo	"	7/8			

TRIBAL ENROLLMENT OF PARENTS

	NAME OF FATHER	YEAR	COUNTY	NAME OF MOTHER	YEAR	COUNTY
1	Louis Keel	1897	Tishomingo	Maulsie Keel	1897	Tishomingo
2	Booker James	Dead	Chick Roll	Martha James	Dead	Chick Roll
3	No. 1			No. 2		
4	No. 1			No. 2		
5	No. 1			No. 2		
6	~~No. 1~~			~~No. 2~~		
7	No. 1			No. 2		
8	No. 1			No. 2		
9	No. 1			No. 2		

(NOTES)

No. 9 Born Nov. 5, 1901; Enrolled December 4, 1901

No. 8 Enrolled Nov. 3, 1899

No. 6 Died Feby 11, 1899; Proof of death filed Feby 19, 1903

Sept. 29, 1898.

RESIDENCE: Tishomingo   COUNTY   CARD NO.

POST OFFICE: Emmet, I.T.   FIELD NO.

NAME	RELATION-SHIP TO PERSON FIRST NAMED	AGE	SEX	BLOOD	TRIBAL ENROLLMENT		
					YEAR	COUNTY	PAGE
1 Collins, Ed	FIRST NAMED	49	M	I.W.	1897	Pickens	79
2 " Louisanna	Dau	16	F	1/8	1897	"	35
3 " Thomas	Son	14	M	1/8	1897	"	35

145

| 4 | " | Edward | | " | || | M | 1/8 | 1897 | | " | | 35 |

TRIBAL ENROLLMENT OF PARENTS

	NAME OF FATHER	YEAR	COUNTY	NAME OF MOTHER	YEAR	COUNTY
1	G.W. Collins	Dead	Non Citizen	Mildred Collins	Dead	Non Citizen
2	No. 1			Elsie Collins	"	Chick Roll
3	No. 1			" "	"	" "
4	No. 1			" "	"	" "

(NOTES)

(No. 1 Dawes' Roll No. 324)

P.O. Nida, I.T.   Sept. 29, 1898.

| RESIDENCE: Tishomingo COUNTY | | CARD NO. |
| POST OFFICE: Emmet, I.T. | | FIELD NO. |

	NAME	RELATION-SHIP TO PERSON FIRST NAMED	AGE	SEX	BLOOD	TRIBAL ENROLLMENT		
						YEAR	COUNTY	PAGE
1	McKinney, Albert Thomas	NAMED	44	M	1/4	1897	Tishomingo	34
2	" Stella DEAD	Wife	24	F	I.W.	1897	"	79
3	" Granville	Son	12	M	1/4	1897	"	34
4	" Tommie	"	5	"	1/8	1897	"	34
5	" Pontie	"	9	"	1/4	1897	"	34
6	" Tishie	Dau	9	F	1/4	1897	"	34
7	" Bertha	"	2	"	1/8			

TRIBAL ENROLLMENT OF PARENTS

	NAME OF FATHER	YEAR	COUNTY	NAME OF MOTHER	YEAR	COUNTY
1	Henry McKinney	Dead	Cherokee Citizen	Sally McKinney	Dead	Chick Roll
2	Ste. Hirowpnous		Non Citizen	Ophelia Hirowpnous	"	Non Citizen
3	No. 1			Evaline McKinney	"	Chick Roll
4	No. 1			No. 2		
5	No. 1			Evaline McKinney	Dead	Chick Roll
6	No. 1			" "	"	" "
7	No. 1			No. 2		

(NOTES)

No. 1 on Chickasaw Roll as A.T. McKinney
No. 2 " " " " Whitey "
No. 7 Affidavit of attending physician to be supplied - Rec'd. Oct. 11, '98.   *(No. 7 Dawes' Roll No. 4752)*
No. 2 died February 13, 1901. See letter of No. 1 in G.O. files, #97193 - 1902
No. 2 Proof of death received and filed Nov. 8, 1902

Sept. 29, '98.

RESIDENCE: Choctaw Nation (3rd Dist) ~~COUNTY~~   CARD NO.

POST OFFICE: Waupaunuka, I.T.   FIELD NO.

NAME	RELATION-SHIP TO PERSON FIRST NAMED	AGE	SEX	BLOOD	TRIBAL ENROLLMENT		
					YEAR	COUNTY	PAGE
1 Keberry, Jonas DEAD	FIRST NAMED	21	M	Full	1893	Pontotoc	P.R.#2 132
2 " ~~Davis~~ VOID	~~Bro~~	~~18~~	"	"	~~1893~~	"	"
3 Billis, Melissa	Wife	23	F	"	1897	Pickens	24
4 " Minnie Bell	Dau of No. 3	3mo	F	1/2			

TRIBAL ENROLLMENT OF PARENTS

	NAME OF FATHER	YEAR	COUNTY	NAME OF MOTHER	YEAR	COUNTY
1	Collin Keberry	Dead	Pontotoc	Rhoda Keberry	Dead	Pontotoc
2	" "	"	"	" "	"	"
3	(Name Illegible)	"	Chick Roll	Winnie	"	Chick Roll
4	William Billis	1896	Choc Roll	No. 3		

(NOTES)

No. 3 on Chickasaw Roll as Nalisa Lewis

No. 3 is now the wife of William Billis on Choctaw Card #4331; See letter of E.J. Ball, Notary Public, June 18, 1901.
    Evidence of marriage requested.

No. 4 Enrolled June 18, 1901.   (No. 4 Dawes' Roll No. 4145)

No. 1 died Sept. 18, 1901; Proof of death filed Oct. 11, 1902.

No. 3 Enrolled March 20, 1899.

    Is not No. 2 a duplicate enrollment of No. 5 on Chickasaw Card #7

    Correct spelling of surname of No. 1 is "Cuberry" See letter of E.J. Ball, filed this day, June 25, 1901.

No. 2 duplicate of No. 5 on Choctaw Field No. 7, Chickasaw

                                        Sept. 29, 1898.

RESIDENCE: Pontotoc   COUNTY   CARD NO.

POST OFFICE: Waupaunuka, I.T.   FIELD NO.

NAME	RELATION-SHIP TO PERSON FIRST NAMED	AGE	SEX	BLOOD	TRIBAL ENROLLMENT		
					YEAR	COUNTY	PAGE
1 Keberry, Jimmie	NAMED	19	M	Full	1897	Pickens	18

TRIBAL ENROLLMENT OF PARENTS

	NAME OF FATHER	YEAR	COUNTY	NAME OF MOTHER	YEAR	COUNTY
1	Collin Keberry	Dead	Pontotoc	Rhoda Keberry	Dead	Pontotoc

(NOTES)

On Chickasaw Roll as James Cuberry.

                                        Sept. 29, 1898.

147

RESIDENCE: Tishomingo COUNTY   CARD NO.

POST OFFICE: Tishomingo, I.T.   FIELD NO.

NAME	RELATION-SHIP TO PERSON FIRST NAMED	AGE	SEX	BLOOD	TRIBAL ENROLLMENT		
					YEAR	COUNTY	PAGE
1 Kingsbery, George H.	NAMED	32	M	1/4	1897	Tishomingo	37
2 " Sallie	Wife	26	F	I.W.	1897	"	79
3 " Minnie H.	Dau	1	"	1/8	1897	"	88
4 " Mamie Nettie	"	2mo	"	1/8			
5 " Robert	Son	2wks	M	1/8			

TRIBAL ENROLLMENT OF PARENTS

	NAME OF FATHER	YEAR	COUNTY	NAME OF MOTHER	YEAR	COUNTY
1	Charley Kingsbery	Dead	Non Citizen	Minerva Kingsbery	1897	Panola
2	Jim Isbon		" "	Lucretia Isbon	Dead	Non Citizen
3	No. 1			No. 2		
4	No. 1			No. 2		
5	No. 1			No. 2		

(NOTES)

No. 2 enrolled Oct. 1, 1900   (No. 2 Dawes' Roll No. 132)
No. 3 on Chickasaw Roll as Minnie Jr.   (No. 3 Dawes' Roll No. 4144)
No. 3 Proof of birth received and filed Sept. 23, 1902
No. 4 Enrolled March 22, 1899.

Sept. 29, '98.

RESIDENCE: Tishomingo COUNTY   CARD NO.

POST OFFICE: Tishomingo   FIELD NO.

NAME	RELATION-SHIP TO PERSON FIRST NAMED	AGE	SEX	BLOOD	TRIBAL ENROLLMENT		
					YEAR	COUNTY	PAGE
1 Boyd, Robert Lewis	NAMED	56	M	1/4	1897	Tishomingo	38
2 " Mollie	Wife	48	F	I.W.	1897	Pickens	79

TRIBAL ENROLLMENT OF PARENTS

	NAME OF FATHER	YEAR	COUNTY	NAME OF MOTHER	YEAR	COUNTY
1	James M. Boyd	Dead	Non Citizen	Nancy Boyd	Dead	Chick Roll
2	Peter McSweeney	"	" "	Jeanna McSweeney	"	Non Citizen

(NOTES)

Affidavit of Reb. Lawrence Smyth, Fort Smith. Ark., who performed marriage ceremony, to be supplied.
Received Oct. 11, 1898.
No. 1 on Chickasaw Roll as R.L. Boyd.   (No. 2 Dawes' Roll No. 131)

Sept. 29, '98.

RESIDENCE: Tishomingo   COUNTY   CARD NO.
POST OFFICE: Baum, I.T.   FIELD NO.

NAME	RELATION-SHIP TO PERSON FIRST NAMED	AGE	SEX	BLOOD	TRIBAL ENROLLMENT		
					YEAR	COUNTY	PAGE
1 Thomas, Tom	NAMED	27	M	1/4	1897	Tishomingo	30
2 " Laura	Wife	28	F	I.W.			

TRIBAL ENROLLMENT OF PARENTS

	NAME OF FATHER	YEAR	COUNTY	NAME OF MOTHER	YEAR	COUNTY
1	Jim Thomas	1897	Tishomingo	Serena Thomas	Dead	Tishomingo
2	Henry Unsell		non citizen	Sally Unsell		non citizen

(NOTES)
No. 1 is husband of Laura Thomas on Chickasaw Card #D.94   (No. 1 Dawes' Roll No. 4143)
No. 1 See his sworn testimony as to the degree of Chickasaw blood possessed by him, filed Oct. 10, 1902.
No. 2 transferred from Chickasaw card #D.94   (No. 2 Dawes' Roll No. 284)
  See decision of March 5, 1904. Mar. 23, 1904

P.O. Address Elmore, I.T. May 5, 1902   Sept. 29/98.

RESIDENCE: Pontotoc   COUNTY   CARD NO.
POST OFFICE: Wynnewood, I.T.   FIELD NO.

NAME	RELATION-SHIP TO PERSON FIRST NAMED	AGE	SEX	BLOOD	TRIBAL ENROLLMENT		
					YEAR	COUNTY	PAGE
1 White, Samuel McKinley	NAMED	44	M	I.W.	1897	Pontotoc	80
2 " Malissa A.	Wife	40	F	1/2	1897	"	60
3 " Lula M.	Dau	20	"	1/4	1897	"	60
4 " Ethel D.	"	18	"	1/4	1897	"	60
5 " Oscar D.	Son	15	M	1/4	1897	"	60
6 " Walter S.	"	13	"	1/4	1897	"	60
7 " Illynoya	Dau	11	F	1/4	1897	"	60
8 " Lucy V.	"	7	"	1/4	1897	"	60
9 " Samuel Benj.	Son	4	M	1/4	1897	"	60
10 " Thomas W.	"	1mo	"	1/4			

TRIBAL ENROLLMENT OF PARENTS

	NAME OF FATHER	YEAR	COUNTY	NAME OF MOTHER	YEAR	COUNTY
1	William White	Dead	Non Citizen	Emaline White	Dead	Non Citizen
2	S Harris	"	Chick Roll	Nancy Harris	"	Chick Roll
3	No. 1			No. 2		
4	No. 1			No. 2		

149

5	No. I			No. 2		
6	No. I			No. 2		
7	No. I			No. 2		
8	No. I			No. 2		
9	No. I			No. 2		
10	No. I			No. 2		

(NOTES)

No. I See decision of June 13, '04.   *(No. I Dawes' Roll No. 390)*
No. I on Chickasaw Roll as S.M. White
No. 2 "   "   " " M.A.   "
No. 4 "   "   " " Ethel B. "
No. 9 "   "   " " Sam   "
No. 4 is now the wife of Jay Cawdell on Chickasaw Card No. 1309. Evidence of marriage filed 11/12, '02
No. 10 enrolled November, 21, 1898.

P.O. Tishomingo, I.T. 11/4/02.   Sept. 29, 1898.

RESIDENCE: Tishomingo **COUNTY**   **CARD NO.**
POST OFFICE: Tishomingo, I.T.   **FIELD NO.**

NAME	RELATION-SHIP TO PERSON FIRST NAMED	AGE	SEX	BLOOD	TRIBAL ENROLLMENT		
					YEAR	COUNTY	PAGE
1 Duncum, John Lawton	NAMED	18	M	1/16	1897	Tishomingo	38
2 " Roy E.	Son	8mo	M	1/32			
3 " Silas Floyd	"	3mo	M	1/32			
4 " Lottie M.	Wife	20	F	I.W.			

TRIBAL ENROLLMENT OF PARENTS

	NAME OF FATHER	YEAR	COUNTY	NAME OF MOTHER	YEAR	COUNTY
1	William Henry Duncum	1897	Tishomingo	Ella Duncum (I.W.)	1897	Tishomingo
2	No. I			Lottie M. Duncum		Non Citizen
3	No. I			" " "		" "
4	Wm Franklin Allison	Dead	Non citizen	Mary F. Allison		Non citizen

(NOTES)

On Chickasaw Roll as J.G. Duncum   *(No. I Dawes' Roll No. 300)*
No. 3 enrolled Aug. 27, 1901   *(No. 3 Dawes' Roll No. 4142)*
Evidence of marriage between No. 1 and mother of children on this card, received and filed Oct. 10, 1902.
No. 2 enrolled Nov. 3, 1899.   *(No. 2 Dawes' Roll No. 4141)*
No. 4 placed hereon in accordance with an order of the Commission of March 22, 1905 holding that application was made for her enrollment within the time provided by the Act of Congress of July 1, 1902 (32 Stat. 641)

P.O. Byrne, I.T.   Sept. 29, '98.

RESIDENCE: Tishomingo COUNTY   CARD NO.
POST OFFICE: Baum, I.T.   FIELD NO.

	NAME	RELATION-SHIP TO PERSON FIRST NAMED	AGE	SEX	BLOOD	TRIBAL ENROLLMENT		
						YEAR	COUNTY	PAGE
1	Bean, Mary	NAMED	35	F	3/4	1897	Tishomingo	33
2	" John	Son	6	M	3/8	1897	"	33
3	" Ben	"	3	"	3/8	1897	"	33
4	" William	"	1mo	"	3/8			
5	" Gregory W.	Hus.	46	M	I.W.			

TRIBAL ENROLLMENT OF PARENTS

	NAME OF FATHER	YEAR	COUNTY	NAME OF MOTHER	YEAR	COUNTY
1	John Thomas	1897	Tishomingo	(Name Illegible)	Dead	Tishomingo
2	George[sic] W. Bean		White man	No. I		
3	" " "		" "	No. I		
4	" " "		" "	No. I		
5	Benjamin Bean		non citizen	Honor Bean	Dead	Non citizen

(NOTES)

No. I *(Illegible)* of Gregory W. Bean, Chickasaw Card No. D.93
No. 2 on Chickasaw Roll as Jack Bean
No. 4 Enrolled Nov. 3, 1899
No. 5 transferred from Choctaw Card D #93 August 10, 1905. See decision of July 25, 1905.

Sept. 29, 1898

RESIDENCE: Tishomingo COUNTY   CARD NO.
POST OFFICE: Belton, I.T.   FIELD NO.

	NAME	RELATION-SHIP TO PERSON FIRST NAMED	AGE	SEX	BLOOD	TRIBAL ENROLLMENT		
						YEAR	COUNTY	PAGE
1	Duncum, William Henry	NAMED	49	M	1/8	1897	Tishomingo	38
2	*(This line left blank on microfilm)*							
3	" William Henry Jr. DEAD	Son	15	M	1/16	1897	"	38
4	" Thomas Brown	"	13	"	1/16	1897	"	38
5	" Charles Lewis	"	10	"	1/16	1897	"	38
6	" Ula	Wife	44	F	I.W.	1897	"	79

TRIBAL ENROLLMENT OF PARENTS

	NAME OF FATHER	YEAR	COUNTY	NAME OF MOTHER	YEAR	COUNTY
1	Wm H. Duncum	Dead	Non Citizen	Mary M. Duncum	Dead	Chick Roll
2	*(This line left blank on micr*	*ofilm)*		Ella Duncum		
3	No. I			Ella Duncum		White woman

151

4	No. 1			" "		" "
5	No. 1			" "		" "
6	Thomas Mobley	Dead	Non Citizen	Ashley Mobley	Dead	Non Citizen

(NOTES)

No. 1 husband of Ella Duncum, Chickasaw Card No. D.92
No. 1 on Chickasaw roll as W.H. Duncum
No. 3 "   "   "   " W.D.   "
No. 4 "   "   "   " T.D.   "
No. 2 "   "   "   " C.D.   "
No. 3 died May 2, 1899; proof of death filed Dec. 8, 1902
    Testimony as to marriage of William Henry Duncum and Ella Duncum, filed with Chickasaw Card D.92
      January 27, 1900
No. 6 transferred from Chickasaw Card #D.92. See decision *(remainder illegible)* *(No. 6 Dawes' Roll No. 189)*

P.O. Byrne, I.T. 12/22/02   Sept. 29, '98.

RESIDENCE: Choctaw Nation (3rd Dist.) ~~COUNTY~~   CARD NO.
POST OFFICE: FIELD NO.

NAME	RELATION-SHIP TO PERSON FIRST NAMED	AGE	SEX	BLOOD	TRIBAL ENROLLMENT		
					YEAR	COUNTY	PAGE
1 Harkins, Annie	NAMED	28	F	1/4			
2 " Willis	Son	5	M	1/8			
3 " Clara	Dau	3	F	1/8			
4 " Lillie	"	11/2	"	1/8			
5 " Lee	Son	10mo	M	1/8			
6 " Grover	"	11days	"	1/8			

TRIBAL ENROLLMENT OF PARENTS

	NAME OF FATHER	YEAR	COUNTY	NAME OF MOTHER	YEAR	COUNTY
1	Henry James		Atoka Co. Choctaw Roll	Lorenna James	Dead	Chick residing in Choc. N. 3rd Dist.
2	William Harkins		Blue Co. Choctaw Roll	No. 1		
3	" "		" "	No. 1		
4	" "		" "	No. 1		
5	" "		" "	No. 1		
6	" "		" "	No. 1		

(NOTES)

All on Choctaw Census Record No. 2, Blue County, Page 250, transferred to Chickasaw Roll by Dawes Commission
No. 1 on Choctaw Roll, 1896, Blue County, No. 5920
No. 2 "   "   " 1896, "   "   " 5921
No. 3 "   "   " 1896. "   "   " 5922

No. 1 husband William M. Harkins on Choctaw Card #4442
No. 6 Born June 13, 1902; Enrolled June 24, 1902.
No. 5 Enrolled Dec. 13, 1899

Sept. 29, '98.

CANCELLED Stamped across card
Transferred to Choctaw Card No. 2403
Oct. 17, 1902

	RESIDENCE: Tishomingo COUNTY					CARD NO.		
	POST OFFICE: Emmet, I.T.					FIELD NO.		
	NAME	RELATION-SHIP TO PERSON FIRST NAMED	AGE	SEX	BLOOD	TRIBAL ENROLLMENT		
						YEAR	COUNTY	PAGE
1	Harkins, Charley	NAMED	26	M	1/4	1897	Tishomingo	34
2	" Lula	Wife	25	F	1/4	1897	"	34
3	" Robert	Son	5	M	1/4	1897	"	34
4	" Nellie Inga	Dau	1/2	F	1/4			

TRIBAL ENROLLMENT OF PARENTS

	NAME OF FATHER	YEAR	COUNTY	NAME OF MOTHER	YEAR	COUNTY
1	George Harkins	Dead	Choctaw Roll	Mary Harkins	1897	Tishomingo
2	Bill Harris		" "	Lucy Harris	Dead	"
3	No. 1			No. 2		
4	No. 1			No. 2		

(NOTES)

No. 2 on Chickasaw Roll as Lela Harkins
No. 4 born June 22, 1901; Enrolled Dec. 27, 1901.

Sept. 29, 1898

	RESIDENCE: Choctaw Nation ~~COUNTY~~					CARD NO.		
	POST OFFICE: South Canadian, I.T.					FIELD NO.		
	NAME	RELATION-SHIP TO PERSON FIRST NAMED	AGE	SEX	BLOOD	TRIBAL ENROLLMENT		
						YEAR	COUNTY	PAGE
1	Cheadle, Lucy B.	NAMED	28	F	1/4			
2	" Jas. Pushmataha	Son	7	M	1/8			
3	" Mary Almeda	Dau	5	F	1/8			
4	" Martin Douglas	Son	3	M	1/8			
5	" George Rector	"	2mo	"	1/8			
6	" Kisko Harkins	"	8mo	"	1/8			

TRIBAL ENROLLMENT OF PARENTS

	NAME OF FATHER	YEAR	COUNTY	NAME OF MOTHER	YEAR	COUNTY
1	George Harkins	Dead	Choc Roll	Mary Harkins	1897	Tishomingo
2	Elias R. Cheadle		" "	No. 1		
3	" " "		" "	No. 1		
4	" " "		" "	No. 1		
5	" " "		" "	No. 1		
6	" " "		" "	No. 1		

(NOTES)

All on Choctaw Census Record No. 2, Page 96, transferred to Chickasaw Roll by Dawes Commission

No. 6 Born Dec. 18, 1901; enrolled Sept. 6, 1902.

No. 2 on Choctaw Roll as James P. Cheadle

No. 3 "   "   "   " Almeda   "

No. 4 "   "   "   " Martin D.   "

No. 5 Affidavit of Physician to be supplied. Rec'd. Oct. 11, 1898.

No. 1 On Choctaw Roll, 1896, Tobucksy County, No. 2364

No. 2 "   "   " 1896   "   "   " 2365, as James P. Cheadle

No. 3 "   "   " 1896   "   "   " 2366, " Almeda M.   "

No. 4 "   "   " 1896   "   "   " 2367, " Martin D.   "

No. 1 is wife of Elias R. Cheadle on Choctaw Card #4679.

Sept. 29, 1898.

CANCELLED Stamped across card

RESIDENCE: Tishomingo   COUNTY   CARD NO.

POST OFFICE: Emmet, I.T.   FIELD NO.

NAME	RELATION-SHIP TO PERSON FIRST NAMED	AGE	SEX	BLOOD	TRIBAL ENROLLMENT		
					YEAR	COUNTY	PAGE
1 Harkins, Mary	NAMED	51	F	1/2	1897	Tishomingo	34

TRIBAL ENROLLMENT OF PARENTS

	NAME OF FATHER	YEAR	COUNTY	NAME OF MOTHER	YEAR	COUNTY
1	Turner Bynum	Dead	Choc Roll	Lucinda Bynum	Dead	Chick Roll

(NOTES)

Sept. 29, '98.

RESIDENCE: Tishomingo   COUNTY   CARD NO.

POST OFFICE: Tishomingo, I.T.   FIELD NO.

NAME	RELATION-SHIP TO PERSON FIRST NAMED	AGE	SEX	BLOOD	TRIBAL ENROLLMENT		
					YEAR	COUNTY	PAGE
1 McLish, Turner Bynum	NAMED	27	M	1/8	1897	Tishomingo	34

Chickasaw Enrollment Cards 1898-1914
Chickasaw by Blood   Volume IV

	TRIBAL ENROLLMENT OF PARENTS					
NAME OF FATHER	YEAR	COUNTY	NAME OF MOTHER	YEAR	COUNTY
1 Ben F. McLish	Dead	Tishomingo	Julia McLish	Dead	Pontotoc

(NOTES)

On Chickasaw Roll as T.B. McLish.

Sept. 29, '98.

RESIDENCE: Tishomingo COUNTY

POST OFFICE: Regan, I.T.

CARD NO.

FIELD NO.

	NAME	RELATION-SHIP TO PERSON FIRST NAMED	AGE	SEX	BLOOD	TRIBAL ENROLLMENT		
						YEAR	COUNTY	PAGE
1	Fisher, Amanda		45	F	Full	1897	Tishomingo	36
2	Greenwood, Alphus DEAD	Son	18	M	"	1897	"	36
3	" Simeon	"	16	"	"	1897	"	36
4	" Emaziah	"	14	"	"	1897	"	36
5	" Lem	"	9	"	"	1897	"	36
6	" Edmon	"	9	"	"	1897	"	36
7	Underwood, Daisy	Dau	6	F	"	1897	"	36
8	" Rosa	"	4	"	"	1897	"	37
9	" Isaac	Son	2	M	"	~~1897~~	"	~~37~~
10	Fisher, Lewis Keel	"	6mo	"	1/2			

	TRIBAL ENROLLMENT OF PARENTS					
NAME OF FATHER	YEAR	COUNTY	NAME OF MOTHER	YEAR	COUNTY
1 Lewis Keel	1886	Tishomingo	Maulsie Keel	1897	Tishomingo
2 Alfred Greenwood	Dead	Chick Roll	No. 1		
3 " "	"	" "	No. 1		
4 " "	"	" "	No. 1		
5 Wilson "	1897	Pontotoc	No. 1		
6 " "	"	"	No. 1		
7 Burney Underwood	1897	"	No. 1		
8 " "	"	"	No. 1		
9 " "	"	"	No. 1		
10 T.J. Fisher		Non Citizen	No. 1		

(NOTES)

No. 3 on Chickasaw Roll as Simon
No. 4 "   "   " " Emazin
No. 3 Father of Eula Greenwood, on Chick Card #723
No. 1 is now the wife of T.J. Fisher - a non Citizen   March 6, 1900
No. 10 enrolled Feby. 1, 1901
No. 2 died January 20, 1901; evidence of death filed Feb'y 18, 1901.

155

No. 9 Proof of birth received and filed Sept. 25, 1902.

(No. 9 Dawes' Roll No. 4140)

Sept. 29, '98.

RESIDENCE: Pickens   COUNTY   CARD NO.

POST OFFICE: Lebanon, I.T.   FIELD NO.

	NAME	RELATION-SHIP TO PERSON FIRST NAMED	AGE	SEX	BLOOD	TRIBAL ENROLLMENT		
						YEAR	COUNTY	PAGE
1	~~Pickens, Thompson~~		~~52~~	~~M~~	~~Full~~	DIED PRIOR TO SEPTEMBER 25 1902 ~~1897~~	~~Pickens~~	9
2	" Ziley	Wife	40	F	"	1897	"	9
3	" Johnie	Son	18	M	"	1897	"	9
4	" Tommie	"	16	"	"	1893	"	P.R.#2 185
5	" Emely	Dau	10	F	"	1897	"	9
6	" Dave	Son	7	M	"	1897	"	9

TRIBAL ENROLLMENT OF PARENTS

	NAME OF FATHER	YEAR	COUNTY	NAME OF MOTHER	YEAR	COUNTY
1	~~O-chan-tub-by~~	~~Dead~~	~~Chick Roll~~	~~En-thi-hee~~	~~Dead~~	~~Chick Roll~~
2	Con-che-tubby	"	" "	*(Name Illegible)*	"	" "
3	No. 1			No. 2		
4	No. 1			No. 2		
5	No. 1			No. 2		
6	No. 1			No. 2		

(NOTES)

No. 2 on Chickasaw Roll as Jily Pickens

No. 5 died in June, 1899

No. 1 died Nov, 1901; Proof of death filed Nov. 8, 1902

Sept. 29, 1898.

RESIDENCE: Tishomingo   COUNTY   CARD NO.

POST OFFICE: Tishomingo, I.T.   FIELD NO.

	NAME	RELATION-SHIP TO PERSON FIRST NAMED	AGE	SEX	BLOOD	TRIBAL ENROLLMENT		
						YEAR	COUNTY	PAGE
1	Maytubby, Joel S.		29	M	1/2	1897	Pontotoc	50

TRIBAL ENROLLMENT OF PARENTS

	NAME OF FATHER	YEAR	COUNTY	NAME OF MOTHER	YEAR	COUNTY
1	Tony Maytubby	Dead	Chick Roll	Nancy Maytubby	Dead	Non Citizen

(NOTES)

Sept. 29, '98.

Chickasaw Enrollment Cards 1898-1914
Chickasaw by Blood   Volume IV

RESIDENCE: Tishomingo   COUNTY   CARD NO.
POST OFFICE: Emmet, I.T.   FIELD NO.

	NAME	RELATION-SHIP TO PERSON FIRST NAMED	AGE	SEX	BLOOD	TRIBAL ENROLLMENT		
						YEAR	COUNTY	PAGE
1	Wolf, Davison	NAMED	46	M	Full	1897	Tishomingo	33
2	" Wicy	Wife	34	F	"	1897	"	33
3	" John	Son	8	M	"	1897	"	33
4	" Abel	"	4	"	"	1897	"	33
5	" Eolins	"	2	"	"	1897	"	33
6	" ~~Solena~~ DEAD	~~Dau~~	~~5mo~~	F	"	DIED PRIOR TO SEPTEMBER 25 1902		
7	" Loman	Son	7mo	M	"			

TRIBAL ENROLLMENT OF PARENTS

	NAME OF FATHER	YEAR	COUNTY	NAME OF MOTHER	YEAR	COUNTY
1	Sho-bah-lok-na	Dead	Chick Roll	Cho-e-whe	Dead	Chickasaw Roll
2	Pos-so-ha	"	" "	Si-ley	"	" "
3	No. 1			No. 2		
4	No. 1			No. 2		
5	No. 1			No. 2		
6	~~No. 1~~			~~No. 2~~		
7	No. 1			No. 2		

(NOTES)

No. 1 on Chickasaw Roll as Lavison Wolf
No. 4 "   "   " " Ebil   "
No. 5 "   "   " " Eaolin   "
No. 7 Enrolled June 27, 1901
No. 6 Proof of birth received and filed Nov. 6, 1902
No. 6 Enrolled Aug. 15, 1899.

Sept. 29, '98.

RESIDENCE: Tishomingo   COUNTY   CARD NO.
POST OFFICE: Davis, I.T.   FIELD NO.

	NAME	RELATION-SHIP TO PERSON FIRST NAMED	AGE	SEX	BLOOD	TRIBAL ENROLLMENT		
						YEAR	COUNTY	PAGE
1	Chigley, Nelson	NAMED	63	M	Full	1897	Tishomingo	27
2	" Julia	Wife	61	F	"	1897	"	27
3	" Mose	Son	25	M	"	1897	"	27
4	" Wyatt	"	23	"	"	1897	"	27
5	Pierce, Eliza	Dau	21	F	"	1897	"	27

6	Cobb, Jim	Nephew	21	M	1/2	1897	"	28
7	" Virginia	Neice[sic]	14	F	1/2	1897	"	28
8	" Calvin	Nephew	12	M	1/2	1897	"	28
9	Wolf, Key	Cousin	12	M	1/2	1897	"	28
10	Pierce, George	Hus of No. 5	23	M	I.W.			

TRIBAL ENROLLMENT OF PARENTS

	NAME OF FATHER	YEAR	COUNTY	NAME OF MOTHER	YEAR	COUNTY
1	Chigley	Dead	Chickasaw Roll	Eu-pul-kee	Dead	Chick Roll
2	Pat-she-kah	"	" "	Kitty	"	" "
3	No. 1			No. 2		
4	No. 1			No. 2		
5	No. 1			No. 2		
6	McKinney Cobb	Dead	Choctaw Roll	June Cobb	Dead	Chick Roll
7	" "	"	" "	" "	"	" "
8	" "	"	" "	" "	"	" "
9	Silas Wolf	"	Chick Roll	(Name Illegible)	"	Non Citizen
10	John Pierce		non citz	Malissa Pierce	"	" "

(NOTES)

No. 7 on Chickasaw Roll as Jennie
No. 9 " " " K. Wolfe
No. 5 is now the wife of George Pierce on Chickasaw Card D.325
No. 10 Transferred from Chickasaw Card D325

Sept. 29, 1898.

RESIDENCE: Pickens COUNTY		CARD NO.
POST OFFICE: Mansville, I.T.		FIELD NO.

	NAME	RELATION-SHIP TO PERSON FIRST NAMED	AGE	SEX	BLOOD	TRIBAL ENROLLMENT		
						YEAR	COUNTY	PAGE
1	Tyubby, Sam		60	M	Full	1897	Pickens	11
2	" Nancy	Wife	0	F	"	1897	"	11
3	McGuire, Elsie	Dau	24	"	"	1897	"	11
4	Tyubby, Noel	Son	21	M	"	1897	"	11
5	Sealy, Esther	Niece in Law	20	F	"	1893	"	P.R.#2 130
6	" Ethel	Gr.Niece in Law	3	F	"	1897	"	28
7	McGuire, Louisa	Gr.Dau	11mo	F	"			
8	Tyubby, Richmon	Son	12	M	"	1897	"	11

| 9 | Russell, Kate | | Dau of No. 3 | 15mo | F | " | | | |

TRIBAL ENROLLMENT OF PARENTS

	NAME OF FATHER	YEAR	COUNTY	NAME OF MOTHER	YEAR	COUNTY
1	Tyubby	Dead	Chick Roll	Che-cah-he	Dead	Chick Roll
2	Ne-ho-o-cho-to-tubby	"	" "	*(Name Illegible)*	"	" "
3	No. 1			Lucy Anna	"	" "
4	No. 1			" "	"	" "
5	Freeman Keel	Dead	Chick Roll	Louisa	"	" "
6	Josh Sealy	"	Tishomingo	No. 5		
7	Sam McGuire			No. 3		
8	No. 1			Louisa Tyubby	Dead	Chickasaw Roll
9	Silas Russell	1897	Tishomingo	No. 3		

(NOTES)

No. 2 also know as Teshohuvye
No. 4 on Chickasaw Roll as Joel
No. 5 "   "   "   " Esther Keel
No. 4 is now the husband of Leah Pickens, on Chickasaw Card #972
As to marriage of these persons, see letter of J.C. McCurtain filed with Chickasaw Case #972, July 17. 1902
No. 8 placed on this card April 24, 1902 from memorandum of *(Illegible)* Bixby of Sept. 29, 1898.
No. 9 Born Sept. 2, 1901; Application made Dec. 24, 1902; proof of birth filed March 6, 1903.

Sept. 29, 1898

| RESIDENCE: Tishomingo | COUNTY | | | | CARD NO. | | |
| POST OFFICE: Mill Creek, I.T. | | | | | FIELD NO. | | |

	NAME	RELATION-SHIP TO PERSON FIRST NAMED	AGE	SEX	BLOOD	TRIBAL ENROLLMENT		
						YEAR	COUNTY	PAGE
1	Henderson, Ceza		31	F	Full	1893	Tishomingo	119
2	" Serena	Dau	6	"	1/2	1893	"	119

TRIBAL ENROLLMENT OF PARENTS

	NAME OF FATHER	YEAR	COUNTY	NAME OF MOTHER	YEAR	COUNTY
1	O-te-mo-non-tubby	Dead	Chick Roll	Shim-mo-ni-ye	Dead	Chick Roll
2	Charley Henderson		Non Citizen	No. 1		

(NOTES)

No. 2 on Chickasaw Roll as Baby Henderson
Nos. 1 and 2 also on 1896 Chickasaw Roll, Tishomingo Co. page 92
See testimony of Susan Allen taken Nov. 13, 1902
No. 1 is the wife of Ben Eyatubby on Chickasaw Card #1347, Nov. 18, 1902.

Sept. 29, 1898.

RESIDENCE: Choctaw Nation   ~~COUNTY~~   CARD NO.
POST OFFICE: Kiowa, I.T.   FIELD NO.

NAME	RELATION-SHIP TO PERSON	AGE	SEX	BLOOD	TRIBAL ENROLLMENT		
					YEAR	COUNTY	PAGE
~~1 Wesley, Abel~~	FIRST NAMED	42	M	~~Full~~	~~1897~~	DIED PRIOR TO SEPTEMBER 25 1902 ~~Chick resid'g in Choc N. 1st Dist.~~	~~74~~

TRIBAL ENROLLMENT OF PARENTS

NAME OF FATHER	YEAR	COUNTY	NAME OF MOTHER	YEAR	COUNTY
~~1 (Name Illegible)~~	~~Dead~~	~~Chick Roll~~	~~Mah-ha~~	~~Dead~~	~~Chick Roll~~

(NOTES)

(Notation Illegible)
No. 1 died May 15, 1900; Proof of death filed Dec. 23, 1900.

Sept. 29, 1898

RESIDENCE: Choctaw Nation   ~~COUNTY~~   CARD NO.
POST OFFICE: Kiowa, Ind. Ter.   FIELD NO.

NAME	RELATION-SHIP TO PERSON	AGE	SEX	BLOOD	TRIBAL ENROLLMENT		
					YEAR	COUNTY	PAGE
1 Cole, John	FIRST NAMED	23	M	I.W.			
2 " Ellen	Wife	22	F	Full	1897	Chick residing in Choc N. 1st Dist.	

TRIBAL ENROLLMENT OF PARENTS

NAME OF FATHER	YEAR	COUNTY	NAME OF MOTHER	YEAR	COUNTY
1 (Name Illegible)	Dead	Non Citizen	Emma Cole	Dead	Non Citizen
2 (Name Illegible)	Dead	Chick Roll	(Illegible) Keel	"	Chick Roll

(NOTES)

(Notation illegible)
Certified copy of divorce proceedings between Benjamin and Ellen Alberson, also affidavits that Ellen Alberson mentioned therein is now Ellen Cole whose name appears hereon filed *(remainder illegible)*

P.O. Blanco, I.T.   Sept. 29, 1898.

RESIDENCE: Tishomingo   COUNTY   CARD NO.
POST OFFICE: Regan, I.T.   FIELD NO.

NAME	RELATION-SHIP TO PERSON	AGE	SEX	BLOOD	TRIBAL ENROLLMENT		
					YEAR	COUNTY	PAGE
1 Brown, Wessen	FIRST NAMED	21	M	Full	1897	Tishomingo	39

2	" Texie	Wife	17	F	I.W.			

TRIBAL ENROLLMENT OF PARENTS

	NAME OF FATHER	YEAR	COUNTY	NAME OF MOTHER	YEAR	COUNTY
1	Mitchell Brown	Dead	Chick Roll	*(Illegible)* Brown	Dead	Chick Roll
2	George Carr		Non Citizen	Susan Carr		Non Citizen

(NOTES)

(Notation illegible)   *(No. 2 Dawes' Roll No. 221)*

P.O. Newton I.T. 10/12/02   Sept. 29, 1898.

RESIDENCE: Pickens   COUNTY   CARD NO.
POST OFFICE: *(Illegible), I.T.*   FIELD NO.

NAME	RELATION-SHIP TO PERSON FIRST NAMED	AGE	SEX	BLOOD	TRIBAL ENROLLMENT		
					YEAR	COUNTY	PAGE
1 Wall, Will		26	M	1/4	1897	Pickens	19

TRIBAL ENROLLMENT OF PARENTS

	NAME OF FATHER	YEAR	COUNTY	NAME OF MOTHER	YEAR	COUNTY
1	*(Illegible)* Wall	Dead	Chick Roll	Minerva Wall	Dead	Chick Roll

(NOTES)

Sept. 29, 1898.

RESIDENCE: Pontotoc   COUNTY   CARD NO.
POST OFFICE: Willis, I.T.   FIELD NO.

NAME	RELATION-SHIP TO PERSON FIRST NAMED	AGE	SEX	BLOOD	TRIBAL ENROLLMENT		
					YEAR	COUNTY	PAGE
1 Carnes, Gincy		20	F	1/2	1897	Pontotoc	50

TRIBAL ENROLLMENT OF PARENTS

	NAME OF FATHER	YEAR	COUNTY	NAME OF MOTHER	YEAR	COUNTY
1	Eli Carnes	Dead	Choctaw Roll	Wincy Carnes	Dead	Chick Roll

(NOTES)

(All notations illegible)

Sept. 29, 1898.

CANCELLED Stamped across card

161

RESIDENCE: Pontotoc   COUNTY   CARD NO.
POST OFFICE: Waupaunuka, I.T.   FIELD NO.

NAME	RELATION-SHIP TO PERSON FIRST NAMED	AGE	SEX	BLOOD	TRIBAL ENROLLMENT		
					YEAR	COUNTY	PAGE
1 Hawkins, *(Illegible)*	NAMED	26	F	Full	1897	Pontotoc	
2 " ~~Bitsey~~	~~Dau~~	~~3mo~~	F	~~1/2~~			
3 Sealey, Julues	Son	I	M	Full			

TRIBAL ENROLLMENT OF PARENTS

	NAME OF FATHER	YEAR	COUNTY	NAME OF MOTHER	YEAR	COUNTY
1	*(Illegible)*Miller	Dead	Chick Roll	Maria Miller	Dead	Chick Roll
2	~~Kingsberry Hawkins~~		~~Choctaw residing in Chickasaw District~~	~~No. I~~		
3	Adam Sealey			No. I		

(NOTES)

No. I wife of Kingsberry Hawkins, Choctaw Roll Card No. 304
No. 2 died Sept. 25, 1899; Proof of death filed Nov. 6, 1902
No. I is now seperated from Kingsberry Hawkins Chickasaw Card # *(illegible)*
No. 3 was born April 22, 1902. Application received Mar. 18, 1905.
   under Act of Congress approved Mar. 3, 1905. Father on 9-60.

Sept. 29, 1898.

RESIDENCE: Pickens   COUNTY   CARD NO.
POST OFFICE: Brownsville, I.T.   FIELD NO.

NAME	RELATION-SHIP TO PERSON FIRST NAMED	AGE	SEX	BLOOD	TRIBAL ENROLLMENT		
					YEAR	COUNTY	PAGE
1 Kaney, Gilbert	NAMED	30	M	Full	1897	Pickens	55
2 " Frances	Wife	31	F	"	1897	"	25
3 Brown, Loman	S.Son	10	M	"	1893	"	P.R.#2 41
4 Frazier, John	Ward	15I"	"	1897	1897	"	55

TRIBAL ENROLLMENT OF PARENTS

	NAME OF FATHER	YEAR	COUNTY	NAME OF MOTHER	YEAR	COUNTY
1	*(Name Illegible)*	Dead	Chick Roll	*(Name Illegible)*	Dead	Chick Roll
2	Jimpson Frazier	"	" "	*(Name Illegible)*	"	" "
3	Thomas Brown	"	" "	No. 2		
4	*(Illegible)*Frazier	"	" "	Betsey Frazier	Dead	Chick Roll

(NOTES)

(All notations illegible)

P.O. Isom Springs, I.T. 10/13/02.   Sept. 28, 1898.

Chickasaw Enrollment Cards 1898-1914
Chickasaw by Blood   Volume IV

RESIDENCE: Tishomingo   COUNTY
POST OFFICE: Sylva, I.T.

CARD NO.
FIELD NO.

	NAME	RELATION-SHIP TO PERSON FIRST NAMED	AGE	SEX	BLOOD	TRIBAL ENROLLMENT		
						YEAR	COUNTY	PAGE
1	Hutchins, Lizzie	NAMED	23	F	Full	1897	Tishomingo	
2	" Lillian May	Dau	1	"	1/2			
3	" Alvie Ross	Son	2mo	M	1/2			
4	" William Andrew	husband	27	M	I.W.			

TRIBAL ENROLLMENT OF PARENTS

	NAME OF FATHER	YEAR	COUNTY	NAME OF MOTHER	YEAR	COUNTY
1	(Name Illegible)	Dead	Tishomingo	Bitsey Newberry	Dead	Chick Roll
2	Wm Andrew Hutchins		White man	No. 1		
3	" " "		" "	No. 1		
4	J.?. Hutchins		Non Citizen	(Illegible) Hutchins		Non Citizen

(NOTES)
No. 1 wife of William Andrew Hutchins, Chickasaw Roll Card No. D.72
No. 1 on Chickasaw Roll as Lizzie Newberry
No. 3 enrolled Nov. 17, 1899
No. 4 transferred from Chickasaw Card #D.72.   (No. 4 Dawes' Roll No. 188)
See decision of May 1, 1902.

Sept. 28, '98.

RESIDENCE: Tishomingo   COUNTY
POST OFFICE: Sylva, I.T.

CARD NO.
FIELD NO.

	NAME	RELATION-SHIP TO PERSON FIRST NAMED	AGE	SEX	BLOOD	TRIBAL ENROLLMENT		
						YEAR	COUNTY	PAGE
1	Alberson, Simon	NAMED	27	M	Full	1897	Tishomingo	27
2	" Elsie	Wife	29	F	"	1897	"	27
3	" (Illegible)	Son	2	M	"	1897	"	88
4	" Margaret	Sister	30	F	"	1897	"	27
5	Owens, Bendie	Sister in Law	17	F	"	1897	"	27
6	Lewis, Hettie	" "	14	"	"	1897	"	27
7	" Maulsie	" "	12	"	"	1897	"	27
8	" Jefferson	Bro in Law	20	M	"	1897	"	27
9	Alberson, Lucy	Dau	2mo	F	"			
10	Pickens, Edmund Hiram	Son of No. 5	2	M	"			

163

11	" George W,	Son of No. 5	8mo	M	"			
12	Alberson, Andy S.	Son	2mo	M	"			

TRIBAL ENROLLMENT OF PARENTS

	NAME OF FATHER	YEAR	COUNTY	NAME OF MOTHER	YEAR	COUNTY
1	*(Illegible)* Alberson	Dead	Chick Roll	Betsey Alberson	Dead	Chick Roll
2	Josiah Lewis	"	" "	Malinda Lewis	"	" "
3	~~No. 1~~			~~No. 2~~		
4	*(Illegible)* Alberson	Dead	Chick Roll	Betsey Alberson	Dead	Chick Roll
5	Josiah Lewis	"	" "	Malinda Lewis	"	" "
6	" "	"	" "	" "	"	" "
7	" "	"	" "	" "	"	" "
8	" "	"	" "	" "	"	" "
9	No. 1			No. 2		
10	Hiram Pickens	"	Chick Card 903	No. 5		
11	" "	"	" " "	No. 5		
12	No. 1			No. 5[sic]		

(NOTES)

No. 1 also known as Listeman.
No. 5 on Chickasaw Roll as Benda Lewis
No. 8 " " " " Looksie "
Josiah Lewis, above, also known as Josiah Calhoun.
No. 4 is wife of Alfred Owens on Chickasaw Card #D.293
No. 9 Enrolled Feby. 24, 1900
No. 5 is now the wife of Alfred Owens, on Chickasaw Card #D.293.
   Evidence of marriage requested July 8, 1902; filed herein Aug. 5, 1902
No. 7 Died Aug. 5, 1900; Enrollment cancelled by Dept Sept. 13, 1904.
No. 4 died Sept. 10, 1900; proof of death filed Oct. 5, 1902.
   Father of No. 12 is No. 1; Mother of No. 12 is No. 2
No. 12 Born July 7, 1902; enrolled Sept. 25, 1902.   *(No. 12 Dawes' Roll No. 4139)*
No. 10 " " 18, 1900; " July 8, 1902
No. 11 " Nov. 20, 1901; " " 8, 1902.
No. 9 died March 29, 1900; *(remainder illegible)*

Sept. 28, '98.

RESIDENCE: Pontotoc COUNTY					CARD NO.			
POST OFFICE: Waupaunuka, I.T.					FIELD NO.			

NAME	RELATIONSHIP TO PERSON FIRST NAMED	AGE	SEX	BLOOD	TRIBAL ENROLLMENT		
					YEAR	COUNTY	PAGE
1 Owens, Solomon	NAMED	27	M	3/4	1897	Pontotoc	56

164

	NAME	RELATION-SHIP	AGE	SEX	BLOOD	YEAR		
2	" ~~Rosa~~	~~Wife~~	17	F	~~Full~~	1897	~~Chick residing in Choc Nation, 3rd Dist~~	65
3	" ~~Sarah~~	~~Dau~~	~~10mo~~	"	~~7/8~~	DIED	PRIOR TO SEPTEMBER 25 1902	
4	" Mary J.	wife	23	F	I.W.			

TRIBAL ENROLLMENT OF PARENTS

	NAME OF FATHER	YEAR	COUNTY	NAME OF MOTHER	YEAR	COUNTY
1	Mason Owens	Dead	Chick Roll	Susan Owens	Dead	Chickasaw Roll
2	~~Coleman Perry~~	~~1897~~	~~Chick resid'g in Choct. N. 1st Dist~~	~~Elsie Perry~~	"	~~Chick resid'g in Choc. N. 1st Dist.~~
3	~~No. 1~~			~~No. 2~~		
4	?uis Williams	Dead	non citizen	Candy Williams		non citizen

(NOTES)

No. 2 on Choctaw Roll as Rosa Perry

(Next 3 notations illegible)

No. 4 placed hereon under order of Commissioner to Five Civilized Tribes of Feby. 26, 1906, holding that
application was made for her enrollment within the time provided by the Act of Congress approved July 1, 1902
Sept. 28, '98.

RESIDENCE: Pontotoc COUNTY   CARD NO.

POST OFFICE: Johnson, I.T.   FIELD NO.

	NAME	RELATION-SHIP TO PERSON FIRST NAMED	AGE	SEX	BLOOD	TRIBAL ENROLLMENT		
						YEAR	COUNTY	PAGE
1	La Count, Benjamin	NAMED	42	M	I.W.			
2	" Minnie Davis	Wife	22	F	1/8	1893	Pontotoc	P.R.#2 60

TRIBAL ENROLLMENT OF PARENTS

	NAME OF FATHER	YEAR	COUNTY	NAME OF MOTHER	YEAR	COUNTY
1	Jas La Count	Dead	Non Citizen	Eliz. La Count	Dead	Non Citizen
2	Joshua Davis	"	Chickasaw Roll	Laura Davis		Chick. Roll

(NOTES)

No. 2 on 1893 Roll as Minnie Davis

No. 1 enrolled Aug. 8, 1899.   *(No. 1 Dawes' Roll No. 738)*

No. 2   "   Sept. 28, 1898.

P.O. Okra, I.T. 10/20/02

RESIDENCE: Pontotoc   COUNTY   CARD NO.

POST OFFICE: Viola, I.T.   FIELD NO.

NAME	RELATION-SHIP TO PERSON FIRST NAMED	AGE	SEX	BLOOD	TRIBAL ENROLLMENT		
					YEAR	COUNTY	PAGE
1 Mosley, Forbus	NAMED	50	M	1/2	1897	Pontotoc	52
2 " Maria	Wife	42	F	1/2	1897	"	52

	TRIBAL ENROLLMENT OF PARENTS						
NAME OF FATHER	YEAR	COUNTY	NAME OF MOTHER	YEAR	COUNTY		
1 Simon Mosley	Dead	Choctaw Roll	Betsey Mosley	Dead	Chickasaw Roll		
2 Jacob Thompson	"	" "	Salina Thompson	"	" "		

(NOTES)

Sept. 28, '98.

RESIDENCE: Pickens   COUNTY   CARD NO.

POST OFFICE: Hewitt, Ind. Ter.   FIELD NO.

NAME	RELATION-SHIP TO PERSON FIRST NAMED	AGE	SEX	BLOOD	TRIBAL ENROLLMENT		
					YEAR	COUNTY	PAGE
1 Snowden, William H	NAMED	56	M	I.W.	1893	Pay Roll No. 1	131

	TRIBAL ENROLLMENT OF PARENTS						
NAME OF FATHER	YEAR	COUNTY	NAME OF MOTHER	YEAR	COUNTY		
1 Jacob Snowden	Dead	Non Citizen	Mary A. Snowden	Dead	Non Citizen		

(NOTES)

(All notations illegible)   *(No. 1 Dawes' Roll No. 546)*

P.O. Pike 9/9-04   Sept. 28/98.

RESIDENCE: Tishomingo   COUNTY   CARD NO.

POST OFFICE: Davis, Ind. Ter.   FIELD NO.

NAME	RELATION-SHIP TO PERSON FIRST NAMED	AGE	SEX	BLOOD	TRIBAL ENROLLMENT		
					YEAR	COUNTY	PAGE
1 Petigrew, John DEAD	NAMED	35	M	Full	1897	Tishomingo	31
2 Grayson, Lizzie	Wife	20	F	"	1897	"	31
3 Petigrew, Oscar	Son	15	M	"	1897	"	31
4 " Viola	Dau	10	F	"	1897	"	31
5 " Arch McCannon	Son	2mo	M	"			
6 " ~~Archie~~	~~Son~~	1	M	"			

166

7	Grayson, Maggie	Dau of No. 2	2mo	F	"		

TRIBAL ENROLLMENT OF PARENTS

	NAME OF FATHER	YEAR	COUNTY	NAME OF MOTHER	YEAR	COUNTY
1	~~Morgan Petigrew~~	~~Dead~~	~~Chickasaw Roll~~	~~Sholakacha~~	~~Dead~~	~~Chickasaw Roll~~
2	Gabriel Brown	1897	Pontotoc	Lucy Brown	1897	Pontotoc
3	No. 1			Mary Petigrew	Dead	"
4	No. 1			Tannie "	"	Tishomingo
5	No. 1			No. 2		
6	~~No. 1~~			~~No. 2~~		
7	Gibson T. Grayson	1897	Pontotoc	No. 2		

(NOTES)

No. 3 on Chickasaw roll as Osacar
No. 5 Affidavit received but returned for correction Dec. 14/99. Child born Oct. 18/99.
No. 2 is now the wife of Gibson T. Grayson on Chickasaw card #41. Evidence of marriage filed May 10, 1902
No. 6 Enrolled Dec. 6, 1900. This notation is an error. See proof of birth Apr. 8, 1902.
No. 1 died Aug. 2, 1899; proof of death filed July 6, 1901.
    Evidence of birth of No. 5 received and filed April 8 1902. Full given name is "Arch McCannon".
No. 7 Born March 10, 1902; enrolled May 10, 1902.

Sept. 28/98.

RESIDENCE:	Tishomingo	COUNTY			CARD NO.			
POST OFFICE:	Emmet, Ind. Ter.				FIELD NO.			

	NAME	RELATION-SHIP TO PERSON FIRST NAMED	AGE	SEX	BLOOD	TRIBAL ENROLLMENT		
						YEAR	COUNTY	PAGE
1	Washington, George	NAMED	25	M	1/2	1897	Tishomingo	35
2	" Kate	Wife	23	F	I.W.	1897	"	79
3	" Johnie Lou	Dau	16mos	"	1/4			
4	" Clela May	Dau	2mos	F	1/4			
5	" Osler Flint	Son	2mos	M	1/4			

TRIBAL ENROLLMENT OF PARENTS

	NAME OF FATHER	YEAR	COUNTY	NAME OF MOTHER	YEAR	COUNTY
1	Geo Washington	Dead	Chickasaw roll	Serena Black		white woman
2	Samuel Maddox	"	non citizen	Elizabeth Maddox		non citizen
3	No. 1			No. 2		
4	No. 1			No. 2		
5	No. 1			No. 2		

(NOTES)

No. 1 Evidence of marriage of parents attached to card No. D.88 1/5/00   *(No. 2 Dawes' Roll No. 737)*
No. 3 Affidavit of attending physician to be supplied. Received Oct. 5/98.

No. 4 Enrolled May 25, 1900.
No. 5 born Dec. 10, 1901. Enrolled Feby. 3, 1902.

Sept. 28/98.

	NAME	RELATION-SHIP TO PERSON FIRST NAMED	AGE	SEX	BLOOD	TRIBAL ENROLLMENT		
						YEAR	COUNTY	PAGE
1	Ayakatubby, Alice	NAMED	21	F	Full	1897	Pontotoc	50
2	Sealy, Rosa	Dau	1	"	"			
3	" Henry	Son	4	M	"	1897	"	50
4	Cowoy, Asaw	Son	1	M	"			

RESIDENCE: Pontotoc   COUNTY   CARD NO.
POST OFFICE: Pontotoc, Ind. Ter.   FIELD NO.

TRIBAL ENROLLMENT OF PARENTS

	NAME OF FATHER	YEAR	COUNTY	NAME OF MOTHER	YEAR	COUNTY
1	Davis Ayakatubby	Dead	Chickasaw roll	Sissy Ayakatubby	Dead	Chickasaw roll
2	Willis Sealy	1897	Pontotoc	No. 1		
3	" "	"	"	"		
4	Billy Cowoy			No. 1		

(NOTES)

No. 1 on Chickasaw roll as Alice Sealy
    Husband and two children on Chickasaw Card #335
No. 3 transferred from Chickasaw card #335 to this card Sept. 4, 1902
No. 4 was born Aug. 27, 1902. application received March 4, 1905,   *(No. 4 Dawes' Roll No. 4976)*
    under Act of Congress approved March 3, 1905
No. 4 illegitimate

Sept. 28/98.

	NAME	RELATION-SHIP TO PERSON FIRST NAMED	AGE	SEX	BLOOD	TRIBAL ENROLLMENT		
						YEAR	COUNTY	PAGE
1	Latta, Emely	NAMED	48	F	Full	1897	Tishomingo	35
2	" Allen	Husband	59	M	I.W.	"	"	"

RESIDENCE: Tishomingo   COUNTY   CARD NO.
POST OFFICE: Emmet. Ind. Ter.   FIELD NO.

TRIBAL ENROLLMENT OF PARENTS

	NAME OF FATHER	YEAR	COUNTY	NAME OF MOTHER	YEAR	COUNTY
1	Robert Colbert	Dead	Chickasaw Roll	Nunnaby	Dead	Chickasaw roll
2	G.W. Latta		Non Citz	Peggy Latta	D'd	Cherokee

(NOTES)

Wife of Allen latta, a Cherokee by blood, but recognized as a Chickasaw by intermarriage

No. 1 on Chickasaw roll as Emely

No. 1 is wife of Allen Latta Chickasaw D.259

No. 2 is a Cherokee, resided since the Civil War in the Chickasaw Nation
    Married a Chickasaw in 1864.

No. 2 transferred from Chickasaw card #D.259   *(No. 2 Dawes' Roll No. 471)*

Sept. 28/98.

RESIDENCE: Pickens   COUNTY   CARD No.

POST OFFICE: Berwyn, Ind. Ter.   FIELD No.

NAME	RELATIONSHIP TO PERSON FIRST NAMED	AGE	SEX	BLOOD	TRIBAL ENROLLMENT		
					YEAR	COUNTY	PAGE
1 Boyd, Thomas	NAMED	19	M	1/8	1897	Pickens	21

TRIBAL ENROLLMENT OF PARENTS

	NAME OF FATHER	YEAR	COUNTY	NAME OF MOTHER	YEAR	COUNTY
1	T.C. Boyd	Dead	Tishomingo	Sarah Boyd (I.W.)	Dead	Tishomingo

(NOTES)

No. 1 said to be in Phillipine Islands with U.S. Army

Sept. 28/98.

RESIDENCE: Pontotoc   COUNTY   CARD No.

POST OFFICE: FIELD No.

	NAME	RELATIONSHIP TO PERSON FIRST NAMED	AGE	SEX	BLOOD	TRIBAL ENROLLMENT		
						YEAR	COUNTY	PAGE
1	Hunnatubby, Solomon	NAMED	65	M	Full	1897	Pontotoc	58
2	" Easter	Wife	62	F	"	1897	"	58
3	Duncan, Eliza	Dau	30	"	"	1897	"	58
4	John, Selion	G.Dau	12	"	1/2	1897	"	58
5	" Nellie	" "	7	"	1/2	1897	"	58
6	Howard, Charlie	" Son	1	M	1/2			
7	Duncan, Frona	G.Dau	1	F	1/2			

TRIBAL ENROLLMENT OF PARENTS

	NAME OF FATHER	YEAR	COUNTY	NAME OF MOTHER	YEAR	COUNTY
1	Hunnatubby	Dead	Chickasaw roll		Dead	Chickasaw roll
2	Simon	"	" "	*(Name Illegible)*	"	" "
3	John Duncan	"	" "	No. 2		
4	(Illegitimate)			No. 3		

169

5	"			No. 3		
6	"			No. 3		
7	"			No. ?		

(NOTES)

No. 4 on Chickasaw roll as Selion Hunnatubby
No. 5 "   "   " " Nellie   "
No. 3 also on 1897 Chickasaw roll as Eliza John, Page 95, Pontotoc Co.
No. 4 "   " 1897   "   "   " Sarah John, "   94   "   "
No. 5 "   " 1897   "   " Page 95
No. 1 Died August 4, 1899. Evidence of death filed March 26, 1901.
No. 7 born March 17, 1902; Application received Apl. 27, 1905,   *(No. 7 Dawes' Roll No. 4965)*
       under Act of Congress. approved March 3, 1905.

Sept. 28/98,

RESIDENCE: Pickens **COUNTY**				CARD No.		
POST OFFICE: Cumberland, Ind. Ter.				FIELD No.		

NAME	RELATION-SHIP TO PERSON FIRST NAMED	**AGE**	**SEX**	**BLOOD**	TRIBAL ENROLLMENT		
					YEAR	**COUNTY**	**PAGE**
1 Bussell, Lucy		11	F	1/2	1897	Pickens	8

TRIBAL ENROLLMENT OF PARENTS						
NAME OF FATHER	**YEAR**	**COUNTY**	**NAME OF MOTHER**	**YEAR**	**COUNTY**	
1 Stephen Bussell	1897	Pickens	Winnie Steele		White woman	

(NOTES)

Mother, Winnie Steele, on Chickasaw Card, No. D.86.

Sept. 28/98.

RESIDENCE: Choctaw Nation ~~COUNTY~~				CARD No.		
POST OFFICE: Waupaunuka, Ind. Ter.				FIELD No.		

	NAME	RELATION-SHIP TO PERSON FIRST NAMED	**AGE**	**SEX**	**BLOOD**	TRIBAL ENROLLMENT		
						YEAR	**COUNTY**	**PAGE**
1	James, Walton		43	M	3/4	1897	Chick residing in Choctaw N. 3rd Dist.	75
2	" Susan	Wife	23	F	Full	1897	" " " "	75
3	" Minnie	Dau	15	"	7/8	1897	" " " "	75
4	" Turner	Son	13	M	7/8	1897	" " " "	75
5	" Felix	"	12	"	7/8	1897	" " " "	75
6	" Moses	"	7	"	7/8	1897	" " " "	75
7	" Zelia	Dau	5	F	7/8	1897	" " " "	75

8	"	Simeon	Son	3	M	7/8			
9	"	Joseph	"	1	"	7/8			
~~10~~	"	~~George D.~~	"	~~10mo~~	"	~~7/8~~	DIED PRIOR TO SEPTEMBER 25 1902		

TRIBAL ENROLLMENT OF PARENTS

	NAME OF FATHER	YEAR	COUNTY	NAME OF MOTHER	YEAR	COUNTY
1	Booker James	Dead	Chickasaw roll	Martha James	Dead	Chickasaw roll
2	James Frazier	1897	Pontotoc	Icy Frazier	"	" "
3	No. 1			No. 2		
4	No. 1			No. 2		
5	No. 1			No. 2		
6	No. 1			No. 2		
7	No. 1			No. 2		
8	No. 1			No. 2		
9	No. 1			No. 2		
~~10~~	No. 1			No. 2		

(NOTES)

No. 10 Died Jan. 11, 1900; Evidence of death *(remainder illegible)*
Evidence of birth of No. 8 received and filed Feby 5, 1903.   *(No. 8 Dawes' Roll No. 4751)*
No. 7 on Chickasaw roll as Eula Janes
Nos 8 and 9 on Choctaw Census Record No. 2, Page 307, Atoka County,
        transferred to Chickasaw roll by Dawes Com.
No. 2 Died July 27, 1901; proof of death filed April 17, 1902.
      Evidence of birth of No. 9 received and filed April 17, 1902.
No. 10 enrolled Nov. 3/99
No. 10 died Jany 11, 1900. Proof of death received and filed Dec. 30, 1902.

P.O. Byrne, I.T. 12/22/02.   Sept. 28/98.

RESIDENCE: Tishomingo	COUNTY					CARD NO.		
POST OFFICE:	Emmet, Ind. Ter.					FIELD NO.		

	NAME	RELATION-SHIP TO PERSON FIRST NAMED	AGE	SEX	BLOOD	TRIBAL ENROLLMENT		
						YEAR	COUNTY	PAGE
1	Melton, George Arnold	NAMED	49	M	I.W.	1897	Tishomingo	79
2	" Mary Jane	Wife	45	F	3/4	1897	"	35
3	Brown, Lena	Ward	17	"	Full	1897	"	35

TRIBAL ENROLLMENT OF PARENTS

	NAME OF FATHER	YEAR	COUNTY	NAME OF MOTHER	YEAR	COUNTY
1	Wm N. Melton	Dead	non citizen	Agnes Melton	Dead	Non-citizen
2	O-kla-non-o-by	"	Chickasaw roll	Rhoda	"	Chickasaw roll

| 3 | Joe Brown | " | Pontotoc | Lizzie Brown | " | Pontotoc |

(NOTES)

No. 1 on Chickasaw roll as G.A. Melton.   *(No. 1 Dawes' Roll No. 36)*

   Marriage license, or certified copy to be supplied. Received Nov. 12/98.

No. 3 is now the wife of Luther J. Horton - non-citizen. Evidence of marriage filed Nov. 8, 1902.

Sept. 28/98

RESIDENCE: Tishomingo   COUNTY   CARD NO.

POST OFFICE: Davis, Ind. Ter.   FIELD NO.

NAME	RELATIONSHIP TO PERSON FIRST NAMED	AGE	SEX	BLOOD	TRIBAL ENROLLMENT		
					YEAR	COUNTY	PAGE
1 ~~Alexander, Chillie~~	NAMED	~~61~~	~~M~~	~~Full~~	~~1897~~	~~Tishomingo~~	~~30~~
2 " Mary Ann	Wife	30	F	"	1897	"	30
3 " Minnie	Dau	13	"	"	1897	"	30
4 " Josie	"	8	"	"	1897	"	30
5 Lacher, Ada	Neice[sic] in las	15	"	"	1897	"	30
6 Nail, Jessie	Neice[sic] in law	6	"	"	1897	"	30

TRIBAL ENROLLMENT OF PARENTS

	NAME OF FATHER	YEAR	COUNTY	NAME OF MOTHER	YEAR	COUNTY
1	~~Is-ta-tubby~~	~~Dead~~	~~Chickasaw roll~~	~~Nutch-u-ma-chey~~	~~Dead~~	~~Chickasaw roll~~
2	Johnie Starr	"	" "	Pun-na-ho-ye	"	" "
3	No. 1			No. 2		
4	No. 1			No. 2		
5	Noah Lacher	Dead	Tishomingo	Minerva Lacher	Dead	Tishomingo
6	Dixon Nail	1897	"	Annie Nail	"	"

(NOTES)

No. 2 on Chickasaw roll as Mayan Alexander

No. 5 " " " Pickens County, page 19 as Ada Leecher

No. 1 Died about 1899; Proof of death filed Oct. 18, 1902.

No. 1 Died Feb. 6, 1899; proof of death filed Oct. 29, 1902.

   Father of No. 6, on Chickasaw Card #897 as Dixon Anpahishcha.

Sept. 28/98.

Chickasaw Enrollment Cards 1898-1914
Chickasaw by Blood   Volume IV

RESIDENCE: Tishomingo   COUNTY   CARD NO.
POST OFFICE: Davis, Ind. Ter.   FIELD NO.

	NAME	RELATION-SHIP TO PERSON FIRST NAMED	AGE	SEX	BLOOD	TRIBAL ENROLLMENT		
						YEAR	COUNTY	PAGE
1	~~James, Simeon~~	NAMED	45	M	~~Full~~	~~1893~~	~~Tishomingo~~	~~120~~
2	" ~~Lowana~~	~~Wife~~	~~40~~	F	~~"~~	~~1893~~	~~"~~	~~120~~
3	" Henry	Son	10	M	"	1893	"	120

TRIBAL ENROLLMENT OF PARENTS

	NAME OF FATHER	YEAR	COUNTY	NAME OF MOTHER	YEAR	COUNTY
1	~~(Name Illegible)~~	~~Dead~~	~~Chickasaw roll~~	~~(Name Illegible)~~	~~Dead~~	~~Chickasaw roll~~
2	~~Chilley Alexander~~	~~1897~~	~~Tishomingo~~	~~Caroline Alexander~~	~~"~~	~~" "~~
3	No. 1			No. 2		

(NOTES)

No. 1 on Chickasaw roll as Simion James
No. 2 "   "   "   " Rena   "
Nos. 1-2-3 also on 1896 Chickasaw Roll, Tishomingo Co, page 92.

Sept. 28/98

RESIDENCE: Pickens   COUNTY   CARD NO.
POST OFFICE: Cumberland, Ind. Ter.   FIELD NO.

	NAME	RELATION-SHIP TO PERSON FIRST NAMED	AGE	SEX	BLOOD	TRIBAL ENROLLMENT		
						YEAR	COUNTY	PAGE
1	Watkins, George W.	NAMED	43	M	I.W.	1897	Pickens	77
2	" Emma A.	Wife	26	F	1/8	1897	"	8
3	" Calvin D.	Son	7	M	1/16	1897	"	8
4	" Oscar Oliver	"	6	"	1/16	1897	"	8
5	" Albert Elverson	"	2	"	1/16	1897	"	8
6	" Onie May	Dau	5mo	F	1/16			

TRIBAL ENROLLMENT OF PARENTS

	NAME OF FATHER	YEAR	COUNTY	NAME OF MOTHER	YEAR	COUNTY
1	John Watkins	Dead	non-citizen	Jane Watkins	Dead	non-citizen
2	Chas. Gooding	"	" "	Monon T. Gooding	1897	Panola
3	No. 1			No. 2		
4	No. 1			No. 2		
5	No. 1			No. 2		
6	No. 1			No. 2		

(NOTES)

No. 2 on Chickasaw roll as Ema Watkins

173

Chickasaw Enrollment Cards 1898-1914
Chickasaw by Blood   Volume IV

No. 3 "   "   "   " Calvin "
No. 4 "   "   "   " Oscar "
No. 5 "   "   "   " Albert E. "
No. 1 Admitted as an intermarried citizen and   *(No. 1 Dawes' Roll No. 323)*
    Nos. 2,3 and 4 as citizens by blood by Dawes Commission in 1896; Chickasaw case #95; No appeal.
No. 6 enrolled Nov. 4/99
No. 6 Died Oct. 19, 1900; proof of death filed Nov. 1, 1902.

Sept. 28/98.

	NAME	RELATION-SHIP TO PERSON FIRST NAMED	AGE	SEX	BLOOD	TRIBAL ENROLLMENT		
						YEAR	COUNTY	PAGE
1	White, Harry Harvel		23	M	1/4	1897	Pontotoc	60
2	" Cora Malissia	Dau	1	F	1/8	~~1897~~	"	~~86~~
3	" Harvel E.	Son	5mo	M	1/8			
4	" Ethel S.	Dau	9mo	F	1/8			
5	" Annie	Wife	21	"	I.W.			

RESIDENCE: Pickens **COUNTY**   CARD NO.
POST OFFICE: Beefcreek, Ind. Ter.   FIELD NO.

TRIBAL ENROLLMENT OF PARENTS

	NAME OF FATHER	YEAR	COUNTY	NAME OF MOTHER	YEAR	COUNTY
1	S.L. White (I.W.)	1897	Pontotoc	Malissa A. White	1897	Pontotoc
2	No. 1			Annie White		white woman
3	No. 1			" "		" "
4	No. 1			" "		" "
5	J.W. Wardwell		Non Citizen	Susan Wardwell		Non Citizen

(NOTES)
No. 5 See decision of June 21, '04.
No. 1 on Chickasaw roll as H.H. White; husband of Annie White, on Chickasaw Card No. D.34.
No. 3 Enrolled May 25, 1900.
No. 4 Born Dec. 1, 1901. Enrolled Sept. 30, 1902.   *(No. 4 Dawes' Roll No. 4138)*
No. 2 Proof of birth received and filed Oct. 29, 1902.   *(No. 2 Dawes' Roll No. 4137)*
    See Chickasaw No. D.34.
No. 5 transferred from Chick D-34 July 7, 1904.   *(No. 5 Dawes' Roll No. 388)*
    See decision of June 21, 1904.

P.O. Wynnewood, I.T.   Sept. 28/98.

RESIDENCE: Tishomingo   COUNTY   CARD NO.
POST OFFICE: Tishomingo, Ind. Ter.   FIELD NO.

NAME	RELATION-SHIP TO PERSON FIRST NAMED	AGE	SEX	BLOOD	TRIBAL ENROLLMENT		
					YEAR	COUNTY	PAGE
1 McGee, Archie	NAMED	31	M	1/2	1897	Tishomingo	37
2 " Minnie	Dau	4	F	1/4	1897	"	37
3 " Isaac	Son	3	M	1/4	1897	"	37

TRIBAL ENROLLMENT OF PARENTS

	NAME OF FATHER	YEAR	COUNTY	NAME OF MOTHER	YEAR	COUNTY
1	Cornelius McGee	Dead	Choctaw roll	Liza McGee	Dead	Chickasaw roll
2	No. 1			Nannie McGee		white woman
3	No. 1			" "		" "

(NOTES)

No. 1 on Chickasaw roll as Arch McGee
No. 1 Died March 20, 1899, proof of death filed Oct. 20, 1902.

Sept.. 28/98.

RESIDENCE: Tishomingo   COUNTY   CARD NO.
POST OFFICE: Emmet, Ind. Ter.   FIELD NO.

NAME	RELATION-SHIP TO PERSON FIRST NAMED	AGE	SEX	BLOOD	TRIBAL ENROLLMENT		
					YEAR	COUNTY	PAGE
1 Robinson, Susan	NAMED	37	F	Full	1897	Tishomingo	33
2 Colbert, Jeff	Son	19	M	"	1897	"	33

TRIBAL ENROLLMENT OF PARENTS

	NAME OF FATHER	YEAR	COUNTY	NAME OF MOTHER	YEAR	COUNTY
1	Cho-co-na-he-cha	Dead	Chickasaw roll	Che-ho-chee	Dead	Chickasaw roll
2	Ben Colbert	1897	Pickens	No. 1		

(NOTES)

No. 2 Administration papers filed by Joseph (Illegible)
No. 2 is now the husband of Lizzie Conway on Chickasaw card #1046 Nov. 7, 1902

Sept. 28/98.

RESIDENCE: Panola   COUNTY   CARD NO.
POST OFFICE: Colbert, Ind. Ter.   FIELD NO.

NAME	RELATION-SHIP TO PERSON FIRST NAMED	AGE	SEX	BLOOD	TRIBAL ENROLLMENT		
					YEAR	COUNTY	PAGE
1 Hendrickson, Susan	NAMED	42	F	Full	1897	Panola	5

| 2 | Bourland, Elsie | | | Dau | 18 | " | 1/2 | 1893 | | " | | 8 |

TRIBAL ENROLLMENT OF PARENTS

	NAME OF FATHER	YEAR	COUNTY	NAME OF MOTHER	YEAR	COUNTY
1	Martin Sheco	Dead	Chickasaw roll	Delphie Sheco	Dead	Chickasaw roll
2	King Perkins	"	Choctaw "	No. 1		

(NOTES)

No. 1 on Chickasaw roll as Susan Hendrix
No. 2 Seperated from her husband Louis Bourland
No. 2 also on 1896 Chickasaw roll, Panola County Page 92
No. 2 on 1893 Chickasaw Pay roll No. 2, Page 8, as Elsie Perkins

Sept. 28/98.

RESIDENCE: Pickens   COUNTY   CARD NO.

POST OFFICE: Cumberland, Ind. Ter.   FIELD NO.

NAME	RELATION-SHIP TO PERSON FIRST NAMED	AGE	SEX	BLOOD	TRIBAL ENROLLMENT		
					YEAR	COUNTY	PAGE
1	Seawright, Lula		17	F	3/8	1897	Pickens	8
2	" Stella Adeline	Dau	2mos	"	3/16			
3	" Ula	Dau	6mos	"	3/16			
4	" Leala	Dau	2mos	F	3/16			

TRIBAL ENROLLMENT OF PARENTS

	NAME OF FATHER	YEAR	COUNTY	NAME OF MOTHER	YEAR	COUNTY
1	Ed Brown	Dead	Cherokee Citz	Elsie Brown	1897	Pickens
2	David Seawright		non citizen	No. 1		
3	" "		" "	No. 1		
4	" "		" "	No. 1		

(NOTES)

No. 1 On Chickasaw roll as Lula Brown
No. 2 Affidavit of attending physician to be supplied. Received Oct. 11/98
    Ula, born Nov. 8/99, on Card No. D.301
    Transferred from Chickasaw card D.301 May 24, 1900
No. 4 born Dec. 6, 1901; Enrolled Feby. 8, 1902.

P.O. Globe, I.T.   Sept. 28/98.

RESIDENCE: Pickens   COUNTY   CARD NO.

POST OFFICE: Cumberland, Ind. Ter.   FIELD NO.

	NAME	RELATION-SHIP TO PERSON FIRST NAMED	AGE	SEX	BLOOD	TRIBAL ENROLLMENT		
						YEAR	COUNTY	PAGE
1	Ross, Ada	NAMED	21	F	5/8	1897	Pickens	8
2	" Homer Wilson	Son	3	M	5/16	1897	"	8
3	" Bessie	Dau	7mos	F	5/16			
4	" Bettie	Dau	1mo	F	5/16			
5	" Thomas Cecil	Son	1mo	M	5/16			

TRIBAL ENROLLMENT OF PARENTS

	NAME OF FATHER	YEAR	COUNTY	NAME OF MOTHER	YEAR	COUNTY
1	Wilson Colbert	Dead	Chickasaw roll	Elsie Brown	1897	Pickens
2	Thomas Ross		Non Citizen	No. 1		
3	" "		" "	No. 1		
4	" "		" "	No. 1		
5	" "		" "	No. 1		

(NOTES)

No. 2 on Chickasaw Roll as Hanna Ross

No. 3 Affidavit of attending physician to be supplied. Received Oct. 21/98.

No. 4 Born Nov. 15, 1899; transferred to this card Feb. 1, 1902

No. 5 Born March 12, 1901; Enrolled April 3, 1902

    Bettis Ross born Nov. 15/9 on Card No. D.304.

Ravia, I.T.   Sept. 28/98.

RESIDENCE: Pickens   COUNTY   CARD NO.

POST OFFICE: Cumberland, Ind. Ter.   FIELD NO.

	NAME	RELATION-SHIP TO PERSON FIRST NAMED	AGE	SEX	BLOOD	TRIBAL ENROLLMENT		
						YEAR	COUNTY	PAGE
1	Brown, Elsie	NAMED	43	F	3/4	1897	Pickens	8
2	" Lela	Dau	16	"	3/8	1897	"	8
3	" John	Son	15	M	3/8	1897	"	8
4	" Edna	Dau	13	F	3/8	1897	"	8
5	" Lucy	"	11	"	3/8	1897	"	8
6	" Willie	Son	5	M	3/8	1897	"	8
7	" Ethel	G.Dau	9mo	F	3/16			
8	Colbert, Frank	Son	23	M	5/8	1897	Pickens	8
9	Seawright, Jack	G.Son	6mo	M	3/16			

177

Chickasaw Enrollment Cards 1898-1914
Chickasaw by Blood   Volume IV

	TRIBAL ENROLLMENT OF PARENTS					
	NAME OF FATHER	YEAR	COUNTY	NAME OF MOTHER	YEAR	COUNTY
1	Jim McCoy	Dead	Chickasaw roll	Sibbie McCoy	Dead	Chickasaw roll
2	Ed Brown	"	Cherokee Citz	No. 1		
3	" "	"	" "	No. 1		
4	" "	"	" "	No. 1		
5	" "	"	" "	No. 1		
6	" "	"	" "	No. 1		
7	Riley Gregory		Non Citizen	No. 2		
8	Wilson Colbert	Dead	Chickasaw roll	No. 1		
9	Wm Z. Searight		Non Citizen	No. 2		

(NOTES)

No. 8 in penitentiary at Columbus, Ohio
No. 2 was married to Wm Zuitman Seawright, a non-citizen and died March 3, 1900
No. 2 Proof of death rec'd and filed Nov. 8, 1902
No. 9 Enrolled April 18, 1900

P.O. Troy, I.T.   Sept. 28/98.

RESIDENCE: Tishomingo COUNTY					CARD NO.			
POST OFFICE: Emmet, Ind. Ter.					FIELD NO.			
NAME	RELATION-SHIP TO PERSON FIRST NAMED	AGE	SEX	BLOOD	TRIBAL ENROLLMENT			
					YEAR	COUNTY		PAGE
1	Latta, George Washington	NAMED	30	M	1/2	1897	Tishomingo	35
2	" Rebecca	Wife	26	F	I.W.	1897	"	79
3	" Johnie	Son	5	M	1/4	1897	"	35
4	" Jeff	"	3	"	1/4	1897	"	35
5	" Fred	"	11mos	"	1/4			
6	" Willie A.	Son	1mo	M	1/4			

	TRIBAL ENROLLMENT OF PARENTS					
	NAME OF FATHER	YEAR	COUNTY	NAME OF MOTHER	YEAR	COUNTY
1	Allen Latta		Cherokee Citz	Emily Latta	1897	Tishomingo
2	Thos. Blankenship		non citizen	Polly Blankenship		Non citizen
3	No. 1			No. 2		
4	No. 1			No. 2		
5	No. 1			No. 2		
6	No. 1			No. 2		

(NOTES)

No. 1 on Chickasaw roll as George W. Latta
No. 2 "   "   "   " Becca Latta   *(No. 2 Dawes' Roll No. 130)*
No. 6 Enrolled June 17, 1901.

P.O. Ada, I.T. 11/11/02   Sept. 28/98.

RESIDENCE: Tishomingo   **COUNTY**   **CARD NO.**

POST OFFICE: Tishomingo, Ind. Ter.   **FIELD NO.**

	NAME	RELATION-SHIP TO PERSON FIRST NAMED	AGE	SEX	BLOOD	TRIBAL ENROLLMENT		
						YEAR	COUNTY	PAGE
1	Taylor, Daniel	NAMED	40	M	I.W.	1897	Tishomingo	83
2	" Vernie Dillard	Wife	19	F	3/16	1897	"	33
3	" Sarah Lucinda	Dau	3	"	3/32	1897	"	33
4	" Daniel Alexander	Son	1	M	3/32	1897	"	35
5	" Leo	Son	1mo	M	3/32			

TRIBAL ENROLLMENT OF PARENTS

	NAME OF FATHER	YEAR	COUNTY	NAME OF MOTHER	YEAR	COUNTY
1	John Taylor	Dead	non Citizen	Sarah Taylor	Dead	non Citizen
2	Ben Dillard	"	Choctaw roll	Nancy Taylor	1897	Tishomingo
3	No. 1			No. 2		
4	No. 1			No. 2		
5	No. 1			No. 2		

(NOTES)

No. 1 on Chickasaw roll as Dan Taylor   *(No. 1 Dawes' Roll No. 129)*
No. 2 "   "   "   " Bennie "
No. 3 "   "   "   " Lucy   "
No. 4 "   "   "   " Dan   " , Jr.   *(No. 4 Dawes' Roll No. 4136)*
No. 4 Proof of birth received and filed Oct. 9, 1902
No. 5 Enrolled July 16, 1901.

P.O. Shego, I.T. 12/2/02
   Sulphur, I.T. 3/15/03   Sept. 28/98.

RESIDENCE: Pickens   **COUNTY**   **CARD NO.**

POST OFFICE: Oakland, Ind. Ter.   **FIELD NO.**

	NAME	RELATION-SHIP TO PERSON FIRST NAMED	AGE	SEX	BLOOD	TRIBAL ENROLLMENT		
						YEAR	COUNTY	PAGE
1	Eastwood, Lewis James	NAMED	39	M	I.W.	1897	Pickens	77

2	"	Emma Luella	Wife	28	F	1/4	1897	"		9
3	"	Arthur Franklin	Son	7	M	1/8	1897	"		9
4	"	~~William Simon~~	"	~~5mos~~	"	~~1/8~~	DIED	PRIOR TO SEPTEMBER 25 1902		
5	Carroll, Joel Henry		StepSon	12	"	1/8	1897	Pickens		9
6	"	James Calvin	" "	10	"	1/8	1897	"		9

TRIBAL ENROLLMENT OF PARENTS

	NAME OF FATHER	YEAR	COUNTY	NAME OF MOTHER	YEAR	COUNTY
1	Lewis Eastwood	Dead	non citizen	Elizabeth Eastwood	Dead	non citizen
2	Joel Kemp	"	Chickasaw Roll	Cath. Sanders	1897	Chick residing in Choctaw N. 3rd Dist.
3	No. 1			Rhoda Eastwood	Dead	Pickens
4	~~No. 1~~			~~No. 2~~		
5	Jim Carroll	Dead	non citizen	No. 2		
6	" "	"	" "	No. 2		

(NOTES)

No. 1 On Chickasaw roll as L.J. Eastwood
No. 2 " " " " Ema "
No. 3 " " " " Arthur "
No. 5 " " " " Joel Carroll
No. 6 " " " " James "
No. 4 Affidavit of attending physician to be supplied. Received Oct. 4/98.
No. 4 Died Sept. 30, 1900; Proof of death filed Nov. 8, 1902
Certified copy of divorce proceeding between No. 2 and her former husband filed Feby, 18, 1903   Date of Application for Enrollment

P.O. Weaverton, I.T.   Sept. 28/98.

RESIDENCE: Tishomingo	COUNTY					CARD NO.		
POST OFFICE: Emmett, Ind. Ter.						FIELD NO.		

	NAME	RELATION-SHIP TO PERSON FIRST NAMED	AGE	SEX	BLOOD	TRIBAL ENROLLMENT		
						YEAR	COUNTY	PAGE
1	Bridges, William Francis		24	M	I.W.			
2	" Nettie	Wife	21	F	1/2	1897	Pontotoc	40
3	" Marion F.	Son	1mo	M	1/4			
4	" Juanita Zelma	1mo	1mo	F	1/4			

TRIBAL ENROLLMENT OF PARENTS

	NAME OF FATHER	YEAR	COUNTY	NAME OF MOTHER	YEAR	COUNTY
1	H.T. Bridges		non citizen	Mary E. Bridges		non citizen
2	Colbert A. Burris	1897	Pontotoc	Laura A. Burris (I.W.)	1897	Pontotoc
3	No. 1			No. 2		
4	No. 1			No. 2		

Chickasaw Enrollment Cards 1898-1914
Chickasaw by Blood   Volume IV

(NOTES)

No. 2 on Chickasaw roll as Nettie Burris   *(No. 1 Dawes' Roll No. 128)*
No. 3 enrolled Nov. 3/99
No. 4 born Jany. 10, 1902; Enrolled Feby 30, 1902

P.O. Hugo, I.T. 12/2/02   Sept. 28/98.

RESIDENCE: Tishomingo **COUNTY**   **CARD NO.**
POST OFFICE: Tishomingo, Ind. Ter.   **FIELD NO.**

	NAME	RELATION- SHIP TO PERSON FIRST NAMED	AGE	SEX	BLOOD	TRIBAL ENROLLMENT		
						YEAR	COUNTY	PAGE
1	Colbert, Margaret	NAMED	50	F	Full	1897	Tishomingo	34
2	Robinson, Eliza	G.Dau	8	"	"	1897	"	33

TRIBAL ENROLLMENT OF PARENTS

	NAME OF FATHER	YEAR	COUNTY	NAME OF MOTHER	YEAR	COUNTY
1	Chickasaw-na-nubby	Dead	Chickasaw roll	La-too-shee	Dead	Chickasaw roll
2	Robinson	"	" "	See-an	"	" "

(NOTES)

Sept. 28/98.

RESIDENCE: Tishomingo **COUNTY**   **CARD NO.**
POST OFFICE: Tishomingo, Ind. Ter.   **FIELD NO.**

	NAME	RELATION- SHIP TO PERSON FIRST NAMED	AGE	SEX	BLOOD	TRIBAL ENROLLMENT		
						YEAR	COUNTY	PAGE
1	Taylor, Nancy	NAMED	39	F	3/8	1897	Tishomingo	33
2	Dillard, Lizzie	Dau	11	"	3/16	1897	"	33
3	" Dick	Son	9	M	3/16	1897	"	33
4	Taylor, Johnie	"	6	"	3/16	1897	"	33
5	" Robert	"	4	"	3/16	1897	"	33
6	" Lula	Dau	2	F	3/16	1897	"	87
7	McCurley, Carrie	"	15	"	3/16	1897	"	33
8	Taylor, John W.P.	Son	2mo	M	3/16			

TRIBAL ENROLLMENT OF PARENTS

	NAME OF FATHER	YEAR	COUNTY	NAME OF MOTHER	YEAR	COUNTY
1	Cubby Love	Dead	Chickasaw roll	Sophie Love	Dead	Chickasaw roll
2	Ben Dillard	"	Choctaw "	No. 1		
3	" "	"	" "	No. 1		
4	John Taylor		Non Citizen	No. 1		

5	" "		" "	No. 1		
6	" "		" "	No. 1		
7	Ben Dillard	Dead	Choctaw roll	No. 1		
8	John C. Taylor		Non Citizen	No. 1		

(NOTES)

No. 7 wife of Anold[sic] McCurley, non citizen; on Chickasaw roll as Carrie Dillard

No. 8 born Dec. 19, 1901; Enrolled Feby 13, 1902

No. 6 Proof of birth received and filed Nov. 13, 1902

No. 6 Affidavits as to birth received and filed Nov. 17, 1902.

See affidavits of Nancy and John Taylor as to correct date of birth of No. 6, filed Jany 28, 1903.

P.O. Sulphur, I.T.   Sept. 28/98.

RESIDENCE: Pontotoc   **COUNTY**   **CARD NO.**

POST OFFICE: Wynnewood, Ind. Ter.   **FIELD NO.**

NAME	RELATION-SHIP TO PERSON FIRST NAMED	AGE	SEX	BLOOD	TRIBAL ENROLLMENT		
					YEAR	COUNTY	PAGE
1 Froman, Perry	NAMED	64	M	I.W.	1897	Pontotoc	80
2 " Levina	Wife	56	F	1/4	1897	"	60
3 " Celescaby	Dau	16	"	1/8	1897	"	60

TRIBAL ENROLLMENT OF PARENTS

	NAME OF FATHER	YEAR	COUNTY	NAME OF MOTHER	YEAR	COUNTY
1	Isaac Froman	Dead	Non Citizen	Frances Froman	Dead	Non citizen
2	Joseph Colbert	"	Chickasaw roll	Ziley Colbert	"	Chickasaw roll
3	No. 1			No. 2		

(NOTES)

No. 2 on Chickasaw roll as Louvina Forman   *(No. 1 Dawes' Roll No. 127)*

No. 3 "   "   "   "   Celescaby   "

                                                                      Sept. 28/98.

RESIDENCE: Tishomingo   **COUNTY**   **CARD NO.**

POST OFFICE: Regan, Ind. Ter.   **FIELD NO.**

NAME	RELATION-SHIP TO PERSON FIRST NAMED	AGE	SEX	BLOOD	TRIBAL ENROLLMENT		
					YEAR	COUNTY	PAGE
1 Moore, Nancy	NAMED	28	F	1/2	1897	Tishomingo	37
2 " Estella	Dau	3	"	3/4	1897	"	37
3 " Ethel	"	11/2	"	3/4	~~1897~~	"	~~87~~
4 Greenwood, Eula	Dau	3mo	F	3/4			

		TRIBAL ENROLLMENT OF PARENTS				
NAME OF FATHER	YEAR	COUNTY	NAME OF MOTHER	YEAR	COUNTY
1 William Moody	Dead	Non Citizen	Sarah Jane Sanders	1897	Tishomingo
2 Cornelius Moore	"	Tishomingo	No. 1		
3 " "	"	"	No. 1		
4 Sim Greenwood	1897	"	No. 1		

(NOTES)

No. 4 Born Nov. 21, 1901; enrolled Feby, 25, 1902.   *(No. 2 Dawes' Roll No. 4134)*
  Father of No. 4 on Chickasaw card #769   *(No. 3 Dawes' Roll No. 4135)*
  See affidavit of Nancy Moore as to degree of Chickasaw blood of Nos. 2 and 3
  filed Nov. 1, 1902.

Sept. 28/98.

RESIGENCE: Choctaw Nation   ~~COUNTY~~   *CARD No.*
POST OFFICE: Hartshorn, Ind. Ter.   *FIELD No.*

NAME	RELATION-SHIP TO PERSON FIRST NAMED	AGE	SEX	BLOOD	TRIBAL ENROLLMENT		
					YEAR	COUNTY	PAGE
1 Carney, William	FIRST NAMED	42	F[sic]	Full	1897	Chick residing in Choctaw N. 1st Dist.	71

		TRIBAL ENROLLMENT OF PARENTS				
NAME OF FATHER	YEAR	COUNTY	NAME OF MOTHER	YEAR	COUNTY
1 Pa-lin-stub-by	Dead	Chickasaw Roll	Tah-ho-nah	Dead	Chickasaw roll

(NOTES)

Sept. 28/98.

RESIDENCE: Pontotoc   *COUNTY*   *CARD No.*
POST OFFICE: Viola, Ind. Ter.   *FIELD No.*

NAME	RELATION-SHIP TO PERSON FIRST NAMED	AGE	SEX	BLOOD	TRIBAL ENROLLMENT		
					YEAR	COUNTY	PAGE
1 Milligan, Ida	NAMED	23	F	1/4	1897	Pontotoc	52
2 " Clell Franklin	Son	3	M	1/8	1897	"	52
3 " Simon James	"	1	"	1/8	~~1897~~	"	~~88~~
4 " Lenora Dell	Dau	2mo	F	1/8			

		TRIBAL ENROLLMENT OF PARENTS				
NAME OF FATHER	YEAR	COUNTY	NAME OF MOTHER	YEAR	COUNTY
1 Simon Mosely	Dead	Choctaw roll	Salina Mosely	Dead	Chickasaw roll
2 J.F. Milligan		non citizen	No. 1		
3 " " "		" "	No. 1		

183

4	" "	"		"	"		No. 1		

(NOTES)

No. 1 on Chickasaw roll as Ida N. Milligan
No. 2 "   "   "   " Clell   "
No. 3 "   "   "   " Simon   "
No. 4 Enrolled Aug. 6, 1900.

Sept. 28/98.

RESIDENCE: Pickens **COUNTY**   **CARD NO.**
POST OFFICE: Ardmore, Ind. Ter.   **FIELD NO.**

NAME	RELATION-SHIP TO PERSON FIRST NAMED	AGE	SEX	BLOOD	TRIBAL ENROLLMENT		
					YEAR	COUNTY	PAGE
1 Moore, Wesley	NAMED	22	M	3/4	1897	Tishomingo	31

TRIBAL ENROLLMENT OF PARENTS

	NAME OF FATHER	YEAR	COUNTY	NAME OF MOTHER	YEAR	COUNTY
1	Wm Moore	Dead	Tishomingo	Jincy Moore	Dead	Tishomingo

(NOTES)

(No. 1 Dawes' Roll No. 4133)

Sept. 28/98.

RESIDENCE: Tishomingo **COUNTY**   **CARD NO.**
POST OFFICE: Regan, Ind. Ter.   **FIELD NO.**

NAME	RELATION-SHIP TO PERSON FIRST NAMED	AGE	SEX	BLOOD	TRIBAL ENROLLMENT		
					YEAR	COUNTY	PAGE
1 Hamilton, Matilda	NAMED	50	F	Full	1897	Tishomingo	37

TRIBAL ENROLLMENT OF PARENTS

	NAME OF FATHER	YEAR	COUNTY	NAME OF MOTHER	YEAR	COUNTY
1	Mack Frazier	Dead	Chickasaw roll	Mary Frazier	Dead	Chickasaw roll

(NOTES)

Sept. 28/98.

RESIDENCE: Tishomingo **COUNTY**   **CARD NO.**
POST OFFICE: Regan, Ind. Ter.   **FIELD NO.**

NAME	RELATION-SHIP TO PERSON FIRST NAMED	AGE	SEX	BLOOD	TRIBAL ENROLLMENT		
					YEAR	COUNTY	PAGE
1 Sealey, Sina	NAMED	40	F	3/4	1897	Tishomingo	35
2 Tyson, Susan	Dau	14	"	5/8	1897	"	35

Chickasaw Enrollment Cards 1898-1914
Chickasaw by Blood   Volume IV

TRIBAL ENROLLMENT OF PARENTS

	NAME OF FATHER	YEAR	COUNTY	NAME OF MOTHER	YEAR	COUNTY
1	Johnson Pickens	Dead	Choctaw roll	Ste-cha-ho-ye	Dead	Chickasaw roll
2	Cubbis Tyson	"	Chickasaw roll	No. 1		

(NOTES)

No. 1 on Chickasaw roll as Sena Sealey

Sept. 28/98.

RESIDENCE: Pontotoc   *COUNTY*   *CARD NO.*

POST OFFICE: Emmet, Ind. Ter.   *FIELD NO.*

	NAME	RELATION-SHIP TO PERSON FIRST NAMED	AGE	SEX	BLOOD	TRIBAL ENROLLMENT		
						YEAR	COUNTY	PAGE
1	Harrell, Tandy Lee	NAMED	26	M	1/8	1897	Pontotoc	50
2	" Sudie	Wife	21	F	I.W.	1897	"	81
3	" Almarine	Dau	2	"	1/16	1897	"	50
4	" Mary Lee	"	9mo	"	1/16			
5	" Bertie Bell	"	1mo	"	1/16			

TRIBAL ENROLLMENT OF PARENTS

	NAME OF FATHER	YEAR	COUNTY	NAME OF MOTHER	YEAR	COUNTY
1	B. Harrell	Dead	Non Citizen	Martha Harrell now Proffitt	1897	Pontotoc
2	Turner Jordan	"	" "	Mary Jordan		non citizen
3	No. 1			No. 2		
4	No. 1			No. 2		
5	No. 1			No. 2		

(NOTES)

No. 1 Surname on Chickasaw roll as Hewald
No. 2   "   "   "   "   " Herald   *(No. 2 Dawes' Roll No. 126)*
No. 3   "   "   "   "   " Hewald
No. 4 Enrolled Nov. 3/99
No. 5 Enrolled Sept. 18, 1901
No. 5 Died Oct. 19, 1901; Proof of death filed Nov. 8, 1902
No. 5 Died Oct. 19, 1901. Enrollment cancelled by Dept. July *(illegible)*

P.O. Wiley, I.T.   Sept. 28/98.

185

RESIDENCE: Pickens   COUNTY   CARD NO.

POST OFFICE: McGee, Ind. Ter.   FIELD NO.

NAME	RELATION-SHIP TO PERSON FIRST NAMED	AGE	SEX	BLOOD	TRIBAL ENROLLMENT		
					YEAR	COUNTY	PAGE
1 Jefferson, Alec	NAMED	3	M	1/2	1897	Pickens	23

TRIBAL ENROLLMENT OF PARENTS

NAME OF FATHER	YEAR	COUNTY	NAME OF MOTHER	YEAR	COUNTY
1 Alex Jefferson	Dead	Pickens	Sarah Jane Roads		non citizen

(NOTES)

On Chickasaw roll as Allie Jefferson.

P.O. Alderson, I.T. 12/24/02   Sept. 28/98.

RESIDENCE: Tishomingo   COUNTY   CARD NO.

POST OFFICE: Ravia, Ind. Ter.   FIELD NO.

NAME	RELATION-SHIP TO PERSON FIRST NAMED	AGE	SEX	BLOOD	TRIBAL ENROLLMENT		
					YEAR	COUNTY	PAGE
1 ~~Underwood, John~~	NAMED	~~70~~	M	~~Full~~	~~1897~~	~~Tishomingo~~	~~36~~
2 " ~~Rachel~~	~~Wife~~	~~70~~	F	"	~~1897~~	"	~~36~~
3 ~~Allen, Nancy~~	~~(none)~~	~~20~~	"	"	~~1897~~	"	~~36~~
4 " Ena	"	4	"	"	1897	"	36

TRIBAL ENROLLMENT OF PARENTS

NAME OF FATHER	YEAR	COUNTY	NAME OF MOTHER	YEAR	COUNTY
1 ~~Im-ma-tub-by~~	~~Dead~~	~~Chickasaw roll~~	~~(Name Illegible)~~	~~Dead~~	~~Chickasaw roll~~
2 ~~A-bi-no-wah~~	"	" "	~~(Name Illegible)~~	"	" "
3 ~~Charley Allen~~	"	" "	Malinda Allen	"	" "
4 Illegitimate			No. 3		

(NOTES)

No. 1 also known as Anoyah.

No. 1 died March 14, 1899 ⎫
No. 2 died Oct. 8, 1900 ⎬ Proof of death filed May 29, 1903.
No. 3 died Aug 4, 1900 ⎭

No. 4 Jerome Brown is guardian. Certified copy of guardianship papers filed June 2, 1903.

186

Chickasaw Enrollment Cards 1898-1914
Chickasaw by Blood   Volume IV

RESIDENCE: Tishomingo   COUNTY   CARD NO.
POST OFFICE: Tishomingo, Ind. Ter.   FIELD NO.

NAME	RELATION-SHIP TO PERSON FIRST NAMED	AGE	SEX	BLOOD	TRIBAL ENROLLMENT		
					YEAR	COUNTY	PAGE
1 Collins, Ben Carter		23	M	1/8	1897	Panola	2
2 " Hettie	Wife	20	F	1/8	1897	Pickens	17
3 " Henry F.	Son	2mo	M	1/8			

TRIBAL ENROLLMENT OF PARENTS

NAME OF FATHER	YEAR	COUNTY	NAME OF MOTHER	YEAR	COUNTY
1 Dan Collins (I.W.)	1897	Panola	Sally Collins	1897	Panola
2 Hobart Heald I.W.	1897	Pickens	Eliza J. Heald	Dead	Pickens
3 No. 1			No. 2		

(NOTES)

No. 1 on Chickasaw roll as Ben C. Collins
No. 2 "   "   " " Hettie Heald
No. 3 Enrolled Nov. 3/99
No. 3 died Jan. 20, 1900. See testimony of Dan Collins Taken at Colbert this 14th of June, 1900.

Sept. 28/98.

RESIDENCE: Tishomingo   COUNTY   CARD NO.
POST OFFICE: Tishomingo, Ind. Ter.   FIELD NO.

NAME	RELATION-SHIP TO PERSON FIRST NAMED	AGE	SEX	BLOOD	TRIBAL ENROLLMENT		
					YEAR	COUNTY	PAGE
1 ~~Hampton, Alice~~		~~25~~	F	~~1/2~~	~~1897~~	~~Tishomingo~~	~~34~~
2 Greenwood, Jackson	Son	4	M	3/4	1897	"	34
3 Colbert, Mary	Dau	1	F	3/4			

TRIBAL ENROLLMENT OF PARENTS

NAME OF FATHER	YEAR	COUNTY	NAME OF MOTHER	YEAR	COUNTY
1 ~~Joe Hampton~~	~~Dead~~	~~Choctaw roll~~	~~Se-ke-lo-ley~~	~~Dead~~	~~Chickasaw roll~~
2 I-to-tub-by	"	Tishomingo	No. 1		
3 Jeff Colbert	1897	"	No. 1		

(NOTES)

No. 1 died in April 1901; Enrollment cancelled by Department *(remainder illegible)*

Sept. 28/98.

RESIDENCE: Tishomingo COUNTY   CARD NO.

POST OFFICE: Davis, Ind. Ter.   FIELD NO.

NAME	RELATION-SHIP TO PERSON	AGE	SEX	BLOOD	TRIBAL ENROLLMENT		
					YEAR	COUNTY	PAGE
1 Gilbert, Lucy	FIRST NAMED	21	F	Full	1893	Tishomingo	P.R.#1 117
2 " Ida	Dau	8	"	"	1893	"	"
3 " Lela	"	4	"	"			
4 " Jennie	"	3	"	"			
5 " Elvie	"	1	"	"			
6 Brown, Florence	"	3 1/2	"	"			

TRIBAL ENROLLMENT OF PARENTS

	NAME OF FATHER	YEAR	COUNTY	NAME OF MOTHER	YEAR	COUNTY
1	Chilley Alexander	1897	Tishomingo	Caroline Alexander	Dead	Tishomingo
2	Siah Gilbert	Dead	"	No. 1		
3	" "	"	"	No. 1		
4	" "	"	"	No. 1		
5	" "	"	"	No. 1		
6	" "	"	"	No. 1		

(NOTES)

No. 1 is now known as Lucy Cunnentubby; see affidavit as to birth of No. 6 filed this date, Nov. 7, 1902.

No. 6 Born Feb. 11, 1900; enrolled Nov. 7, 1902   *(No. 3 Dawes' Roll No. 4130)*

No. 1 is now husband of Palmer Cunnentubby on Chickasaw Card 942.

(No. 4 Dawes' Roll No. 4131)   *(No. 6 Dawes' Roll No. 4132)*

Sept. 28/98

RESIDENCE: Tishomingo COUNTY   CARD NO.

POST OFFICE: Davis, Ind. Ter.   FIELD NO.

NAME	RELATION-SHIP TO PERSON FIRST	AGE	SEX	BLOOD	TRIBAL ENROLLMENT		
					YEAR	COUNTY	PAGE
1 Alexander, Lizzie	NAMED	45	F	Full	1897	Tishomingo	31

TRIBAL ENROLLMENT OF PARENTS

	NAME OF FATHER	YEAR	COUNTY	NAME OF MOTHER	YEAR	COUNTY
1	Morgan Petigrew	Dead	Chickasaw roll	Sholakacha	Dead	Chick roll

(NOTES)

Sept. 28/98

RESIDENCE: Pickens COUNTY						CARD NO.		
POST OFFICE: Cumberland, Ind. Ter.						FIELD NO.		

NAME	RELATION-SHIP TO PERSON FIRST NAMED	AGE	SEX	BLOOD	TRIBAL ENROLLMENT		
					YEAR	COUNTY	PAGE
1 Allen, Emeline	NAMED	67	F	1/8	1897	Pickens	25

	TRIBAL ENROLLMENT OF PARENTS						
NAME OF FATHER	YEAR	COUNTY	NAME OF MOTHER	YEAR	COUNTY		
1 Christopher Moore	Dead	non citizen	Catherine Moore	Dead	Chickasaw roll		

(NOTES)

On Chickasaw roll as Emoline Allen.

Sept. 28/98.

RESIDENCE: Tishomingo COUNTY						CARD NO.		
POST OFFICE: Regan, Ind. Ter.						FIELD NO.		

NAME	RELATION-SHIP TO PERSON FIRST NAMED	AGE	SEX	BLOOD	TRIBAL ENROLLMENT		
					YEAR	COUNTY	PAGE
1 Brown, Martha	NAMED	50	F	Full	1897	Tishomingo	37

	TRIBAL ENROLLMENT OF PARENTS						
NAME OF FATHER	YEAR	COUNTY	NAME OF MOTHER	YEAR	COUNTY		
1 Nu-ko-i-che	Dead	Chickasaw roll	Mollie Ann	Dead	Chickasaw roll		

(NOTES)

Sept. 28/98.

RESIDENCE: Pontotoc COUNTY						CARD NO.		
POST OFFICE: Emmet, Ind. Ter.						FIELD NO.		

NAME	RELATION-SHIP TO PERSON FIRST NAMED	AGE	SEX	BLOOD	TRIBAL ENROLLMENT		
					YEAR	COUNTY	PAGE
1 Wolf, Malinda	NAMED	22	F	Full	1897	Pontotoc	59
2 " Sallie	Dau	3	"	1/2	1897	"	59
3 " Jim	Son	7mo	M	1/2			

	TRIBAL ENROLLMENT OF PARENTS						
NAME OF FATHER	YEAR	COUNTY	NAME OF MOTHER	YEAR	COUNTY		
1 Amos Hamilton	Dead	Tishomingo	Sally Hamilton	Dead	Pontotoc		
2 Esau Wolf		Cherokee Citz	No. 1				
3 " "		" "	No. 1				

(NOTES)

P.O. Fillmore, I.T.

Sept. 28/98.

RESIDENCE: Choctaw Nation ~~COUNTY~~					CARD NO.			
POST OFFICE: Stringtown, Ind. Ter.					FIELD NO.			

NAME	RELATION- SHIP TO PERSON FIRST NAMED	AGE	SEX	BLOOD	TRIBAL ENROLLMENT		
					YEAR	COUNTY	PAGE
1 Billie, Simon	NAMED	40	M	1/2			
2 " Nancy	Wife	26	F	1/2			

TRIBAL ENROLLMENT OF PARENTS

	NAME OF FATHER	YEAR	COUNTY	NAME OF MOTHER	YEAR	COUNTY
1	Alexander Billie	Dead	Choctaw roll	Ah-lo-we-che	Dead	Chickasaw roll
2	Thomas Noah	1896	" "	Asey Noah	"	" " "

(NOTES)

No. 1 on Choctaw Census Record No. 2 Page 76, Jack Fork Co. transferred to Chickasaw roll by Dawes Com.

No. 2 on 1893 Choctaw Pay Roll Page 82 No. 733 Jacks Fork Co, as Nancy Watson,
    transferred to Chickasaw roll by Dawes Com.
    On Choctaw Roll, 1896, Jacks Fork County, No. 1892 as Simon Billy

No. 1 has a child, by former Choctaw wife, on Choctaw Card No. 1963.

Sept. 28/98.
No. 2 - May 23/99.

CANCELLED Stamped across card

RESIDENCE: Choctaw Nation ~~COUNTY~~					CARD NO.			
POST OFFICE: Stringtown, Ind. Ter.					FIELD NO.			

NAME	RELATION- SHIP TO PERSON FIRST NAMED	AGE	SEX	BLOOD	TRIBAL ENROLLMENT		
					YEAR	COUNTY	PAGE
1 Moore, Christopher D.	NAMED	32	M	1/2			
2 ~~Williams, Amanda~~	~~Orphan~~	1	F				

TRIBAL ENROLLMENT OF PARENTS

	NAME OF FATHER	YEAR	COUNTY	NAME OF MOTHER	YEAR	COUNTY
1	Dallas Moore	Dead	Choctaw roll	Mary Bond Moore	1897	Chick residing in Choctaw N. 3rd Dist.
2	~~J.B. Williams~~		~~Jack Fork County Choctaw Roll~~	~~Carrie Williams~~	~~Dead~~	" " " "

(NOTES)

Husband of Tennessee Moore, Choctaw roll, Card No. 300.

No. 1 on Choctaw Census Record No. 2, Jack Fork Co., Page 357. as C.D. Moore,
    transferred to Chickasaw roll by Dawes Com.

No. 1 is now the husband of Ida Bob on Choctaw card #1834, April 19, 1902

No. 1 on Choctaw Roll, 1896, Jacks Fork County, No. 8861, as C.D. Moore

No. 2 on *(remainder illegible)*

Dec. 2, 99; No. 2 Enrolled on Chickasaw card #1436 by father.

Sept. 28/98.

CANCELLED Stamped across card

RESIDENCE: Tishomingo **COUNTY**   **CARD NO.**
POST OFFICE: Regan, Ind. Ter.   **FIELD NO.**

	NAME	RELATION-SHIP TO PERSON FIRST NAMED	AGE	SEX	BLOOD	TRIBAL ENROLLMENT		
						YEAR	COUNTY	PAGE
1	Sanders, Sarah Jane	NAMED	60	F	Full	1897	Tishomingo	33
2	Fletcher, Joe	Son	11	M	"	1897	"	33

TRIBAL ENROLLMENT OF PARENTS

	NAME OF FATHER	YEAR	COUNTY	NAME OF MOTHER	YEAR	COUNTY
1	No-ki-e-che	Dead	Chickasaw roll	Mollie Ann	Dead	Chickasaw roll
2	Tom Fletcher	1897	Pickens	No. 1		

(NOTES)

No. 1 on Chickasaw roll as Sealy

Sept. 28/98.

RESIDENCE: Tishomingo **COUNTY**   **CARD NO.**
POST OFFICE: Emmet, Ind. Ter.   **FIELD NO.**

	NAME	RELATION-SHIP TO PERSON FIRST NAMED	AGE	SEX	BLOOD	TRIBAL ENROLLMENT		
						YEAR	COUNTY	PAGE
1	Miller, Eli	NAMED	23	M	Full	1897	Tishomingo	33
2	" Sarah	Wife	20	F	"	1897	"	33
3	" Annie	Dau	1	"	"			
4	" Mulbert	Son	5mo	M	"			
5	" Stella	Dau	5mo	F	"			

TRIBAL ENROLLMENT OF PARENTS

	NAME OF FATHER	YEAR	COUNTY	NAME OF MOTHER	YEAR	COUNTY
1	John Miller	Dead	Chickasaw roll	Wicey Miller	1897	Tishomingo
2	Wallace John	"	Pontotoc	Jane John	Dead	Pontotoc
3	No. 1			No. 2		
4	No. 1			No. 2		
5	No. 1			No. 2		

(NOTES)

No. 4 Enrolled Aug. 14/99
No. 5 Enrolled June 27, 1901.

Sept. 28/98.

191

RESIDENCE: Tishomingo   **COUNTY**

POST OFFICE: Emmet, Ind. Ter.

CARD NO.

FIELD NO.

	NAME	RELATION-SHIP TO PERSON FIRST NAMED	AGE	SEX	BLOOD	TRIBAL ENROLLMENT		
						YEAR	COUNTY	PAGE
1	Wolf, Delphia	NAMED	65	F	Full	1897	Tishomingo	33
2	Carney, Gilbert	Son	11	M	"	1897	"	34

TRIBAL ENROLLMENT OF PARENTS

	NAME OF FATHER	YEAR	COUNTY	NAME OF MOTHER	YEAR	COUNTY
1	Ni-he-che	Dead	Chickasaw roll	Che-ho-che	Dead	Chickasaw roll
2	Charley Carney	"	Pontotoc	No. 1		

(NOTES)

No. 2 on Chickasaw roll as Cubert Carney

Sept. 28/98

RESIDENCE: Tishomingo   **COUNTY**

POST OFFICE: Emmet, Ind. Ter.

CARD NO.

FIELD NO.

	NAME	RELATION-SHIP TO PERSON FIRST NAMED	AGE	SEX	BLOOD	TRIBAL ENROLLMENT		
						YEAR	COUNTY	PAGE
1	Beam, Andrew	NAMED	22	M	Full	1897	Tishomingo	33
2	" Sinie	Wife	23	F	Full	1897	"	33

TRIBAL ENROLLMENT OF PARENTS

	NAME OF FATHER	YEAR	COUNTY	NAME OF MOTHER	YEAR	COUNTY
1	Landers Bean	Dead	Panola	Lucy Beam	Dead	Pontotoc
2	Daniel Colbert		Pontotoc	Delphia Wolf	1897	Tishomingo

(NOTES)

No. 2 on Chickasaw roll as Sena Colbert

See affidavit of No. 2 as to degree of her Chickasaw blood filed Feby. 9, 1903

Sept. 28/98

RESIDENCE: Pickens   **COUNTY**

POST OFFICE: Willis, Ind. Ter.

CARD NO.

FIELD NO.

	NAME	RELATION-SHIP TO PERSON FIRST NAMED	AGE	SEX	BLOOD	TRIBAL ENROLLMENT		
						YEAR	COUNTY	PAGE
1	Jefferson, Martin	NAMED	18	M	Full	1897	Tishomingo	18
2	" ~~Sylvia~~	~~Wife~~	~~19~~	~~F~~	~~"~~	~~1897~~	~~Pickens~~	~~8~~

TRIBAL ENROLLMENT OF PARENTS

	NAME OF FATHER	YEAR	COUNTY	NAME OF MOTHER	YEAR	COUNTY
1	Alex Jefferson	Dead	Pickens	Bicey Jefferson	Dead	Pickens
2	~~Overton Keel~~	"	"	~~Lizzie Keel~~	"	"

(NOTES)

No. 2 on Chickasaw roll as Sylia Keel

Sept. 28/98.

RESIDENCE: Pickens COUNTY   CARD NO.

POST OFFICE: Willis, Ind. Ter.   FIELD NO.

	NAME	RELATION-SHIP TO PERSON FIRST NAMED	AGE	SEX	BLOOD	TRIBAL ENROLLMENT		
						YEAR	COUNTY	PAGE
1	~~Keel, Simon~~	NAMED	~~77~~	M	~~Full~~	~~1897~~	~~Pickens~~	~~8~~
2	Courtney, Ziley	Neice[sic]	44	F	"	1897	"	8
3	" Peter	G.Neph.	8	M	"	1897	"	8
4	Pickens. William	G.G.Son	2	"	"	~~1897~~	"	~~87~~

TRIBAL ENROLLMENT OF PARENTS

	NAME OF FATHER	YEAR	COUNTY	NAME OF MOTHER	YEAR	COUNTY
1	~~E-la-hu-tubby~~	~~Dead~~	~~Chickasaw roll~~	~~To-wah-ne~~	~~Dead~~	~~Chickasaw roll~~
2	Peter Courtney	"	" "	Liney Courtney	"	" "
3	Amos Kaney	"	" "	No. 2		
4	Ben Pickens	"	Pickens	Lucy Pickens	1893 Dead	Pickens

(NOTES)

No. 3 on Chickasaw roll as Pitman Courtney

No. 4 Affidavits of T.W. Williams, Margaret Carney, Janey Archison and Ziley Courtney, as to birth
filed Oct. 10, 1902.

(No. 4 Dawes' Roll No. 4129)

Sept. 28/98.

RESIDENCE: Choctaw Nation ~~COUNTY~~   CARD NO.

POST OFFICE: McAlester, Ind. Ter.   FIELD NO.

	NAME	RELATION-SHIP TO PERSON FIRST NAMED	AGE	SEX	BLOOD	TRIBAL ENROLLMENT		
						YEAR	COUNTY	PAGE
1	Phillips, Thomas Jefferson	NAMED	59	M	I.W.	1897	Chick residing in Choctaw N. 1st Dist.	82
2	" William Thomas	Son	20	"	1/32	1897	" " " "	68
3	" Charles Rooks	"	18	"	1/32	1897	" " " "	68
4	" Rolla H.	"	16	"	1/32	1897	" " " "	68

5	"	John E.	"	13	"	1/32	1897	"	"	"	"	68
6	"	Annie Louisa	Dau	11	F	1/32	1897	"	"	"	"	68
7	"	George E.	Son	8	M	1/32	1897	"	"	"	"	68
8	"	William Ross	Gr.Son	3wks	"	1/64						
9	"	Nettie A.	Wife of No. 2	22	F	I.W.						

TRIBAL ENROLLMENT OF PARENTS

	NAME OF FATHER	YEAR	COUNTY	NAME OF MOTHER	YEAR	COUNTY
1	Joseph Phillips	Dead	Non Citizen	Mary Phillips	Dead	Non Citizen
2	No. 1			Mary E. Phillips	"	Chick residing in Choctaw N. 1st Dist.
3	No. 1			" " "	"	" " " "
4	No. 1			" " "	"	" " " "
5	No. 1			" " "	"	" " " "
6	No. 1			" " "	"	" " " "
7	No. 1			" " "	"	" " " "
8	No. 2			Nettie A. Phillips		Intermarried
9	(Name Illegible)		non citizen	(Name Illegible)		non citizen

(NOTES)

No. 1 on Chickasaw roll as T.J. Phillips   *(No. 1 Dawes' Roll No. 322)*
No. 2 "   "   " " W.T. "
No. 3 "   "   " " Chas. R. "
No. 6 "   "   " " Louisa "
No. 2 is now the husband of Nettie A. Phillips on Chickasaw Card #D.347 Aug. 12, 1901
No. 8 Born Aug. 12, 1902. enrolled Aug. 28, 1902.
         See testimony of No. 1 taken October 16, 1902.
(Other notations illegible)

P.O. of No. 2 is ~~Juanita~~, IT
         Chickasha, I.T.   Sept. 28/98.

RESIDENCE: Pickens	COUNTY					CARD NO.			
POST OFFICE: Oakland, Ind. Ter.						FIELD NO.			

	NAME	RELATION-SHIP TO PERSON FIRST NAMED	AGE	SEX	BLOOD	TRIBAL ENROLLMENT		
						YEAR	COUNTY	PAGE
1	Lewis, Isaac Overton		42	M	1/16	1897	Pickens	12
2	*(This line left blank on microfilm)*							
3	Reirdon, Claudie Ella	Dau	14	F	1/32	1897	Pickens	12
4	Lewis, Quincy Hardy	Son	11	M	1/32	1897	Pickens	12
5	" William Chesley	"	6	"	1/32	1897	Pickens	12

6	" Dixie Ellen	Dau	4	F	1/32	1897	Pickens		12
7	" Alta	"	2	"	1/32	1897	Pickens		12
8	" General Fitzhugh Lee	Son	6mo	M	1/32				
9	" Lillian Madill	Dau	1mo	F	1/32				
10	Reirdon, Thelma O.	G.dau	6wks	F	1/64				
11	Reirdon, Joseph P.	husband of No. 3	27	M	I.W.				

TRIBAL ENROLLMENT OF PARENTS

	NAME OF FATHER	YEAR	COUNTY	NAME OF MOTHER	YEAR	COUNTY
1	L.W. Lewis	Dead	non citizen	Elzira Love Lewis	Dead	Chickasaw roll
2						
3	No. 1			Rebecca J. Lewis	Dead	non citizen
4	No. 1			" " "	"	" "
5	No. 1			Mary L. Lewis		white woman
6	No. 1			" " "		" "
7	No. 1			" " "		" "
8	No. 1			" " "		" "
9	No. 1			" " "		" "
10	Joe Reirdon			No. 3		
11	Chas Reirdon		non citizen	Louisa Reirdon		non citizen

(NOTES)

No. 1 on Chickasaw roll as I.O. Lewis
No. 3 "   "   " " Claudie "
No. 4 "   "   " " J.H. "
No. 5 "   "   " " W.C. "
No. 6 "   "   " " Dixie "
No. 7 "   "   " " Alty "
No. 8 Affidavit of attending physician to be supplied. Received Oct. 4/98.
No. 1 husband of Mary L. Lewis, Chickasaw Card No. D.84.
No. 11 transferred from Chickasaw card #D.256. March 29, 1903.
    See decision of March 13, 1903.
Wife of No. 1 is on Chick Card #1699.
For evidence of marriage of No. 1 to Mary L. Lewis see card No. D.84
No. 3 is now the wife of Joseph P. Reirdon on Chickasaw Card D.258. Evidence of marriage filed in that case.
No. 9 Enrolled Aug. 6, 1900.
No. 10 Enrolled Dec. 6, 1900.

Sept. 28/98.

RESIDENCE: Tishomingo COUNTY   CARD NO.

POST OFFICE: Buckhorn, Ind. Ter.   FIELD NO.

	NAME	RELATION-SHIP TO PERSON FIRST NAMED	AGE	SEX	BLOOD	TRIBAL ENROLLMENT		
						YEAR	COUNTY	PAGE
1	Holcomb, Sparrell Harvey	NAMED	45	M	I.W.			
2	Holcomb, Fannie E.		26	F	1/16	1897	Tishomingo	31
3	" Millard Fillmore	Son	9	M	1/32	1897	"	31
4	" Pleasant	"	7	"	1/32	1897	"	31
5	" Martha Easter	Dau	3	F	1/32	1897	"	31

TRIBAL ENROLLMENT OF PARENTS

	NAME OF FATHER	YEAR	COUNTY	NAME OF MOTHER	YEAR	COUNTY
1	L.L. Holcomb	Dead	Non Citizen	Martha Holcomb	Dead	Non Citizen
2	Taylor Cummings	Dead	non citizen	now Lowrance Mary E. Cummings	1897	Tishomingo
3	Sparrell H. Holcomb		white man	No. 1		
4	" " "		" "	No. 1		
5	" " "		" "	No. 1		

(NOTES)

No. 2 wife of Sparrell Harvey Holcomb, Chickasaw Card No. D.83
No. 3 on Chickasaw roll as Willard F. Holcomb
No. 4 "   "   " " Pleas   "
No. 5 "   "   " " Mattie E.   "
No. 1 transferred from Chickasaw Card #D.83   (No. 1 Dawes' Roll No. 187)
    See decision May (illegible)

Sept. 28/98

RESIDENCE: Choctaw Nation ~~COUNTY~~   CARD NO.

POST OFFICE: Hartshorn, Ind. Ter.   FIELD NO.

	NAME	RELATION-SHIP TO PERSON FIRST NAMED	AGE	SEX	BLOOD	TRIBAL ENROLLMENT		
						YEAR	COUNTY	PAGE
1	Carter, Casey	NAMED	47	F	Full	1897	Chick residing in Choctaw N. 1st Dist.	68
2	Nail, Silas W.	Son	26	M	1/2	1897	" " " "	68
3	Carter, Ida	Dau	10	F	1/2	1897	" " " "	68
4	" Williston	Cousin	7	M	1/2	1897	Pontotoc	52
5	Camp, Calvin	"	23	"	Full	1897	Chick residing in Choctaw N. 1st Dist.	67
6	" Sissy	"	17	F	"	1897	" " " "	67
7	" Nancy	"	13	"	"	1897	" " " "	67

	Name		Age	Sex	Blood	Year	County				Page
8	" Lyman	"	10	M	"	1897	"	"	"	"	67
9	Jefferson, Tecumseh	"	2	"	1/2	1897	"	"	"	"	67
10	Bee, Dollie	Dau of No. 7	1	F	1/4						
11	McClish, Ruben	Son of No. 6	2	M	Full						

TRIBAL ENROLLMENT OF PARENTS

	NAME OF FATHER	YEAR	COUNTY	NAME OF MOTHER	YEAR	COUNTY
1	Jim-o-na-cha	Dead	Chickasaw roll	Chim-mon-ney	Dead	Chickasaw roll
2	Winon nau	"	Choctaw "	No. 1		
3	Jesse Carter		Choctaw roll Tobucksy Counry	No. 1		
4	Robert Carter	Dead	Choctaw roll	Liza Ann Carter	Dead	Chickasaw roll
5	Isom Camp	"	Chickasaw roll	Betsey Camp	"	" "
6	" "	"	" "	" "	"	" "
7	" "	"	" "	" "	"	" "
8	" "	"	" "	" "	"	" "
9	Julius Bond	"	Choctaw "	No. 6		
10	William Bee		"	No. 7		
11	Buddie McClish	1896	Gaines	No. 6		

(NOTES)

No. 4 on Chickasaw roll as Willis Carter
No. 8   "   "   "   " Simon Camp
No. 1 Died October 28, 1899; Evidence of her death filed May 9, 1901.
  She was the wife of Jesse Carter on Choctaw Card #3232.
No. 7 is now wife of William Bee on Choctaw card #3157. Evidence of marriage filed Dec. 1, 1902
No. 10 born March 3, 1901; enrolled Dec. 1, 1902   *(No. 10 Dawes' Roll No. 4128)*
No. 11 Born Feby. 24, 1900. Application for enrollment received Aug. 5, 1901.   *(No. 11 Dawes' Roll No. 4967)*
  and returned for identification of mother.
No. 11 Enrolled Aug. 1, 1904.

P.O. Alderson, I.T. 12/23/02.   Sept 28/98.

RESIDENCE: Tishomingo COUNTY					CARD NO.			
POST OFFICE: Dougherty, Ind. Ter.					FIELD NO.			

NAME	RELATION-SHIP TO PERSON FIRST NAMED	AGE	SEX	BLOOD	TRIBAL ENROLLMENT		
					YEAR	COUNTY	PAGE
1 James, Fulsom	FIRST NAMED	40	M	Full	1893	Tishomingo	P.R.#1 120

2	Naponahoyah	Sister	65	F	"	1893	"	P.R.#1 127
3	James, Nelson	Nephew	10	M	"	1893	"	P.R.#1 108

TRIBAL ENROLLMENT OF PARENTS

	NAME OF FATHER	YEAR	COUNTY	NAME OF MOTHER	YEAR	COUNTY
1	Le-con-etch-ey James	Dead	Chickasaw roll	Pid-ley	Dead	Chickasaw roll
2	(Name Illegible)	"	" "	Ful-la-ma-ho-ke	"	" "
3	Solomon James	"	" "	Elsie James	"	" "

(NOTES)

No. 2 on Chickasaw roll as Napona
No. 1 also on 1897 roll, Page 92, Tishomingo Co
No. 3 on 1893 Chickasaw pay roll #11 paage 108 as Nelson Burris
    Also see Nelson Burris page 3, above roll and
        Nelson Burris " 51 " "
No. 2 on colored card Oct. 22/98.

P.O. Davis. I.T. 2/1-04   Sept. 27/98.

RESIDENCE: Tishomingo **COUNTY**   **CARD NO.**
POST OFFICE: Mill Creek, Ind. Ter.   **FIELD NO.**

	NAME	RELATION-SHIP TO PERSON FIRST NAMED	AGE	SEX	BLOOD	TRIBAL ENROLLMENT		
						YEAR	COUNTY	PAGE
1	Quincy, Thomas	NAMED	27	M	Full	1897	Tishomingo	31

TRIBAL ENROLLMENT OF PARENTS

	NAME OF FATHER	YEAR	COUNTY	NAME OF MOTHER	YEAR	COUNTY
1	William Quincy	Dead	Chickasaw	Naht-ke	Dead	Chickasaw roll

(NOTES)

No. 1 on Chickasaw roll as Thomas Quincey

Sept. 27/98.

RESIDENCE: Pontotoc **COUNTY**   **CARD NO.**
POST OFFICE: Emmet, Ind. Ter.   **FIELD NO.**

	NAME	RELATION-SHIP TO PERSON FIRST NAMED	AGE	SEX	BLOOD	TRIBAL ENROLLMENT		
						YEAR	COUNTY	PAGE
1	Proffitt, Abraham M.	NAMED	38	M	I.W.	1897	Pontotoc	81
2	" Martha A.	Wife	56	F	1/4	1897	"	50
3	Hearrell, Jesse B.	StepSon	29	M	1/8	1897	"	50
4	" Alice	" Dau	23	F	1/8	1897	"	50

5	"	~~Daisy~~	" "	~~18~~	F	1/8	~~1897~~	"	~~50~~
6	"	~~Ada~~	" "	~~16~~	"	1/8	~~1897~~	"	~~50~~

TRIBAL ENROLLMENT OF PARENTS

	NAME OF FATHER	YEAR	COUNTY	NAME OF MOTHER	YEAR	COUNTY
1	Turner Proffitt		non citizen	Jane Proffitt		non citizen
2	Louis Walker	Dead	Choctaw roll	Mary Walker now Cheadle	Dead	Chickasaw roll
3	J.B. Hearrell	"	non citizen	No. 2		
4	" " "	"	" "	~~No. 2~~		
5	" " "	"	" "	~~No. 2~~		
6	" " "	"	" "	~~No. 2~~		

(NOTES)

No. 3   on Chickasaw roll as Jessie B. Hewald
Nos. 4,5,&6   "   "   "   "   "Hewald"
No. 1   "   "   "   "   A.M. Proffitt
No. 2   "   "   "   "   M.A. Phrofet
No. 5   transferred to Chickasaw Card No. 1515 with her husband Thomas M. Hunnicutt, at Durant I.T. 8/17, 1899.
No. 6   was transferred to card No. 1516 with husband Abner M. Blocker - Aug. 17, 1899
Aug. 16/99   No. 4 has been placed upon Card No. 1500 with her husband William H. Murray.
No. 1   Died Nov. 27, 1900;   proof of death filed Nov. 10, 1902.

P.O. Wiley, I.T. 11/6/02.   Sept. 27/98.

RESIDENCE: Pickens   **COUNTY**   **CARD NO.**

POST OFFICE: Oakland, Ind. Ter.   **FIELD NO.**

	NAME	RELATION-SHIP TO PERSON FIRST NAMED	AGE	SEX	BLOOD	TRIBAL ENROLLMENT		
						YEAR	COUNTY	PAGE
1	Chastain, John Boone	NAMED	37	M	I.W.	1897	Pickens	77
2	" Mary	Wife	41	F	Full	1897	"	12
3	" Alec	Son	11	M	1/2	1897	"	12
4	" Jessie	Dau	10	F	1/2	1897	"	12

TRIBAL ENROLLMENT OF PARENTS

	NAME OF FATHER	YEAR	COUNTY	NAME OF MOTHER	YEAR	COUNTY
1	Elijah Chastain		non-citizen	Elizabeth Chastain		non citizen
2	Cornelius McGee	Dead	Chickasaw Roll	Eliza McGee	Dead	Chickasaw roll
3	No. 1			No. 2		
4	No. 1			No. 2		

(NOTES)

No. 1 on Chickasaw roll as Boone Chastine.

11/5/02   P.O. Randolph, I.T.   Sept. 27/98.

RESIDENCE: Pontotoc COUNTY					CARD NO.		
POST OFFICE: Boggy Depot, Ind. Ter.					FIELD NO.		
	NAME	RELATIONSHIP TO PERSON FIRST NAMED	AGE	SEX	BLOOD	TRIBAL ENROLLMENT		
						YEAR	COUNTY	PAGE
1	Wolfe, Jonas		68	M	Full	1897	Pontotoc	58
2	" Lizzie	Wife	45	F	"	1897	"	58
3	" Solbun	Ward	7	M	"	1897	"	58

TRIBAL ENROLLMENT OF PARENTS

	NAME OF FATHER	YEAR	COUNTY	NAME OF MOTHER	YEAR	COUNTY
1	I-yo-co-mah-tubby	Dead	Chickasaw roll	Tal-le-mah-he	Dead	Chickasaw roll
2	En-cush-tam-by	"	" "	Cha-ko-nah	"	" "
3	Henry Wolfe	"	Pontotoc	Lottie Wolfe	"	Panola

(NOTES)

No. 1 Died Jany. 14, 1900. Proof of death filed Aug. 19, 1901.
(Other notations illegible)

Sept. 27/98.

RESIDENCE: Tishomingo COUNTY					CARD NO.		
POST OFFICE: Hickory, Ind. Ter.					FIELD NO.		
	NAME	RELATIONSHIP TO PERSON FIRST NAMED	AGE	SEX	BLOOD	TRIBAL ENROLLMENT		
						YEAR	COUNTY	PAGE
1	Frazier, Newton Galloway		48	M	Full	1897	Tishomingo	29
2	McLish, Wm Bourland	Ward	13	"	"	1897	"	29
3	Harris, Hettie	Mother	70	F	"	1897	"	27

TRIBAL ENROLLMENT OF PARENTS

	NAME OF FATHER	YEAR	COUNTY	NAME OF MOTHER	YEAR	COUNTY
1	Jackson Frazier	Dead	Chickasaw Roll	Hettie Frazier now Harris	1897	Tishomingo
2	Holmes McLish	"	" "	Sis McLish	Dead	Pickens
3	*(Name Illegible)*	"	" "	*(Name Illegible)*	"	Chickasaw Roll

(NOTES)

No. 1 on Chickasaw roll as Newton G. Frazier
No. 2 " " " " William McLish
No. 1 Died in Feby. 1902; proof of death filed May 1, 1902.

Sept. 27/98.

Other Books and Series by Jeff Bowen

1901-1907 Native American Census Seneca, Eastern Shawnee, Miami, Modoc, Ottawa, Peoria, Quapaw, and Wyandotte Indians (Under Seneca School, Indian Territory)

1932 Census of The Standing Rock Sioux Reservation with Births And Deaths 1924-1932

Census of The Blackfeet, Montana, 1897- 1901 Expanded Edition

Eastern Cherokee by Blood, 1906-1910, Volumes I thru XIII

Choctaw of Mississippi Indian Census 1929-1932 with Births and Deaths 1924-1931 Volume I

Choctaw of Mississippi Indian Census 1933, 1934 & 1937, Supplemental Rolls to 1934 & 1935 with Births and Deaths 1932-1938, and Marriages 1936-1938 Volume II

Eastern Cherokee Census Cherokee, North Carolina 1930-1939 Census 1930-1931 with Births And Deaths 1924-1931 Taken By Agent L. W. Page Volume I

Eastern Cherokee Census Cherokee, North Carolina 1930-1939 Census 1932-1933 with Births And Deaths 1930-1932 Taken By Agent R. L. Spalsbury Volume II

Eastern Cherokee Census Cherokee, North Carolina 1930-1939 Census 1934-1937 with Births and Deaths 1925-1938 and Marriages 1936 & 1938 Taken by Agents R. L. Spalsbury And Harold W. Foght Volume III

Seminole of Florida Indian Census, 1930-1940 with Birth and Death Records, 1930-1938

Texas Cherokees 1820-1839 A Document For Litigation 1921

Choctaw By Blood Enrollment Cards 1898-1914 Volumes I thru XVII

Starr Roll 1894 (Cherokee Payment Rolls) Districts: Canadian, Cooweescoowee, and Delaware Volume One

Starr Roll 1894 (Cherokee Payment Rolls) Districts: Flint, Going Snake, and Illinois Volume Two

Starr Roll 1894 (Cherokee Payment Rolls) Districts: Saline, Sequoyah, and Tahlequah; Including Orphan Roll Volume Three

Other Books and Series by Jeff Bowen

Cherokee Intruder Cases Dockets of Hearings 1901-1909 Volumes I & II

Indian Wills, 1911-1921 Records of the Bureau of Indian Affairs Books One thru Seven;

Native American Wills & Probate Records 1911-1921

Turtle Mountain Reservation Chippewa Indians 1932 Census with Births & Deaths, 1924-1932

Chickasaw By Blood Enrollment Cards 1898-1914 Volume I, II & III

Visit our website at **www.nativestudy.com** to learn more about these and other books and series by Jeff Bowen